Werner Schroeter

Edited by Roy Grundmann

Österreichisches Filmmuseum
SYNEMA – Gesellschaft für Film und Medien

For David Pendleton

A book by SYNEMA ☰ Publikationen
Werner Schroeter
Volume 32 of FilmmuseumSynemaPublikationen

FilmmuseumSynemaPublikationen is a book series jointly conceptualized by Austrian Film Museum and SYNEMA – Gesellschaft für Film und Medien.

This volume was published in collaboration with Filmmuseum München, Germany, and with the support of Boston University and the Goethe-Institut, Boston.

Copy editor: Catherine A. Surowiec
Design and layout: Gabi Adébisi-Schuster
Project coordination: Eszter Kondor (Austrian Film Museum)
Cover photo: Werner Schroeter (1970s) © bpk / Roswitha Hecke
Printed and published in Vienna, Austria
Printed by Donau Forum Druck Ges.m.b.H.
Printed on paper certified in accordance with the rules of the Forest Stewardship Council.

ISBN 978-3-901644-74-0

Österreichisches Filmmuseum (Austrian Film Museum) and SYNEMA – Gesellschaft für Film & Medien are supported by Bundeskanzleramt Österreich/Kunst und Kultur – Abt. (II/3) Film and by Kulturabteilung der Stadt Wien.

Table of Contents

Roy Grundmann

The Passions of Werner Schroeter

An Introduction

"Counterdesigns to reality"—these are the words used to characterize director Werner Schroeter's works in the documentary *Mondo Lux* (2010), made by his longtime collaborator Elfi Mikesch shortly before Schroeter's death. As an artist, Schroeter explains on camera, he must create his own world that stands in opposition to the reality around him. Artificial as that world may seem, it liberates the artwork from the constraints of imitation and furnishes the artist with self-knowledge. The notion that an *oeuvre* is a reflection of its creator is by no means new. Schroeter, however, is a particularly good example. In his case, the person becomes identical with the work and its theatricality. This observation comes from the critic Dietrich Kuhlbrodt, who in an early assessment of Schroeter identifies theatricality as the key to understanding his films.[1] It enables Schroeter to turn his work into both a conduit for exalted feelings and a display of them. It stimulates our senses and our imagination and it invites affective engagement rather than intellectual decoding.[2]

Schroeter's consummate theatricality is far from indiscriminate. Kuhlbrodt, whose assay of Schroeter's first decade still provides a useful primer, breaks it down into a catalogue of strategies and devices adopted for specific purposes. Foremost is Schroeter's prioritization of gestures over words. Ranging from the smallest, most minimal to the grandest, most exalted expressions, gesture carries performance's full affective charge. In most of Schroeter's films and all of his stage work, theatricality is near-synonymous with female performance—of such historical and literary figures as Lucrezia Borgia, Emilia Galotti, or Miss Julie, of mythical characters like Kriemhild and the Virgin Mary, and of cultural archetypes such as the whore or the gypsy. Transcending their respective plots, Schroeter's heroines display dignity in their suffering and invite intense empathy and identification with their strength, even in death.[3] As canonized characters ripe for reinterpretation, they help Schroeter appropriate any literary text, any popular type, for his own agenda, which includes foregrounding the individual's rebellion against social hypocrisy and self-serving patriarchal mores. But Schroeter also conceives of gestures as going beyond specific semantic and symbolic functions. In his films the gestural does not neatly align with principles

1 Dietrich Kuhlbrodt, "Erfahrene Erfahrung: Über den Umgang mit Werner Schroeter, will sagen seinen Filmen," in Sebastian Feldmann, et al., eds., *Werner Schroeter* (Munich: Hanser Verlag, 1980), p. 7.

2 Kuhlbrodt, p. 7.

3 Kuhlbrodt, pp. 8, 13, 23.

of realism. Never less than ambiguous—and quite often enigmatic or opaque—gestures retain an autonomous force that directs spectators towards the realm of emotions, desires, and preverbal fantasies.[4] At the same time, this force does not reveal an interior state. The gestures in Schroeter's films, as Alice Kuzniar has argued, signify the state of passion as such. They constitute "a cinema of pure external signs or symptoms without an etiology."[5]

The autonomy of the gestural realm, which Kuhlbrodt describes as the "reduction of all reality particles to their mimetic value,"[6] is cognate to several other qualities he identifies in Schroeter's work: the decomposition of space (using real, found spaces as settings for stylized performances) and of time (transforming these performances' sequential flow into charged simultaneity); the asynchronicity of sound and image (the music we hear is rarely that to which Schroeter's performers sing and dance); the breakdown of high and low art (Schroeter's films include both opera and pop, both "high" drama and "low" melodrama); the extensive use of citation and bricolage (processes that seize on found materials that they reassemble / recirculate in new form); and the inscription of cultural consumption in the act of production (performing, or putting something out there, is always an act of listening, of taking something in).[7]

This set of observations shall serve as an entry into the work of one of the most complex and elusive filmmakers of his generation. First, however, Schroeter must be situated within his historical context. What is it that has made him so elusive? Indeed, the term "his generation" already proves problematic, because it runs the risk of implying membership in an artistic cohort with which he had little in common.

Schroeter was born within a few years of Werner Herzog and the same year as Rainer Werner Fassbinder and Wim Wenders—three of the most prominent filmmakers of the New German Cinema. Fassbinder and Wenders became his personal friends. But friendship and other affinities aside (Fassbinder, like Schroeter, was gay and cast him in two of his films), Schroeter's position in the New German Cinema was marginal. He dropped out of film school during his first semester, and the films he made from 1968 to 1976, during the first nine years of his creative trajectory, hardly fit the feature-film mold successfully deployed by the New German Cinema in the 1970s. While that Cinema's most visible filmmakers enjoyed

4 Kuhlbrodt, p. 23. This observation was made by several critics already in the early 1970s. Kuhlbrodt credits the critic Jörg Peter Feurich in a review published in *Filmkritik* (Munich), no. 180 (December 1971), p. 654.

5 Alice A. Kuzniar, *The Queer German Cinema* (Stanford, CA: Stanford University Press, 2000), Chapt. 4, "The 'Passionate Evidence' of Werner Schroeter's *Maria Malibran* and *Der Rosenkönig*," pp. 113–138; quote from p. 117. Taking a psychoanalytic approach to Schroeter's aesthetic, Kuzniar argues, via the Lacanian concept of the *objet petit a* (pp. 126–129), that Schroeter's images of vibrancy and fullness signify love and passion as prohibited, lost, and impossible, while at the same time putting themselves in place of such loss. This way Schroeter's images signify passion as such. Its purity and tragic impossibility are two sides of the same coin. This, as Kuzniar goes on to argue, is what makes Schroeter's aesthetic resonate with queer experience beyond his casting of androgynes and transvestites.

6 Kuhlbrodt, p. 33. [Author's translation]

7 Kuhlbrodt, pp. 10–16, 25–27.

The young
Werner Schroeter

breakout success on the international art-film circuit before being recognized at home, Schroeter's wider success, slower to come and always more relative than that of his compatriots, cannot be mapped in quite the same way onto the geopolitics of national cinema and the international film festival circuit. If anything, it was vertical, starting at German underground film festivals that were of marginal interest to most Germans, then moving to *Das kleine Fernsehspiel* (The Little Teleplay), a late-night television slot broadcast nationally but of interest only to a small group of critics and afficionados.

During the same time, Schroeter also began to be recognized abroad, but it was by institutional insiders, such as Pierre-Henri Deleau of the Quinzaine des Réalisateurs, the experimental wing of the Cannes Film Festival, and Henri Langlois of the Cinémathèque Française. When Schroeter in the late 1970s and early 1980s won wider acclaim with four feature films, *Nel regno di Napoli* (*The Kingdom of Naples*, 1978), *Palermo oder Wolfsburg* (*Palermo or Wolfsburg*, 1980), *Tag der Idioten* (*Day of the Idiots*, 1981), and *Liebeskonzil* (*Lover's Council*, 1982), the New German Cinema was in its final phase. By the time he returned to feature filmmaking with *Der Rosenkönig* (*The Rose King*), released in 1986, it was history.

To be able to appreciate Schroeter's work, considering his membership in the New German Cinema's "queer wing"—including Ulrike Ottinger and Rosa von Praunheim—is more illuminating. This wing had strong roots in experimental and non-fiction film and shared Schroeter's interest in performance—an interest that most of its members would retain even after moving into feature filmmaking, and that, along with an interest in developing a queer aesthetic, accounts for this wing's peripheral position in a national cinema shaped by bourgeois tastes and consumption habits.[8] It bears noting that many of the qualities Kuhlbrodt identifies in Schroeter's early work are classic characteristics of Queer Cinema. Schroeter's casting, choreography, and *mise-en-scène* are queer through and through: several of his films unapologetically eroticize the male body; his gender non-conforming performers embody and enact transgressive desires—their slow, drawn-out movements, stylized embraces, ritualistic kisses, and obsession with blood and tears expand the codes of the erotic and reformulate traditional human relations;[9] and his

8 Von Praunheim made the first gay political advocacy documentary in Germany, *It Is Not the Homosexual Who Is Perverse, But the Situation in Which He Lives* (1971), and went on to make many films about gay culture, gay sex, and AIDS. Ottinger became famous for *Madame X: An Absolute Ruler* (1977) and other films that had radically lesbian-feminist politics. Both filmmakers were long considered by the established press to be "minor" examples of the New German Cinema. For a detailed positioning of Schroeter and his queer peers in the context of the New German Cinema, see Caryl Flinn, *The New German Cinema: Music, History and the Matter of Style* (Berkeley: University of California Press, 2003), p. 178. Flinn argues that the elements of kitsch and camp that inhere in this queer wing's style faced resistance in the New German Cinema's anti-formalist climate. For a book-length study of queerness in German film, see Kuzniar.

9 On the *Grand Guignol* qualities of Schroeter's style, which shows the influence of one of his literary idols, Comte de Lautréamont and his sextet of prose cantos, *Les Chants de Maldoror*, see James Quandt, "Magnificent Obsession," in *Artforum* (New York), vol. 50 no. 9 (May 2012), pp. 252–262.

films break down normative standards of beauty and behavior, creating, among other things, a jarring contrast to the real-life settings in which Schroeter positions them. Finally, their suffused emotionality enables Schroeter's films to mobilize affective registers vital to a queer culture frequently under attack by normative, homophobic society. All these qualities make Schroeter's cinema exemplary of a specifically queer kind of world-making.[10]

This queer vision comprises biographical as well as cultural-historical factors. Schroeter had a lonely childhood during which he suffered more than his share of homophobic violence, yet the support of his mother helped him get to a point in his late teenage years when he was able to move into communities that mirrored his own sexual and artistic proclivities. Von Praunheim and Schroeter were lovers for five months following their encounter in December 1967 at the 4th Festival International du Cinéma Expérimental in Knokke-le-Zoute, Belgium.[11] Their affair led to a life-long friendship and an initially close collaboration.[12] Schroeter credits their relationship with launching his career as a filmmaker, which he soon organized around a group of friends and collaborators, notably Christine Kaufmann, Carla Aulaulu, and Magdalena Montezuma, all of whom would appear regularly in his early films (Montezuma until her untimely death in 1984).[13]

Schroeter and his entourage were but a small segment of an emerging counterculture led by a spirit of artistic and sexual experimentation

10 A good summary of the thematic and stylistic concerns of contemporary queer cinema can be found in Rosalind Galt and Karl Schoonover, *Queer Cinema in the World* (Durham, NC: Duke University Press, 2017).

11 See Xavier García Bardón, "EXPRMNTL. An Expanded Festival. Programming and Polemics at EXPRMNTL 4, Knokke-le-Zoute, 1967," in *Cinema Comparat/ive Cinema*, vol. 1 no. 2 (Spring 2013), pp. 57–58. Available at: www.ocec.eu/cinemacomparativecinema/index.php/en/15-n-2-forms-in-revolution/133-exprmntl-an-expnded-festival-programming-and-polemics-at-exprmntl-4-knokke-le-zoute-1967. The festival gave Schroeter his first exposure to American underground cinema, particularly Gregory Markopoulos's *Twice a Man* (1963). Indeed, its fourth edition boosted the European experimental film scene, because, like the 1966 Mixed Arts Festival in New York, it provided a forum for filmmakers to meet artists of various disciplines. See also Birgit Hein's brief account of the festival in *Film im Underground* (Frankfurt am Main: Ullstein, 1971), pp. 133–136.

12 See Walter Schobert's biographical sketch of Schroeter's first ten years in Sebastian Feldmann, et al., eds., *Werner Schroeter* (Munich: Hanser Verlag, 1980), p. 193. Schroeter collaborated with von Praunheim on the film *Grotesk—Burlesk—Pittoresk* (1968). He also performed in von Praunheim's film *Schwestern der Revolution* (Sisters of the Revolution, 1969), and assisted von Praunheim with other projects.

13 Details of Schroeter's visit to Knokke and the productive years that followed it are relayed in his autobiography *Tage im Dämmer, Nächte im Rausch* (Berlin: Aufbau Verlag, 2011), pp. 51–59. Schroeter credits von Praunheim (born Holger Mischwitzky) with motivating him to channel his creative energy into concrete endeavors. While Schroeter met Carla Aulaulu through von Praunheim (who also married her), he had already met Montezuma (born Erika Kluge) in the mid-1960s in Heidelberg (Schroeter, *Tage im Dämmer*, p. 44). Schroeter was fascinated by her moodiness and gave her the name under which she would become known. The name comes from one of the characters in a book Schroeter was reading when he met Kluge, *Little Me*, by Patrick Dennis, which was a fictional, parodistic biography of a character named Maybelle Schlumpfert, a celebrity-obsessed wannabe film and television star. Schlumpfert's nemesis is named Montezuma (Schroeter, p. 44).

that redefined beauty in erotic terms and celebrated sex for its own sake—that is, for the purpose of pleasure and personal fulfillment. But it was not merely its celebration of unconventional or taboo forms of sexuality that made this new bohemia queer. As queer theorist José Esteban Muñoz has pointed out with regard to the alternative art scene of New York's Greenwich Village in the 1960s, the spirit of bohemia entailed a rejection not only of bourgeois sexual mores, but also of how bourgeois society understood work, productivity, and professional accomplishment in the industrial age[14]—a mindset Herbert Marcuse in his influential analysis of late capitalist society, *Eros and Civilization*, has famously characterized as "the performance principle."[15] Guided as it is by Marcuse's critical framework, Muñoz's assessment of queer art's capacity to disrupt the performance principle can also be applied to Schroeter's queer bohemian approach to art and life. In his early films we see a similar rejection—or "great refusal," in Marcuse's terms—of industrial society's (and industrial cinema's) idealization of functionality, and a rejection, too, of the notion of time defined by productivity and efficiency.

From this perspective, many of the qualities identified by early formalist approaches to Schroeter, such as Kuhlbrodt's, acquire a distinctly queer character and charge. The distention of time, for example, that characterizes the rejection of normative industrial time in Schroeter's films is not the result of an orthodox minimalism, but of bohemian languor and queer decadence. Frequently swooning, daydreaming, or inhabiting some form of trance or exuberant state, Schroeter's performers extend their queer eros to all aspects of human relations. They live by what they feel. And once one understands their use of gestures to be synecdochic of the *mise-en-scènes* that engulf them, one is moved to ascribe a specifically queer character to Schroeter's images. Gestures and images that a formalist perspective would neutrally describe as fragmented can be understood to constitute what Muñoz, discussing 1960s queer performance art, terms "landscapes of ornamentation."[16] Their ornate excess makes the artist's use of the everyday and the ephemeral readable as an act of resistance against "the coercive practicality of the performance principle."[17] In this realm a performer's failures may hold utopian potential in their very rejection of perfectionism, which may be read not as a botched act but as a politically salutary enactment of difference.[18]

The applicability of this queer theoretical framework to Schroeter becomes even more evident when one considers that Muñoz developed it in part through an engagement with Andy Warhol's work, which was also influential on Schroeter. Most films Schroeter made before *Nel regno di Napoli* are nearly plotless ex-

14 José Esteban Muñoz, *Cruising Utopia* (New York: NYU Press, 2008), pp. 133–136.

15 Herbert Marcuse, *Eros and Civilization: A Philosophical Inquiry into Freud* (Boston: Beacon Press, 1974 [1st ed. 1955]), pp. 35, 44–48.

16 Muñoz, p. 141.

17 Muñoz, p. 135.

18 Muñoz, p. 154. Muñoz draws on the theory of Ernst Bloch for his definition of utopia.

plorations of the time-based qualities of performance, assisted or enhanced by a number of technical/aesthetic devices familiar from Warhol's films. These include a static or minimally moving camera, long takes, and even dual-screen projection, while retaining a central interest in performance. As is typical of many marginal cinemas, performance in Schroeter is enabled by the goodwill of the members of the artist's circle—almost never is there any financial compensation. This liminal artisanal mode often triggers a blurring of life and art, which in turn produces a particular kind of performer, a personality whose character, persona, and relationship to the filmmaker and to other performers and crew become part of their impromptu performances.

When Schroeter describes his performers Aulaulu and Montezuma as stars, he uses the term with an irony reminiscent of Warhol's concept of "superstars."[19] The affinity with Warhol's cinema inevitably culminates in Schroeter's casting of Warhol performer Candy Darling in *Der Tod der Maria Malibran* (*The Death of Maria Malibran*, 1971). It should be pointed out, however, that there are also several profound differences between Schroeter's and Warhol's cinema. Warhol's New York studio space, the famous Factory—a social hub as much as an artist's workspace—helped enable a close link between Warhol's performative personalities, the films they appeared in, and the social scenes of which they were a part. The effects of this synergy fully unfolded by virtue of Warhol's trademark extension of a camera take to the full length of a reel, which turned the performances of Warhol's superstars into "seamless expressions of their own charged social space."[20]

By contrast, Schroeter's itinerant mode of filmmaking made for a much smaller, more hermetic scene of collaborators, a small traveling stock company. Their performances were closely shaped by the artistic, musical, and literary tastes of their director—notably Schroeter's passion for opera and his great interest in the canon of bourgeois tragic drama, which he frequently asked his performers to recite. Their off-camera lives had fewer ways of filtering into their on-camera work than was the case with Warhol's performers. Rather than evolving organically into a sustained act lasting the duration of a full reel, performance in Schroeter functions like *bricolage* assembled by the filmmaker according to his personal interests and pre-conceived plans. It is part of a set of practices characteristic of Underground Cinema in general.

19 Schroeter, *Tage im Dämmer*, p. 59. Schroeter (p. 56) compares Aulaulu's self-styled persona to Marilyn Monroe, and argues that she and Montezuma nicely complemented one another. He describes Aulaulu as the "comedian with the philosophical profile *vis-à-vis* the philosopher Montezuma with the tragic face." [Author's translation] At the same time, he does not regard his performers as commercial stars in the traditional sense. See also Quandt, "Magnificent Obsession," for an evocative description, particularly of Montezuma's acting style.

20 Callie Angell, "'Our Movies': Art-Making, Personality, and Social Space in Warhol's Factory," in Debra Miller, ed., *Out of the Shadow: Artists of the Warhol Circle Then and Now* (Newark, DE: University Gallery, University of Delaware, 1996), pp. 62–63.

UNDERGROUND BEGINNINGS: 1968–1969

In 1968 Schroeter made numerous 8mm films. Many were homages to one of Schroeter's great idols, Maria Callas. For these films, Schroeter processed found art of the diva—press images, stills from opera sets, and cover art from Callas's recordings—into a variety of densely textured films that use their found materials to great effect.[21] These early films already allow us to glean what Marc Siegel in his essay in the present volume terms "the diva's dialectic": in an articulation of fandom characteristic of gay culture, Schroeter's seizing on the death of grand-opera divas such as Callas and Maria Malibran constitutes the ultimate expression of a life lived without compromise—that is, passionately, and, more often than not, tragically. Other films of that same year consisted of what Schroeter himself has described as "film *collages*."[22] The *collage* structure—edited-together scenes of Kaufmann, Aulaulu, Montezuma, and others listening and singing to music, reciting text, or improvising mythical or dramatic characters—carried over into a new group of films whose greater length and structural complexity was enabled by Schroeter's acquisition of a 16mm camera. These were *Aggression* (1968), *Neurasia* (1968), *Argila* (1969), and *Eika Katappa* (1969).[23]

Aggression is an interesting early example of Schroeter's repurposing of real space. But rather than functioning, in the manner of his future films, as a stage for stylized performances or enactments of dramatic figures, the parks, cafés, stairwells, and restroom entrances Schroeter uses for this film are claustrophobic backdrops for various acts of sexual harassment suffered by a young woman (Heidi Lorenzo) at the hands of an unidentifiable man. While the camera never loses sight of the woman's anguished face, the man is shown only from the back, as he pushes up against her, lies on top of her in bed, or manhandles her from just beyond the frame. The film humanizes the female victim while turning her male aggressor into an impersonal yet real threat.[24]

Schroeter then complicates this binary through several devices: a female voice-over monotonously recites text fragments. We don't know whether it is the voice of the woman we see on screen, but some of the text passages we hear seem to describe the on-screen woman's emotional attachment to the male aggressor, bringing to mind the phenomenon of victims'

21 Schroeter in his autobiography (p. 55) explicitly likens the found materials he processed via enlargement, double exposure, split screen, and text bubbles to a form of recycled waste. Citing the critic Frieda Grafe's labeling of them as "*Kulturschutt*" (cultural rubble), Schroeter (p. 61) thus places himself in the tradition of underground filmmakers like Kenneth Anger, Bruce Conner, and Jack Smith.

22 Schroeter, *Tage im Dämmer*, p. 54. The German term used by Schroeter is *Filmcollagen*.

23 *Aggression* is included on the DVD of *Willow Springs* and *Tag der Idioten*, *Argila* on the DVD of *Eika Katappa* and *Der Tod der Maria Malibran*, both issued by Filmmuseum München. *Neurasia* awaits preservation.

24 This choreography accounts for the fact that the identity of the actor who performed the part of the male aggressor remained unidentified for many years. Sebastian Feldman, in his annotated filmography for the volume he co-edited on Schroeter, mentions Knut Koch as a possibility, but adds a question mark. See Feldmann, "*Aggression*," in Feldmann et. al., p. 197. This question mark has finally been removed. See Stefan Drössler's updated filmography in this volume.

dependency on their abusers.[25] Other statements consist of *petit-bourgeois* platitudes leveled against the counterculture. The voice-over laments a loosening of social mores and urges that society rebuild itself on liberal yet Christian values. This was conservative middle-class culture's characteristic response to the sexual revolution and the advent of Women's Lib. The repetitive reciting of these lines suggests that the woman shown on screen may have internalized the very ideology that oppresses her. As it rotates through the same scenes of attacks against the woman, the film turns into a powerful essay on the vicious cycle of sexual aggression. Violence, as the final scene of the woman standing before her attacker's lifeless body suggests, begets more violence, cathartic as it may be in some instances.[26] The film's highly stylized nature underscores the real-life syndrome its title invokes.

Schroeter's next two films, *Neurasia* and *Argila*, garnered him recognition at the West

Aggression (1968, top)
Neurasia (1968, middle and bottom)

25 The disembodied female voice is a central feature of Schroeter's use of sound in many of his films. It is a mark of his fragmented aesthetics, but can more specifically be related to the phenomenon of the disembodied voice that is valorized by feminists for eluding the semantic constraints of the patriarchal symbolic.

26 Sebastian Feldman mentions Rudolf Thomé's short films of late-1960s bohemian Munich in conjunction with *Aggression*. *Aggression* also merits discussion in relation to feminist filmmaking of the period. While the final scene retains some ambiguity as to who caused the man's death, the implication that it was the woman, who may have acted in a sudden but completely calm manner, makes for an intriguing comparison with, for instance, Chantal Akerman's *Jeanne Dielman, 23, quai du Commerce, 1080 Bruxelles* (1975), notwithstanding the formal differences between both films.

German festival for experimental film, Hamburger Filmschau, in 1969. *Neurasia* consists of a series of *tableaux* of Aulaulu, Montezuma, Rita Bauer, and Steven Adamczewski performing songs, dancing, and gesticulating in a slow, ritualistic manner on makeshift sets, some of which cast dramatic shadows. Montezuma mostly strikes moody, at times haughty, poses. Aulaulu blissfully enacts a Marilyn Monroe-type musical performance, while Bauer and Adamczewski sit silently on the side, reminiscent of certain performers in some of Warhol's *tableaux*, with Bauer observing the action topless from the margins of the stage and Adamczewski strumming his guitar. These acts share a ludic spirit in their unrehearsed play of gestures. In Schroeter's films, *bricolage* is a sensual process that makes viewers feel the performers' passion and engagement. Schroeter's cinema of stylized if deliberately amateurish or imperfect gestures and fleeting allusions to popular culture has a long tradition in queer circles—for instance, in the experimental wing of the downtown New York dance scene (exemplified by such dancers as Freddy Herko),[27] but also in mundane acts of queer fandom as practiced, for instance, by gay men re-enacting their favorite movie scenes. The way Adamczewski and Montezuma handle Aulaulu as she collapses in performed hysteria is reminiscent of feverish Hollywood melodramas that queer audiences re-perform in a utopian spirit, refusing to separate victimization and suffering from resistance and survival.[28]

The improvised nature of the performances in *Neurasia* belies the film's intricately crafted structure, which was shaped by the music Schroeter chose for his cast to perform to, and by his editing, which gave him ultimate control over the duration and sequencing of the takes. The carefully edited structure of Schroeter's cinema becomes even more evident in his next film, *Argila*, through the elaborate visual effects achieved by its double-screen projection. According to his autobiography, the reason Schroeter conceived *Argila* as a double-screen film was to give spatial expression to the relationship triangle between a young man (Sigurd Salto), a woman his age (Magdalena Montezuma), and an older woman (Gisela Trowe). Their various on-screen constellations are doubled by the projection, whereby the image projected on the left side is re-projected on the right in flipped form and with approximately 30 seconds delay.[29] Schroeter leaves the flipped and re-projected sequence intact, but adds two vectors of asymmetry. A time delay between both projections creates an undulating visual tension between both sides. At times, we see both images mirroring each other in startling symmetry. At other times, when the right image has not yet "caught up" with the left one, there is a visual dialogue, with one image seemingly commenting on the other. This contrast is enhanced by the fact that the left reel is printed in black & white, and the right in color.

27 See, for example, Muñoz's discussion of Herko's "flawed" performances (Muñoz, pp. 147–168).

28 However, Schroeter stated that the only film he was truly influenced by was Carl Theodor Dreyer's *La Passion de Jeanne d'Arc* (*The Passion of Joan of Arc*, 1928), whose style is referenced in *Les Flocons d'or*.

29 Schroeter, *Tage im Dämmer*, p. 63.

Argila (1969)

Argila is thus only intermittently symmetrical. Images mirror each other just long enough to produce the impression that, as Schroeter puts it, each character is his or her own mirror image, his or her own "counterfigure."[30] Retarding narrative flow to give the impression of simultaneity, Schroeter complements the film's queer visuals with a queer temporality that foregrounds the emotional and situational—that is, ultimately melancholic—nature of love stories. According to Schroeter, the delayed second image registers as the memory of the first. Thus fusing two temporal levels into one, Schroeter effectively identifies cinema's presentness to always already carry its own past.[31] The sound, however, does not replicate the visual logic of the double projection. It draws on both reels, but never at the same time. While the image comprises the temporal dimension of present and past, the sound, according to Schroeter, adds a third one—that of the future—whereby, as he states in his comments on the film, all three levels are fused into the dimension of the eternal.[32]

Argila's double projection inevitably invites comparison to Warhol's double-screen films, particularly to *The Chelsea Girls* (1966). Similarities, however, remain limited.[33] In contrast to *The Chelsea Girls*, *Argila*'s two images overlap slightly in the middle. *Argila* consists of only two reels, which, once started, unspool side by side in fixed relation. *The Chelsea Girls* comprises twelve separate reels that, while locked into sequence by Warhol's instructions, require discrete handling by the projectionist, making each screening a uniquely timed event. Of course, any double-screen film amplifies interpretive possibilities. The fact, however, that each reel in Warhol's film consists of a full camera take instead of separate takes edited together as in *Argila* makes Warhol's film fundamentally performance-based, whereas performance in *Argila* is but one vector. A densely crafted essay that includes recitations of pre-selected text passages from Lautréamont, Schroeter's film only comes together in the editing phase. As such, the film should be placed within a tradition of experimental cinema that regards film first and foremost as a mental structure whose individual particles have spatio-temporal equivalence.[34]

30 Schroeter, p. 63. The term "counterfigure" is my own translation of Schroeter's term "*Gegenfigur*."

31 Schroeter, p. 63. See also Feldmann, "*Argila*," p. 116. According to Feldmann, spectators want to follow the left image for narrative clues but get distracted by the lusciousness of the color image. Anxiety develops that one misses something on one side while being pulled to the other. This pull towards the sensuous, we may add, is another instance of Schroeter queering spectatorship.

32 Schroeter does not say how his use of sound achieves this effect, but the asynchronicity between image and sound is notable. Also, of the two voices Schroeter records for the film, only one belongs to an on-screen performer, Gisela Trowe. The other is unidentifiable.

33 While Schroeter credits the Knokke film festival with exposing him to underground filmmakers, it is not clear which Warhol films he may have been familiar with at the time of making *Argila*. Of Warhol's two double-screen films, it is highly unlikely Schroeter would have been familiar with the first, *Inner and Outer Space* (1965). It is possible he would have heard or read about *The Chelsea Girls*, even if he may not have seen it at that point. From the late 1960s/early 1970s onwards, some of Warhol's later films, such as *Lonesome Cowboys* (1967) and *Blue Movie* (1968), were distributed theatrically in Germany.

34 One approach to this type of cinema is through philosophy—specifically Gilles Deleuze's theory of the crystal

Eika Katappa is the final film of this phase of Schroeter's career, and already constitutes something of an early peak—a summary of the various artistic techniques he had developed as a filmmaker in less than two years. Like Schroeter's previous films, *Eika Katappa* is highly structured. However, its internal architecture is not immediately apparent because spontaneity and improvisation are integral to its artistic concept. Its multiple sets and locations are made up of at best loosely scheduled way stations of a three-month road trip, during which Schroeter shot the film with nothing but a brief handwritten treatment that he kept rewriting on the journey as a tenuous guide.[35] Schroeter only met several of its cast members during the trip and spontaneously invited them to be part of the project. The film is subdivided into nine fairly lengthy segments separated only by brief moments of black leader that lack chapter headings (for clarity's sake, however, the following discussion will refer to them via chapter numbers). Their respective themes are a kaleidoscope of Schroeter's life-long obsessions: love, death, suffering, and the climactic moments of his favorite operas—all performed with pathos and exalted gestures, accompanied by an eclectic soundtrack featuring opera as well as German and international pop music.[36]

Chapter 1 revolves around the topic of religious martyrdom, which has long resonated in gay culture and also courses through Schroeter's later work, including *Der Rosenkönig*. First we see Montezuma as the stigmata-bearing nun Therese von Konnersreuth. Then Schroeter dramatizes the suffering, death, and funeral procession of St. Sebastian.[37] Chapter 2, set at a Heidelberg amphitheater, a quarry, and a cathedral, re-enacts parts of the Nibelungen myth that focus on the death of Siegfried (Sigurd Salto) and his being mourned by Kriemhild (Magdalena Montezuma).[38] Chapter 3 places the theme of death, suffering, and salvation in a modern context through the portrait of a tragic star (Carla Aulaulu), who turns from a vivacious performer into a mechanical wind-up doll before dying a tragic death on the road. Her final words, an indication of queer bohemia's rejection of the performance principle and a testimony to the queer spirit of survival,

image. For a detailed discussion of Schroeter's cinema within a Deleuzian framework, see Michelle Langford, *Allegorical Images: Tableau, Time and Gesture in the Cinema of Werner Schroeter* (Bristol, UK: Intellect, 2006).

35 Schroeter, pp. 65–67. Schroeter cut his seven hours of footage down to a version that ran 144 mins.

36 Schroeter, pp. 65–71. Schroeter's autobiography has a detailed description of the making of the film.

37 See Feldmann, "*Eika Katappa*," pp. 123–132. Feldmann's description, which supports my summary of the nine chapters of *Eika Katappa*, draws on Schroeter's own summary of the film, published in Eva M. J. Schmid and Frank Scurla, eds., *Werner Schroeter. Filme 1968–1970* (documentation issued by Volkshochschule Recklinghausen/Studienkreis Film-Filmclub Ruhr-Universität Bochum, 1970). See Feldmann also for a detailed listing of the various music pieces used by Schroeter for the soundtrack.

38 This segment exemplifies Schroeter's eclectic use of music in his early films, ranging from opera to German pop music (*Schlager*). For a detailed discussion of this topic, see Caryl Flinn's essay in this volume. For a discussion of Schroeter's use of the music of Caterina Valente in this segment of *Eika Katappa*, and for a larger discussion of Valente's music, see Roy Grundmann, "Mehr als nur eine Geschmacksfrage: Über die widersprüchliche Valenz der Valente," in *Montage AV* (Marburg: Schüren), vol. 26 no. 2 (2018), pp. 206–227.

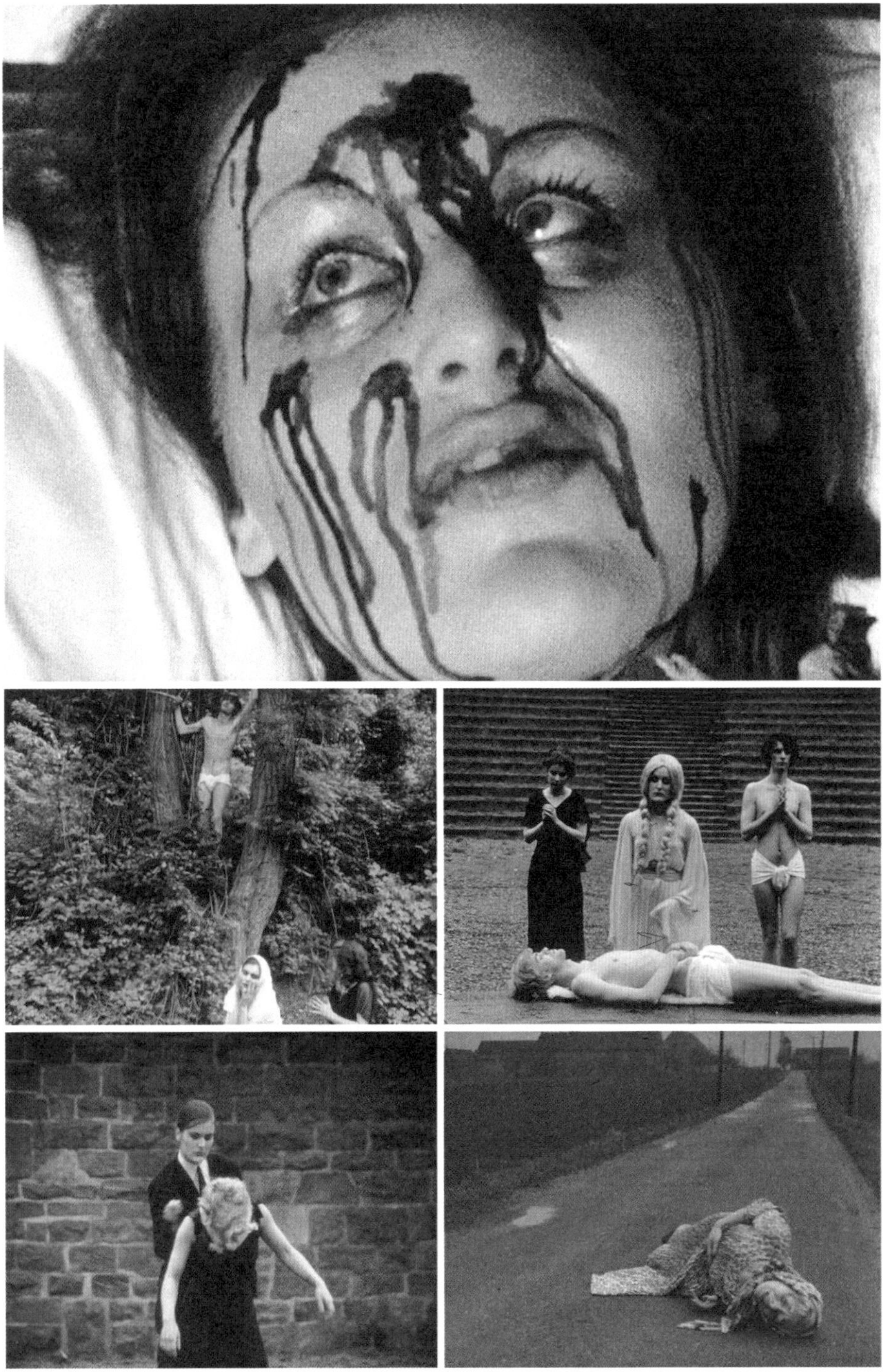

Eika Katappa (1969)

Eika Katappa

deaths, are intended to dramatize the dehumanizing nature of modern life.[40] This segment also uses prominent outdoor locations in the city of Rome, whose eternal splendor it recasts in a menacing light.[41] Chapter 6 is devoted to another opera, Puccini's *Tosca*. As with his treatment of *Rigoletto*, Schroeter presents key moments of the text out of order (the segment starts with Tosca's suicide) and emphasizes the topics he deems most important[42]—in this case, not Tosca's love for Cavaradossi, who is executed, but her relationship to Scarpia, whom she kills personally. As with the *Rigoletto* segment, Schroeter uses mostly outdoor locations, which stand in for some of the opera's original setting, including Castel Sant'Angelo, for which Schroeter had no shooting permit.[43]

Chapter 7 is set in and around Naples, where Schroeter was joined by von Praunheim, who assisted him with the filming. For the segment's main story he cast local Neapolitans. It centers on a handsome youth, Mario, who whisks

are "life is very precious—even right now."[39] In Chapter 4, Montezuma, in a cross-dressing part reminiscent of queer German cinema of the Weimar period, plays the title character of Giuseppe Verdi's opera *Rigoletto*, a hunchbacked jester, whose daughter ends up sacrificing her life in a web of intrigues involving her father and the lecherous Duke for whom he works. Chapter 5, which is the film's centerpiece, does not refer to a specific text or myth. Its scenes, which are set against urban and industrial backdrops and mostly feature young men standing in isolation or dying various

39 The segment's music includes waltzes and Ophelia's coloratura aria from the 1868 opera *Hamlet* by Ambroise Thomas. A scene in a shabby contemporary bar features original dialogue and music from the soundtrack of the 1962 German crime thriller *Das Gasthaus an der Themse* (*The Inn on the River*, dir. Alfred Vohrer), including a Mackie Messer-type *moritat* breathily intoned by Elisabeth Flickenschildt that is noticeably—that is, nearly as artificially as in Schroeter's own films—post-dubbed.

40 The image on page 23 that shows Sigurd Salto against an industrial backdrop is actually taken from the film's final segment, which reiterates the visual theme of Chapter 5.

41 Feldmann (p. 125) compares Schroeter's depiction of Rome to Luis Buñuel's indictment of the city as site of death and suffering from his film *L'Age d'or* (1930).

42 Feldmann, p. 129.

43 Feldmann, p. 129.

another youth, Carlo, away from his family against the objections of Carlo's father. The scene in which the father finds his son's lifeless body lying on the Riviera di Chiaia once again demonstrates Schroeter's knack for staging his stylized but small-scale dramas in prominent locations. The soundtrack, too, gestures towards collapsing art and life. Schroeter once again draws upon classical music, this time by Richard Strauss (*Im Abendrot* and *Vier letzte Lieder*, both settings of verses by Joseph von Eichendorff) and by Wolfgang Amadeus Mozart (Piano Concerto no. 17 in G major); but he also uses unsubtitled sync sound in the confrontation between Carlo and his father.[44] The scene showing Mario setting out for Capri to lay Carlo's body to rest is reminiscent of queer filmmaker Gregory Markopoulos's depiction of New York Harbor in *Twice a Man* (1963), and demonstrates the influence of American underground film on Schroeter. Chapter 8, for which Robert van Ackeren did the camerawork, is an homage to yet another opera, Verdi's *La Traviata*. Gisela Trowe is the aging prostitute Violetta, whose decline is visually paralleled by the burning candle positioned next to her. This and the previous segment exemplify particularly well queer art's non-normative perception of time. The slow, drawn-out character of the scenes that show Mario's passage to Capri and his handling of Carlo's corpse on the pasture reference a mythological timelessness that sidesteps normal concepts of time, while the prominent display of the flickering candle in the segment about Violetta allegorizes the cruelties that attach themselves to the passing of time in a patriarchal culture that treats women like mere tools and objects. Chapter 9 has been characterized as a fireworks-like finale, in which visual motifs from the previous segments recur.[45] These, however, are no mere repetitions of previous scenes, but consist of alternate takes featuring new angles and different groupings of shots. The segment has a tongue-in-cheek quality. Schroeter uses pop music ("Save the Last Dance for Me"), and

Eika Katappa

44 Feldmann, p. 130.
45 Kuhlbrodt, p. 24.

with deadpan wit films himself directing the actor playing Mario in Chapter 7.

GETTING DOWN TO BASICS: ART, POLITICS, AND STATE-SPONSORED UNDERGROUND FILMS

If negative utopia (as understood by Theodor W. Adorno) is founded on the insight that it is impossible to live right in a false society, positive utopia insists on precisely this possibility. Schroeter's determination to find dignity in suffering and beauty in ugliness has earned him the reputation of being a proponent of positive utopia.[46] But the question of utopia, to the extent that "utopianism" refuses to engage with the real world, begs another: what is Schroeter's relation to politics? Can a cinema that lacks concrete political agendas and frowns on *realpolitik* be called political? For some critics, the answer is Yes. The way Schroeter's theatricality stresses emotions and gestures, the way he puts existing space at the service of his own universe, is said to activate animistic energies that, in our repressive society, enable a widening of existence—a free space in which one can live one's life.[47] Schroeter's counterdesigns to reality create blueprints for living that go beyond the realm of the individual. They furnish their own *Basiskultur*.[48] This view is confirmed by Gertrud Koch, whose essay in this volume historicizes Schroeter's cinema of gestures in the context of late 1960s cine-club revivals of silent films.[49] Far from constituting a strictly archivist or aestheticist revival, such events, as Koch reminds us, were part and parcel of the rapidly politicizing film scene of the late 1960s. Koch's essay gives insight into this link by discussing the animistic energies and emancipatory effect of the cinema of gestures that, as she argues, Schroeter's work shares with silent films. By the mid- to late-1970s, after the generation of '68 had undergone a sense of ideological calcification, watching a Schroeter film was considered to be politically revivifying. For Koch, the exalted mimeticism of Schroeter's films brought back memories of cinephile dinner parties during which the guests, inspired by party music, began to gesticulate in the manner of silent film actors, potentially producing a new lexicon of human interaction. For others, such as Kuhlbrodt, the way Schroeter extracts art's various components from their traditional contexts for audiences to re-experience them in more sensual ways triggered emotions and memories of political activism—moments at which, in Kuhlbrodt's recollection, one used to link arms on the street during political rallies.[50]

46 According to Kuhlbrodt (p. 24), Schroeter is in search of utopia within one's own self. See also my own discussion of *Poussières d'amour* in this volume, which is inspired by queer theory's attention to utopia, specifically to Ernst Bloch's writings.

47 Kuhlbrodt, pp. 24–25.

48 Kuhlbrodt (p. 36) juxtaposes Schroeter's cinema with politically programmatic films that demand intellectual rather than aesthetic processing.

49 See also Schroeter, p. 61. Schroeter himself points out that his films triggered associations with silent cinema. He cites the German critic Frieda Grafe, who characterized *Neurasia* in the influential journal *Filmkritik* as a "silent film with music," seizing on the same asynchronicity that was part of the experience of watching a silent film with musical accompaniment. See Frieda Grafe, "Schauplatz für Sprache: *Neurasia*," in *Filmkritik* (Munich), no. 159 (March 1970), pp. 136–137.

50 Kuhlbrodt, p. 35.

But the mnemonic impulse Schroeter's films are apt to generate is strictly associative. It brings back the feeling of being at rallies, rather than furnishing recollections of a specific rally.[51] For better or worse, it is precisely Schroeter's distance from organized activism that shaped his own politics. Instead of using cinema for political manifestos or retreating into the formal orthodoxy of political modernism, Schroeter's militancy consisted of elevating the personal to the political in a consequential manner. One may call him an anarchist of the imagination.[52] The comparison to anarchism, with its valorization of radical heterogeneity, its distrust of organized politics of any kind, and its interest in ritualistic performance and alternative base cultures, is by no means far-fetched. Anarchism's most visible mouthpiece in the West German left scene was the journal *Unter dem Pflaster liegt der Strand*, a title that translates as "under the pavement lies the beach"—a motto Schroeter himself embraced in word and deed.[53] There is a photograph (see p. 195) that shows him "getting down to basics," lying on a street paved with cobblestones shooting a film on location in the early 1980s. Serendipitous as it may be for the present argument, the image perfectly exemplifies Schroeter's subversiveness, a quality he once described with the ambiguous word *untergründig*—a slightly poetic adjectival form of the German noun *Untergrund*. While referring to the state of being "underground," it also means "subversive" in a broader and at once more literal sense.

The term, discussed by several contributors to this volume, was used by Schroeter in reference to his friend and colleague Fassbinder's attack on Schroeter's critics, who disparaged his films as "mere" underground works that fail to appeal to a mass audience. One indication of how right Fassbinder was in his insistence of a more elastic definition of the term is the fact that, within a year and a half after first picking up a camera, Schroeter found himself travers-

51 Linking Schroeter's gestural cinema to memories of political activism seems rather subjective, yet queer theory, too, has recently begun to mine the gestural in this regard. Muñoz discusses the seemingly apolitical 1960s downtown New York dance scene regarding its potential for sponsoring collectively conceived utopias. One glimpses an intersection between queer theory's interest in dance's utopian impulse and the mnemonic operations Schroeter's cinema has triggered in theorists such as Koch and Kuhlbrodt. Both camps seem to reference a community-shaping experience just out of reach, whether that is because it is already lost or has yet to occur.

52 Towards the end of *Auf der Suche nach der Sonne* (1986), a documentary Schroeter made together with Juliane Lorenz about Ariane Mnouchkine and the Théâtre du Soleil, we hear Schroeter stating in voiceover: "Artists and anarchists—they are in agreement about their refusal to bow to the unbearability of the existing order. They have the courage to break with convention, to break the norm." [Author's translation]

53 The slogan "Unter dem Pflaster liegt der Strand" is commonly attributed to the Situationist movement and has been translated into English with various modifications. The slogan is used as the original German title for a 1975 film by New German Cinema director Helma Sanders-Brahms. However, that film's English-language release title is listed by www.filmportal.de as *Under the Beach's Cobbles*, while its DVD release title was *Under the Pavement Lies the Strand*. Culturally and etymologically, the word "Pflaster" is closely associated with the pre-modern practice of using cobblestones for paving streets. While the image of Schroeter lying on a cobblestone street while shooting a film fits nicely with this older meaning of the word "Pflaster," I have used the more common translation "pavement" as the main reference for the slogan.

ing multiple segments of the cultural sphere: he recruited his cast and crew from the bohemian scene that also fêted him at alternative cine-clubs;[54] by mid-1969, he was receiving recognition at official, if still alternative, film festivals, such as the Hamburger Filmschau. The same year he also garnered the Josef-von-Sternberg-Preis awarded by the Mannheim-Heidelberg International Film Festival in the category "Most Original Film"; and in 1970, he was invited to a subsection of the Cannes Film Festival with *Eika Katappa*.

Earlier in 1970 he attracted support from West German television, which was state-sponsored and acted as a financing agent within the labyrinthine scene of German film subsidy. But that Schroeter gradually was embraced more widely did not entail any large-scale changes in his aesthetics. The agreement he had with his sponsoring network ZDF (Zweites Deutsches Fernsehen, literally "Second German Television") was to retain complete artistic freedom in return for staying within the minuscule budgets he was given. And while, beginning with *Nel regno di Napoli*, his films can no longer be called "underground," in the sense of the mode of production that characterized a work such as, say, *Eika Katappa*, or with regard to the ethos promulgated by the Knokke film festival, many of their qualities remained *untergründig* in one way or another.

While retaining the basic qualities of his earlier films, Schroeter introduced several innovations into the first three films he made with funding from ZDF's *Das kleine Fernsehspiel*. *Der Bomberpilot* (The Bomber Pilot, 1970) was the first Schroeter film to tell a linear story. In *Salome* (1971), for the first time he observed the unity of time, place, and action. *Macbeth* (1971) was his first exposure to making a film with magnetic tape instead of film.

If *Der Bomberpilot* tells a recognizable story, it bears noting that the latter is still rather fragmented, as well as satirical to the point of being absurdist. It focuses on the personal and professional travails of three German women trying to take their career ambitions from Nazi-era Germany to post-World War II America and back to Adenauer Germany. Its found settings, improvised cabaret numbers, and eclectic use of opera, marching music, and high-pitched amateur renditions of Austrian waltzes make the film classic Schroeter—"a not entirely respectable Nazi operetta," as some called it at the time.[55] The three heroines have unshakable confidence in their versatile talents: Carla (Carla Alulaulu) sings operetta and works in a patisserie, Mascha (Mascha Rabben) is a back-to-nature *art nouveau* dancer, and Magdalena (Magdalena Montezuma) is a restorer of church murals, snake dancer, and part-time evening-school teacher for the *Reich*. These diverse skills, so the trio somehow comes to believe, make them ideally poised to aid the project of racial integration in Eisenhower America.

The zeal with which they move from Nazi

54 See Schroeter, p. 60. One such club was run by Ulrike Ottinger in Konstanz.

55 According to Schroeter (p. 81), the label came about in response to him calling Luchino Visconti's *La caduta degli dei / The Damned* "eine seriöse Nazi-Operette" ("a respectable Nazi operetta"), in a review for *Filmkritik*.

settings to American high-school classrooms and back to U.S. airbase cabarets, and the fun Schroeter allows them to have through it all, raised eyebrows. Was *Der Bomberpilot*, in its front-and-center celebration of the human spirit and will to survive, sufficiently aware of the very contradictions it sought to comically exploit? Could the director of avant-garde operas and underground romps be trusted with "historical" material?[56] *Der Bomberpilot* is not a message film. It lacks didactic details about the Nazi period. Schroeter retroactively compared his film to Fassbinder's *Die Ehe der Maria Braun* (*The Marriage of Maria Braun*, 1978), with whose title figure his characters share a determination to reinvent themselves without bothering to examine their past.[57] While their story, in contrast to Fassbinder's mainstream melodrama, does not end fatally, Schroeter misses no opportunity to turn *Der Bomberpilot* into a comical record of their conceits, failures, and what one may call a salutary ineptitude to be efficient Nazi women.[58] The film hides its history lesson in its exaggerated irony, which facilitates its critique while at the same time enabling Schroeter to stay committed to depicting women as suffering martyrs. When Magdalena hears of Hitler's death, she tries to drown herself. The scene parodies several films of Nazi star Kristina Söderbaum, whose characters' resolve to drown themselves to preserve their purity earned her the moniker "Reichs-Water-corpse."[59]

But it is Schroeter's appropriation of real spaces—the gall with which he infiltrates a U.S. Army base and an American high school in Germany, and makes these sites stand in for stateside locations, the slyness with which he recruits their staff for cameos while leaving them in the dark about what kind of film they will be in—that is perhaps the best example of Schroeter being *untergründig*. These scenes in *Der Bomberpilot* foreground not only the *frisson* of their representational context, but the medium itself, whose degraded materiality they make palpable, evoking Frieda Grafe's term "cultural rubble." Straddling home-movie and candid-camera aesthetics, the humorous contrast Schroeter creates between his entourage and the guileless cameo players he recruits harbors its own poetics. Polysemic and opaque at once, these scenes insinuate an underlying continuity between Germany and America.

The effect becomes more concrete towards the end of the film. The late success that *Der Bomberpilot*'s heroines get to enjoy as showgirls performing Wagner, B-movie snake dances, sailor songs, and Zarah Leander-type *Schlager* for American GIs stationed abroad in the late 1960s, when West Germany, with its business

56 Feldmann, "*Der Bomberpilot*," p. 132.
57 Schroeter, p. 80.
58 Michelle Langford makes a similar point when describing the gestures of the heroines as "faulty" in a way that makes viewers skeptical they could ever have performed according to Nazi rules. See Langford, p. 22.
59 For a discussion of this scene's use of sound, see Flinn, pp. 253–254. While I agree with Flinn that Magdalena's putative investment in Aryan purity is not supported by the film's soundtrack, I believe the scene's rather overt allusion to Söderbaum and her roles is still readable as foregrounding Nazi culture's racially motivated sacrificial ideologies.

Der Bomberpilot (1970): Carla Aulaulu, Mascha Rabben and Magdalena Montezuma

leaders and senior administrators (many of them former Nazis), had long been re-embraced by the U.S., seems to prove our heroines right, though not exactly for the reasons they think. Celebrating themselves as the stars of their own German-American variety show in the era of NATO, their *bric-à-brac* cabaret is really a showcase of degraded fragments of hegemonic culture that actually fail to add up to any grand synthesis. Their "de-natured *Gesamtkunstwerk*"[60] becomes an illuminating index both of how individuals cast about in oppressive systems (or careen from one system to another) and of the systems themselves. By getting down to basics, Schroeter unearths a substrata of reality that comprises the underlying conditions of fascism stretching from one continent to another. This approach puts *Der Bomberpilot* closer to films like Jean-Pierre Gorin's documentary *Poto and Cabengo* (1980) than to melodramatic treatments about Germans' inability to mourn history. And it places Schroeter's cinema in the service of a radical materialist historiography worthy of Walter Benjamin.

Reading his films through Benjamin's concept of allegory has become an important contribution to critical discourse on Schroeter, pioneered by Michelle Langford. Benjamin's notion of allegory, with its focus on the fragment, the ruin, and decay, with its attention to the subversion of hierarchies and to conflicting temporalities, and with its identification of melancholy as allegory's central mode and mood, provides a rich set of concepts to apply to Schroeter's artistic approach and his aesthetics, so Langford argues in her book *Allegorical Images: Tableau, Time and Gesture in the Cinema of Werner Schroeter* (2006).[61] Langford discusses several of these aspects in her analysis of *Salome* in the present volume. Focusing on Schroeter's elaborate *collage* of musical pieces and on his cinematographic and choreographic use of the film's location, the temple ruins of Baalbek,

60 See Langford, pp. 9–10, and Flinn, p. 256. Langford credits Ekkehard Pluta with coining this term specifically in relation to Schroeter's filmmaking. The question of a non-synthesizing aesthetic is raised in detail in Flinn's reading of the film. She argues that its featuring of "materialized kitsch" helps audiences engage taboo memories and desires relating to the Nazi period and its aesthetics. Describing what she terms Schroeter's homeopathic introjection of kitsch, Flinn states: "What happens is less a control over undesirable aspects of the past than a momentary embrace, a way of *bringing them into relationship with our present identity.*"

61 Langford, p. 55. See also Flinn, p. 180, for a discussion of links between allegory and queerness.

Lebanon, Langford theorizes the film's vision of chaos and decline as a potentially liberating allegory of decay. She draws an analogy with how Benjamin conceives of the filmic medium—as an explosive device capable of shattering the prison of alienated industrial modernity, "so that now, in the midst of its far-flung ruins and debris, we calmly and adventurously go travelling."[62]

Benjamin's vision may well have inspired cinematographer Robert van Ackeren, whose camera slowly and deliberately scans the ruin set of *Salome*. Indeed, Benjamin's description of the experience afforded by cinema at the peak of modernity evokes spectatorship in all of Schroeter's films. They offer their viewers the unique opportunity to discover, as if for the very first time, the cultural debris Schroeter so sensuously seizes upon. Benjamin's image of the drifting melancholy traveler can be related to Schroeter even more literally. A self-styled dandy and *flâneur* since his teenage years, Schroeter used a fair portion of the funding he received from ZDF to set several of his films in far-flung locations. He had already begun this practice with the pre-ZDF *Eika Katappa*. As became evident with that film's road-movie production mode, traveling to and around foreign locations was a personally enriching experience for Schroeter. In some instances, such travels even became a temporary distraction from the film shoot.[63] Erratic and meandering as his trips often were, they were always an integral part of his cinema, with the physical journey frequently shaping the artistic process of the project at hand, and, in some cases, its semantics. After making *Salome* in Lebanon, Schroeter shot his next film, *Macbeth* (1971), in Germany. But as that film was part of a twin commission that included a second adaptation of Shakespeare's play, directed by Rosa von Praunheim, Schroeter followed von Praunheim to England and Cornwall to assist with the shoot, before making his own version in a Frankfurt TV studio. For *Der Tod der Maria Malibran* (*The Death of Maria Malibran*, 1972), Schroeter and Montezuma traveled to New York for what Schroeter characterized as preparatory work for the film. While the trip facilitated the encounter with and eventual casting of Warhol star Candy Darling, that meeting was not part of the trip's original purpose, and the film itself was shot in Germany and Austria rather than New York.[64]

Like most of Schroeter's films, *Der Tod der Maria Malibran* and *Macbeth* mobilize the trope of the journey in literal and allegorical ways. Both films are about the dissolution of external as well as internal (mental) boundaries[65]—a process indicative of Schroeter's rejection of

62 Langford, p. 153. Langford cites Benjamin's famous essay "The Work of Art in the Age of Mechanical Reproduction," in *Illuminations*, trans. Harry Zohn (London: Fontana Press, 1992), p. 229.

63 Langford (p. 153) links this meandering pattern to the aimlessness of the *flâneur* as described by Benjamin and Baudelaire.

64 Schroeter, pp. 101–105.

65 Kuzniar (p. 116) argues that in Schroeter's cinema "the possibility of a coherent, communicable selfhood—the linchpin of bourgeois ideology—dissolves, with ecstasy taking its place as an antithetical state into which one falls. The mesmerized same-sex gazes of Schroeter's characters [...] bear witness to and instigate a queer transport that disarticulates individuality."

Der Tod der Maria Malibran (1972)

stable hierarchies and readable as a call to embark on an adventurous journey of self-discovery, a painful and bewildering but ultimately thrilling process of personal reinvention. In *Macbeth*, Schroeter portrays schizophrenia as a force that notably precedes the character of Lady Macbeth rather than being exclusively associated with her.[66] In *Der Tod der Maria Malibran* it is less madness than the ecstasy of blind passion that is at the center of the film.[67] To stage it Schroeter picked the dark, cavernous space of a grotto as its setting, which, along with the rooms of a Munich villa used for other scenes, foil any attempt at orienting oneself.[68] As in *Eika Katappa*, the sets—which also included carefully selected outdoor locations, such as the hill behind Munich's Olympic Stadium—visually accentuate the expressive gestures of Montezuma, Darling, and Ingrid Caven, which, as Koch and Siegel point out in their essays, are central to Schroeter's cinema. As Siegel goes on to argue concerning *Der Tod der Maria Malibran*, this aesthetic facilitates an inherently queer vision of diva life, through which Schroeter captures the emotional essence (rather than the biography) of his subject, one of the 19th century's most revered opera stars.[69]

Having gone over-budget for *Der Tod der Maria Malibran*, Schroeter owed ZDF a follow-up film, to be made for half the money. He proposed a small avant-gardist cinematic essay about Marilyn Monroe, but by the time he boarded a plane bound for Los Angeles with the advance in his pocket he had abandoned that idea. The trip was motivated by personal reasons that Schroeter, however, did not disclose

66 Feldmann, "*Macbeth*," p. 144. This non-pathologizing diffusion of madness also characterizes several of Schroeter's later films.

67 See Kuzniar, pp. 120–124, for a discussion of blindness and the unreturned gaze.

68 Feldmann, "*Der Tod der Maria Malibran*," pp. 148–150.

69 Feldmann, p. 149. Some parts of the film explicitly reference the trope of the journey that dramatizes the self as being cast into a world of loss and solitude. Schroeter uses Johannes Brahms' *Alto Rhapsody*, a musical setting of Goethe's poem "Harzreise im Winter" (Winter Journey through the Harz Mountains). For a detailed discussion of Maria Malibran as a rebellious queer woman, see Kuzniar's discussion of Schroeter's use of the singer's biography (Kuzniar, p. 119).

to his sponsor. In California he continued his own journey of self-discovery, which involved learning how to drive and going on the road.[70] When he and his crew did get around to making their film, the result, *Willow Springs* (1973), reflected their unbound thirst for freedom no less than the challenges they incurred to quench it, which stranded them penniless in an inhospitable hamlet in the Mojave desert after which the film is named. *Willow Springs*, as Christine N. Brinckmann argues in her essay in this volume, is neither purely situational in the manner of some of Schroeter's earlier films, nor is there a clearly identifiable forward-moving narrative. It develops its own rhythm, something Brinckmann terms "leaping and lingering," as it moves from one staged *tableau* to another, coming to rest long enough to build atmosphere and allow the relations between its trio of female protagonists, who lure men into their ramshackle house to kill them, to achieve a rich associative density.

A trip is also what enabled Schroeter's next film, *Der schwarze Engel (The Black Angel,* 1974). In 1973 the Goethe Institute in Mexico City invited Schroeter to attend a retrospective of his work and to make a film as part of the Institute's effort to sponsor Mexican-German cultural dialogue. Schroeter was fascinated by Mexico, both for its ancient civilizations and for the rawness of its contradictions as a modern developing country. After touring Mayan ruins, he decided to volunteer with the Red Cross of Mexico City, for which he rode in an ambulance for several weeks.[71] Both influences are visible in the film, but their unresolved co-existence indicates that Schroeter, as he himself admitted, was unable to fully think through the contradictions he found[72]—not to speak of the contradictions of a European director making a film about a culture and people he was bound to remain foreign to, no matter how much he revered that culture and how aware he may have been about his own European background.

Der schwarze Engel features two protagonists, an American blonde (Ellen Umlauf), who in her cliché tourist role obsesses about Mexican folklore, and a black-clad German voyager (Montezuma), whose ambition, however idealistic, to arrive at a "deeper" understanding of the country, aims to facilitate the spectator's transcultural engagement with its myths. Through the interplay of these two characters, Schroeter seeks to capture the complexity of Mexico in a kind of stereoscopic vision. The film also includes footage of a found character, a deaf-mute named Carlos, who, reminiscent of many of the characters in Werner Herzog's cinema, remains enigmatic. In atypical manner, Schroeter includes copious statistical data about modern Mexico's socio-economic problems. But his *collage* approach is of limited use as a meditation on the relation between the film's main themes and the location, Mexico. Schroeter himself called the film "meine mexikanische Katastrophe."[73]

70 For further details, see Schroeter's chapter on the making of the film in his autobiography, pp. 112–118.
71 Schroeter, pp. 137–139.
72 See Feldmann's cogent commentary on the film (Feldmann, pp. 158–164).
73 Schroeter, p. 137.

Der schwarze Engel (1974): Magdalena Montezuma and Ellen Umlauf

This unresolved tension, as Caryl Flinn argues in her essay in this book, is not only part of the film's image world, but also reverberates through Schroeter's music selection. And, as Flinn goes on to demonstrate, it would remain a formal and thematic challenge for Schroeter in his forthcoming projects, particularly *Palermo oder Wolfsburg*. Flinn's essay initiates discussion on an important subject that awaits further debate, particularly within queer studies. On one hand, the closely twined activities of traveling and art-making place Schroeter in a long tradition of European writers, painters, and, more recently, filmmakers, who have sought artistic inspiration from non-European cultures. This tradition has been central especially to queer cinema history, from Eisenstein to Pasolini and from Ulrike Ottinger to Matthias Müller. The globetrotting gay filmmaker is to be distinguished from the "global gay," the well-heeled gay traveler in the age of commercialized mass tourism who is content to experience what is now called "the Global South" through alienated and ultimately exploitative capitalist models of travel. On the other hand, Schroeter's self-proclaimed "Mexican catastrophe" indicates that certain differences that are inherent in white privilege seem to exist even in liminal art-making. If the image of the Benjaminian *flâneur* is still applicable to global queer cinema in the era of late capitalism, it may be so only if equipped with certain caveats acknowledging and addressing white privilege.

Schroeter's next film, *Les Flocons d'or* (1976) has him at his creative peak as a maker of avant-garde / underground films and it also caps that period.[74] He used the modest prize money he received from the 1974 Avant-garde Festival in Toulon for *Willow Springs* to embark on the project. Aesthetically as uncompromising as any of Schroeter's previous films, and once again replicating his artisanal production mode, *Les Flocons d'or* is nonetheless something of a different beast. It took two years to make and required international financing partners (ZDF in Germany and the prominent French art-film company Les Films du Losange), costing well over 100,000 Marks. In addition to featuring Schroeter regulars Montezuma, Caven, Kaufmann, Umlauf, and Ila von Hasperg, the film boasts a cast of art-cinema stars, including Andréa Ferréol, who had already made *La*

74 Schroeter, p. 159. Upon completion of the film in 1976, Schroeter abandoned making films in this vein, both for creative reasons and because these types of productions demanded that cast and crew donated their time and money, which became unsustainable.

Grande Bouffe (*Blow Out*, 1973); Udo Kier, who was appearing in Warhol/Morrissey films; and Bulle Ogier, who had been in *Céline et Julie vont en bateau* (*Celine and Julie Go Boating*, 1974) by Jacques Rivette, a filmmaker whose interest in performance intersects with Schroeter's. The international scope of its cast and production reflects the fact that by the mid-1970s Schroeter had successfully established himself outside Germany. Many of the actors and resources for *Les Flocons d'or* came from France. Notwithstanding its scale and star power, however, *Les Flocons d'or* remained firmly destined for a late-night slot on German television.[75]

Les Flocons d'or (1976):
Carlos Clarens, Magdalena Montezuma, Rainer Will

Schroeter described the film as the final part of an unofficial trilogy that included *Der Tod der Maria Malibran* and *Willow Springs*, in which he sought to combine human tragedy and comedy.[76] The film had four episodes, framed by a prologue and an epilogue: episode 1, "En Cuba," is a 1940s-style fantasy in which Montezuma plays the French spouse of a land baron addicted to heroin; episode 2, "Un Drame de rail," shot at the Bochum railroad yard, is about a woman's romance with a foreign worker that is foiled by her mother; episode 3[77] features Ferréol as a borderline-mad recluse in search of spiritual release; and in episode 4, "Réalité—Vérité!," Udo Kier plays a murderer and sex offender who is chased by an angel of death (Montezuma). The prologue and epilogue, which feature Montezuma as a dark goddess watching Kier build a house of cards, has a fatalist atmosphere that alludes to the proximity of love and death (the homology of both words in French is frequently remarked upon by critics), which Schroeter musically underscores with the "Melons! Coupons!" card trio from Bizet's *Carmen*.

But *Les Flocons d'or* is as notable for the virtuoso way in which it weaves its performances into settings that reference elaborately construed genres. The dialogue-heavy Cuban episode pays homage to Latin American *telenovelas*, but the *mise-en-scène* is cinematic. Montezuma as the alternately distressed and melancholic lady of the house is placed in ornate *tableaux* suggesting a golden cage. Rainer Will plays a Tadzio-like filial character whom Schroeter places in

75 For a detailed account of the production, see Schroeter's autobiography, pp. 154–159.

76 Schroeter, p. 155.

77 While the film's other main episodes are each clearly titled, the third one is marked by two different intertitles following each other within a few minutes, "Cœur brisé" (broken heart) and "Ame meurtrière" (murderous soul).

Les Flocons d'or

symbolically fraught relation to both Montezuma's character and her husband (Carlos Clarens). The visual splendor of the family rooms alternates with visceral close-ups of syringes about to penetrate human skin, and the final scene stages the addict's death as a horror-movie orgy of blood that also alludes to fellatio.

Episode 2 has a poetic realism comparable to French pre-war cinema.[78] Though filmed in color, its images look faded compared to the saturated hues of the previous episode. Schroeter upends a rote story in Fassbinder-like manner: Ferréol's character, Joselle, has an affair with railroad worker Reza that is forbidden by her foster mother and condemned by her sister, Marie (Montezuma), until Reza shockingly sides with the mother out of jealousy over Marie and Joselle's reconciliation. This plot is vividly enacted in the style of silent cinema, replete with slow, "floating" (i.e., unsutured) images and histrionic gestures that undermine the functionality of industrial narrative cinema. The logic of this approach is extended to the film's use of the empty railroad yard. With much of the drama filmed directly on or beside the train tracks, Schroeter's visuals make realism and poetry mutually enhancing coefficients. They transform the derelict environment into a scenario of melancholic decay that allegorizes industrial society and, by extension, its structuring of human relations.

At the same time, by finding beauty in the very fallowness of the industrial structures he films, Schroeter suggests the ruin as a utopian site. Moments of melodrama, like Marie's breakdown or the image of the face of the temporarily detained Joselle behind the window, alternate with references to Schroeter's earlier films that insert glimpses of utopian freedom into the characters' lives. Schroeter visualizes the bond between both sisters by quoting the scene from *Eika Katappa* that symbolizes Mario and Carlo's bond through the "beaking" of the cranes. Such serendipitous poetry performed upon industrial objects "festoons" them, subverting industry's functionality. As

78 See Feldmann, "*Flocons d'or. Goldflöckchen*," p. 172, where he compares it to Jean Renoir's *La Bête humaine* (1938).

Muñoz puts it: "The desire to render the world as ornamented is the desire to see past the limits of the performance principle."[79] Joselle's dream of her and Reza frolicking on a railroad push trolley allegorizes the film camera itself; Joselle's defiantly self-absorbed reverie (the intertitle reads "Je suis libre") on the train tracks exemplifies Schroeter's credo that utopia can spring from the most desolate situations—in Joselle's case, a symphony between love, passion, and dream life (both actual and cinematic) in the face of death.

In the third episode, the narrative recedes, in the manner of *Willow Springs*, in favor of a mood-oriented dramatization of a triangle relationship between Ferréol's manic/melancholic recluse, who, over losing a lover, has retreated to the country with her dogs, and two other women, Bulle Ogier's "murderous soul" *femme fatale* whom Ferréol's character seeks out as an oracle, and Montezuma's similarly dark spirit, who follows Ferréol in pursuit of "living victims for her ravenous soul."[80] Schroeter, to dazzling effect, over-exposes the black & white film stock and achieves a completely new kind of poetics. Whereas episode 2 references a specific historical style, this episode's crisp yet chimeric-looking visuals amplify what Siegfried Kracauer famously identified as the affinities of the photographic medium. The realism inherent in film's capturing of the unstaged, of motion, and of the space beyond the frame, is enhanced, paradoxically, by the overexposure,

Les Flocons d'or

which, however, also abstracts the image into a flat, densely textured surface. Schroeter underscores the artifice through intertextual hints, ranging from early cinema's self-referential framing—as first seen in the Lumières' *Sortie d'usine* (*Workers Leaving the Factory*, 1895) to Dada's cheekily erotic girl-on-a-swing fantasies. One interior set is in the style of Carl Theodor Dreyer (p. 36, bottom left image), but Schroeter also makes astute use of the Avignon location. It is vaguely reminiscent of Hollywood biblical epics, while it also helps him claim real-life public space as a stage for his feverish fantasies.

79 Muñoz, p. 143.
80 Schroeter, quoted in Feldmann, p. 173.

Les Flocons d'or

The title of episode 4 translates as "Reality or Truth?" It subverts the *Heimat* film genre with a tale about a man who, traumatized by childhood and marriage, becomes a child molester. Here, too, film-historical references abound, beginning with the performance of Udo Kier, which vaguely invokes Chaplin and Peter Lorre. His character's name, Franz, alludes to Fassbinder anti-heroes, epitomized by *Berlin Alexanderplatz*'s Franz Biberkopf. Schroeter uses elements from melodrama, New Wave cinema, and contemporary media culture. Franz's loved ones make "diagnostic" statements about him in the style of talking-head interviews. But, as reverse cutting reveals, the place of the camera is not occupied by a TV news team but by another protagonist. Blithely irreverent to the gravity of the topic of child molestation, Schroeter resists moralizing. Instead of using a protagonist-versus-antagonist structure, Schroeter has all characters share the same space. Following his pursuit by Montezuma's "Angel of Death", Franz commits suicide on the mountain, perverting the genre's disingenuous idealization of settings of natural splendor. But Schroeter also parodies certain films of the New German Cinema that were trying to revise classic *Heimat* films by vulgarizing regionally specific characters through hyper-realist use of dialect. By contrast, Schroeter's characters' pronunciation is deliberately fake. *Les Flocons d'or* would be Schroeter's last, and most epic, celebration of artifice within an Underground mode of production.

THEATRICAL FEATURE FILMS AND WIDER RECOGNITION

With his theatrical features *Nel regno di Napoli* (1978) and *Palermo oder Wolfsburg* (*Palermo or Wolfsburg*, 1980) Schroeter took his filmmaking to a new level. This was fueled as much out of a perceived need to evolve artistically as it was by bitterness over not having received any revenue from his films. Theatrical distribution had been foreclosed to them. While retaining some elements from his earlier work, Schroeter conceived *Nel regno di Napoli* from the start as a predominantly realist narrative for which he wrote a full script. And while this film, too, had a low budget, it was produced and promoted according to industry norms.[81] As Gerd Gemünden argues in his essay on Schroeter's two Italian feature films in this volume, Schroeter's decision to film the saga of an Italian family spanning the years 1945–1972 as a linear narrative and according to principles associated with neo-realism did not keep him from infusing it with melodramatic flourishes and visual distanciation devices, such as the announcements of each year in garish pink figures, all of which made French critics call it "*écriture baroque.*"

Closer to Pasolini and Buñuel than Rossellini and De Sica, *Nel regno di Napoli* became Schroeter's calling card as a director of theatrically distributed art cinema. *Palermo oder Wolfsburg*, made directly after *Nel regno di Napoli* and

81 Schroeter, p. 178. Schroeter attributes its success at the Taormina Film Festival in part to the fact that it was professionally promoted. He was able to use the promotion budget for Fassbinder's *Die Ehe der Maria Braun*, which had been withdrawn from the festival.

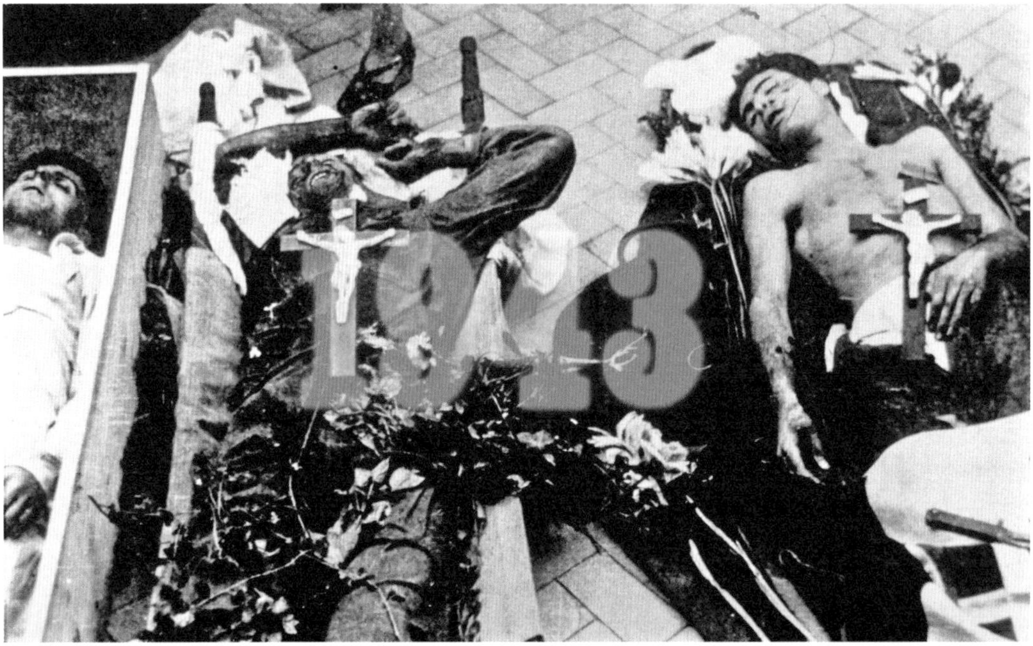

Nel regno di
Napoli (197

Palermo ode
Wolfsburg
(1980)

with the same producer (and, again, with ZDF money), became an even bigger critical success. It tells the story of Nicola, a young Sicilian who comes to Germany to work in the Volkswagen (VW) automobile plant in Wolfsburg, with a mixture of realism and stylization. After finding the story in a discarded newspaper, Schroeter enlisted Italian social-realist writer Giuseppe Fava (who later was killed by the Mafia for his critical stance against them) to write the script.[82] But he supplemented the realist depiction of Nicola's Sicilian backstory, his journey to Wolfsburg and alienated existence at VW, and his ill-fated love for a German woman whose friends he ends up killing, with a heavily stylized courtroom drama that ends with Nicola's own admission of guilt. The ending produces what Gemünden terms "enlightened victimology," by facilitating spectatorial identification with Nicola's tragedy without pandering to mainstream morality.

Palermo oder Wolfsburg earned Schroeter the Golden Bear at the 1980 Berlin Film Festival, the first ever awarded to a German director, and further boosted his reputation as one of the New German Cinema's most original voices.[83] It would be misleading, however, to attribute Schroeter's relatively sturdy cinematic output in the 1980s to his new-found prestige. According to Schroeter's own account, his productivity, which continued apace with three critically praised theatrical features—*Tag der Idioten* (*Day of the Idiots*, 1981), *Liebeskonzil* (*Lover's Council*, 1982), and *Der Rosenkönig* (*The Rose King*, 1986)—and five non-fiction films (to be discussed in the next section), defied the odds he found himself battling, especially early in the decade when he suffered several professional setbacks. In 1980, following a controversial interview he gave to the German weekly *Die Zeit*, the federal state of Bavaria campaigned to have him fired from the production of Richard Strauss's opera *Salome*, which he was scheduled to direct in Augsburg. Schroeter lost the job, but rather than protesting his dismissal, he took the moral high ground by letting his mistreatment stand as evidence of a culture war that was intensifying ahead of federal elections in West Germany. Yet, the widening row between theater management, regional politicians, and nationally renowned cultural critics inevitably reinforced his status as an *enfant terrible*. Already immersed in preparations for an adaptation of Jean Genet's novel *Querelle*, Schroeter was fired from the project by the film's producers, who regarded him as a liability in their funding efforts.[84]

Several other film projects also fell through, for a variety of reasons,[85] but amidst these setbacks Schroeter was approached by a Czech producer and a German journalist-turned-scriptwriter to shoot a feature film set in an insane asylum on location in Prague. He was able to cast recently befriended international art-film star Carole Bouquet. The result was *Tag der Idioten (Day of the Idiots)*, a drama questioning the institutional division between sanity

82 Schroeter, pp. 193–194.
83 Schroeter, p. 199.
84 Schroeter, pp. 213–219. As is well known, the film ended up being directed by Rainer Werner Fassbinder; it would be Fassbinder's final completed film.
85 Schroeter, p. 216.

and insanity. Schroeter's reasoning about what had attracted him to *Querelle* can be extended to *Tag der Idioten*—indeed, to the remaining theatrical feature films of his career. As an outlaw, Genet's anti-hero lives with the very freedom society does not permit itself, and for which it punishes those who dare to revel in it. For Schroeter, the twin qualities of being an outcast and being free enjoin the homosexual with three other figures who would figure prominently in his remaining films—the criminal, the artist, and the insane.

Schroeter has stated that he always felt close to the inner psychic worlds of mad people. They constitute concretely lived transgression, which he has identified as his own motif and reservoir.[86] In *Tag der Idioten*, Bouquet plays Carole Schneider, an eccentric but perfectly sane woman who rebels against society by provoking her own institutionalization in an insane asylum. The story affords Schroeter the opportunity to depict Carole's female ward as a cross-section of the characters his films, plays, and operas typically revolve around. Critic Wolfram Schütte called the film "an allegorical panorama of deeply hurt, crushed women,"[87] who, apart from functioning as clinical case studies of abused victims, personify literary and historical figures like Ophelia and Mary Stuart, not to speak of patriarchy's longstanding victims and outcasts like the betrayed woman and the prostitute.[88] What Schroeter makes Carole share with these women, Schütte argues, is a search for love, which, however, she finds neither inside nor outside institutional confines.[89]

But despite the affinity Carole feels to her inmates, her story departs from the logic of the self-elected outcast exemplified by Genet's characters and by Schroeter's own world of bohemia. Schroeter goes to some length to portray life in the asylum as a place of great imagination, but he does not romanticize it.[90] At the same time, the film makes clear that its protagonist has no place in the world outside. On a temporary leave from the asylum, Carole intrudes on a ballroom dancing rehearsal for a society event, and is depicted as being literally crushed by the formal rigidity of the ritual (and what it represents socially).

Ultimately, *Tag der Idioten* posits the asylum and the world outside as two broken halves of the same whole. Hence, Carole's rebellion has little that inspires, that carries forward. It is as if Schroeter had decided to exchange his trademark positive utopia for its negative counterpart. The film features many scenes staging madness as *Grand Guignol*, some of which, such as the shower sequence between the inmates, have a notably queer, fleetingly utopian feeling to them. Yet, the most intriguing shots are

86 Schroeter, p. 216.
87 Wolfram Schütte, "Werner Schroeter," trans. Jeremy Roth and John King (Goethe-Institut München, 1988/1991). Reprinted in DVD liner notes, *Willow Springs & Tag der Idioten* (Filmmuseum München, 2014).
88 Schütte, *Willow Springs & Tag der Idioten* DVD liner notes.
89 Schütte, *Willow Springs & Tag der Idioten* DVD liner notes.
90 Schütte, *Willow Springs & Tag der Idioten* DVD liner notes. For Schütte the aesthetics of the scene of the inmates' group shower have an operatic feel. The scene, we may add, is not devoid of a certain queer eroticism, because of the palpably anarchic pleasure the women feel in their bodies.

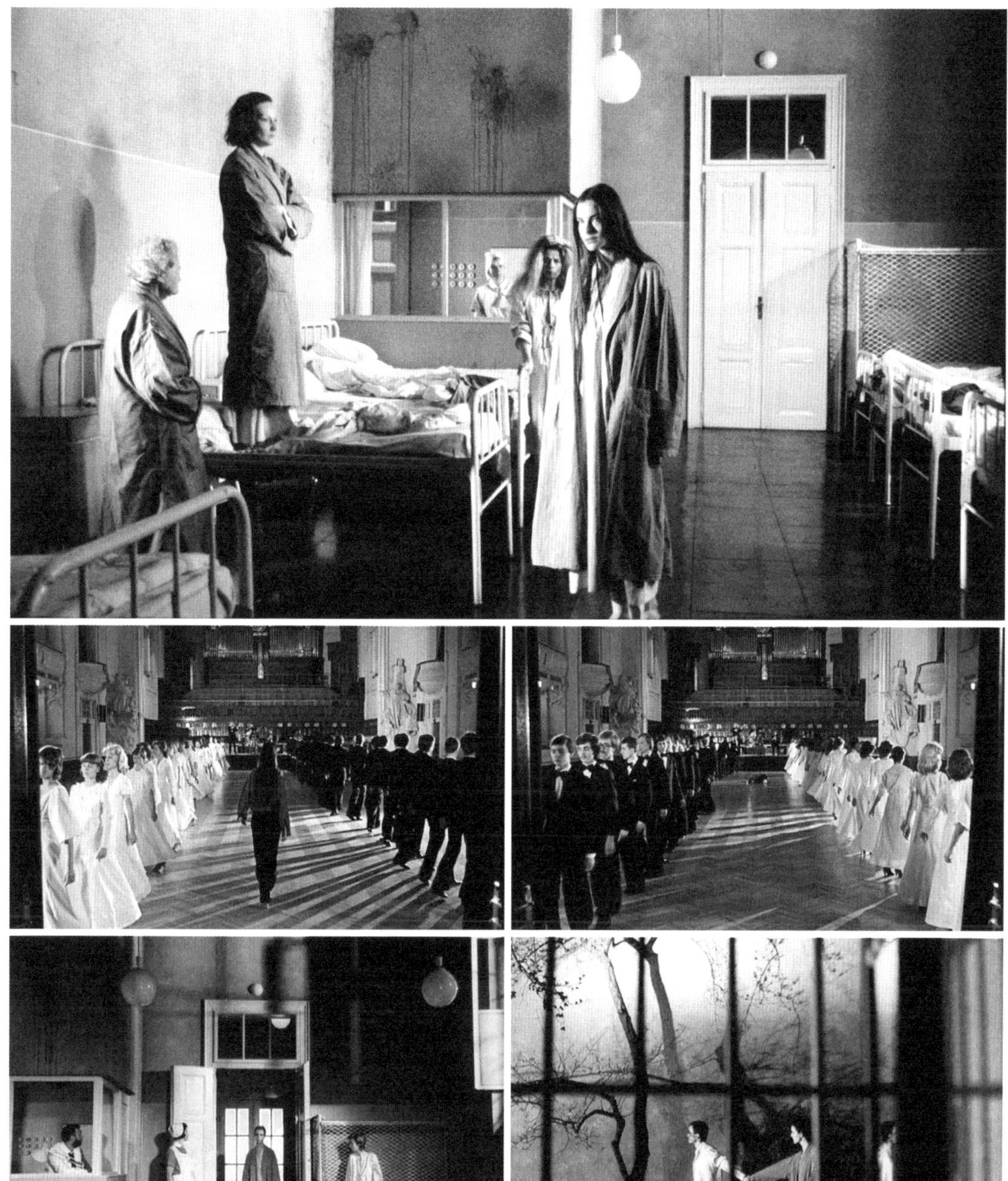

Tag der Idioten (1981)

those that position Carole next to open doors, in door frames, and in anterooms or gardens, showing her poised to take advantage of her ability to traverse the institution's boundaries in either direction. But in the context of her resounding failure to find happiness on either side, these shots ultimately mean the opposite of what they, at first glance, seem to signal.

Its visually baroque illustration of the cultural logic guiding normative society's relation to its outsiders made *Tag der Idioten* a template for Schroeter's remaining features. The film's refusal to afford its protagonist her personal utopia in the interstices of the system places it on the bleaker side of Schroeter's *oeuvre*. But its conceptual binaries of sane/insane, inside/outside, law/outlaw—even though they are disqualified as truth categories by the film—would, in various iterations, also come to shape *Der Rosenkönig*, *Malina* (1991), *Deux* (2002), and *Nuit de chien* (2008). It is as if Schroeter felt that these binaries are the most apposite tropes for the cinema's most luxurious variant, 35mm film, which necessitates the costliest, most heavily industrialized mode of production to yield the largest, brightest, and clearest image suffused with the deepest hues and darkest shades. Schroeter, in other words, may have realized that the limpidity of the feature film, whose institutional dimension turned the filmmaker into a purveyor of "above ground" art-house fare shown at prestigious festivals and reviewed by the mainstream press, at once enabled and commanded him to render his universe in either/or terms.

Once the "underground" is pulled "above ground," it loses its opacity. Either it melts into the brightness that exposed it, or its otherness gets frozen and put on display. The latter seems to have been the case with Schroeter, who cultivated his status as public provocateur with two films that were quickly deemed blasphemic. Schroeter took an acting part, playing a bishop, in Herbert Achternbusch's *Das Gespenst* (The Ghost, 1982), a low-budget farce about Christ stepping down from the cross and bumbling through Bavaria. The film drew the ire not only of the Church, but of the Minister of the Interior, who denied Achternbusch completion funding.

Next, Schroeter made a screen adaptation of *Liebeskonzil*, Oskar Panizza's late-19th century anti-Catholic stage satire, infamous in its day, that depicts an outbreak of syphilis as a punishment that God commissions the devil to inflict on the court of the debaucherous Pope Alexander VI (the father of Lucrezia Borgia, whose fate Schroeter had already dramatized in a stage farce).[91] With this film, scandal was likewise pre-ordained. The play had earned its author a jail sentence and ruinous legal bills. Not performed for 70 years after its premiere, it resurfaced in 1969 in Paris and then again in 1981 in Naples, where it was seen by Schroeter's producer Peter Berling, who arranged for Schroeter to film the Teatro Bellini production. Schroeter decided to further sharpen the adaptation's satirical tone in his German-language overdub shown at the Berlin Film Festival,

91 See Schroeter, pp. 213–214, for a discussion of the Achternbusch film, and pp. 227–230 for a discussion of *Liebeskonzil*.

Liebeskonzil (1982)

Werner Schroeter on the set of *Liebeskonzil*

where the film was promoted with a poster depicting a satyr with an erection (the figure exists in the film as a small prop in the background). Cowed by Church protests, the film's distributor tried to change the ad campaign, to which Schroeter responded by publishing various materials that had gone into the creation of the film. This strategy of reframing obscenity as art—or, if you wish, declaring obscene art culturally valuable—illustrates the dynamics that contain transgression by transforming it into cultural discourse.

Schroeter's next theatrical feature, *Der Rosenkönig*, thematizes the binary between the law and its transgression through a mythopoeic portrayal of male homosexuality. Filmed on location in Portugal, the film is about the attraction of Albert (Mostéfa Djadjam), a young gardener who cultivates roses, to another youth, Fernando (Antonio Orlando), whom he imprisons in order to transform him into an erotic object of a higher order. Drawing on gay mythology and cultural studies' theorization of the homosexual as a sad young man, Michelle Langford analyzes Albert's treatment of Fernando as a Christ figure.[92] Albert cuts up Fernando's body both literally, by making incisions in his flesh, and figuratively, by subjecting him to a melancholy gaze whose idealization of its object—because it implies reassemblage into illusory wholeness—entails its violation.[93] In what Langford terms "a kind of allegorical montage upon the body itself, a montage that brings together his obsession with creating the perfect rose and his own homoerotic desires,"[94] Albert places roses into Fernando's wounds, a procedure that allegorically reenacts the cultivation of roses by way of grafting (that is, inserting one stem into another).[95] Schroeter deploys homosexuality as a trope to reframe the law / outlaw binary as the perversion of nature by culture.[96] The film's luscious, symbolical *mise-en-scène* situates the body's fragmentation within the tradition of western art and religion. This tradition, as Langford astutely points out,[97] conceals or disavows the very violence of the process. In turn, Schroeter brings it out into the open—without, however, appearing to be able to alter its basic terms.

For his contribution to this book, David Pendleton had planned to offer a reading of *Der Rosenkönig* that, drawing on Michel Foucault's and Georges Bataille's respective concepts of extreme, quasi-ecstatic experience, intended to wrest the film from its overdetermined Christian hermeneutics. Such an approach would argue against reading Fernando's possible death at film's end as the subject's mystical union with God (with Albert acting as catalyst to

92 Langford, p. 157.
93 Langford, p. 158.
94 Langford, p. 158.
95 Langford, p. 158. For a discussion of the relationship between allegory and queerness in particular, see Flinn (p. 180), who argues that allegory, because it exists independently of a referent or interpretive endpoint and hides as much as it discloses, is "a crucial piece of nonheterosexual interpretive economies."
96 Placing the film in the context of Fassbinder and Genet's universes, Kuzniar (p. 136) argues that the film locates male homosexuality's central binary in its "willingness to admit a link between physical attraction and mutilation, between aggression and beauty."
97 Langford, p. 159.

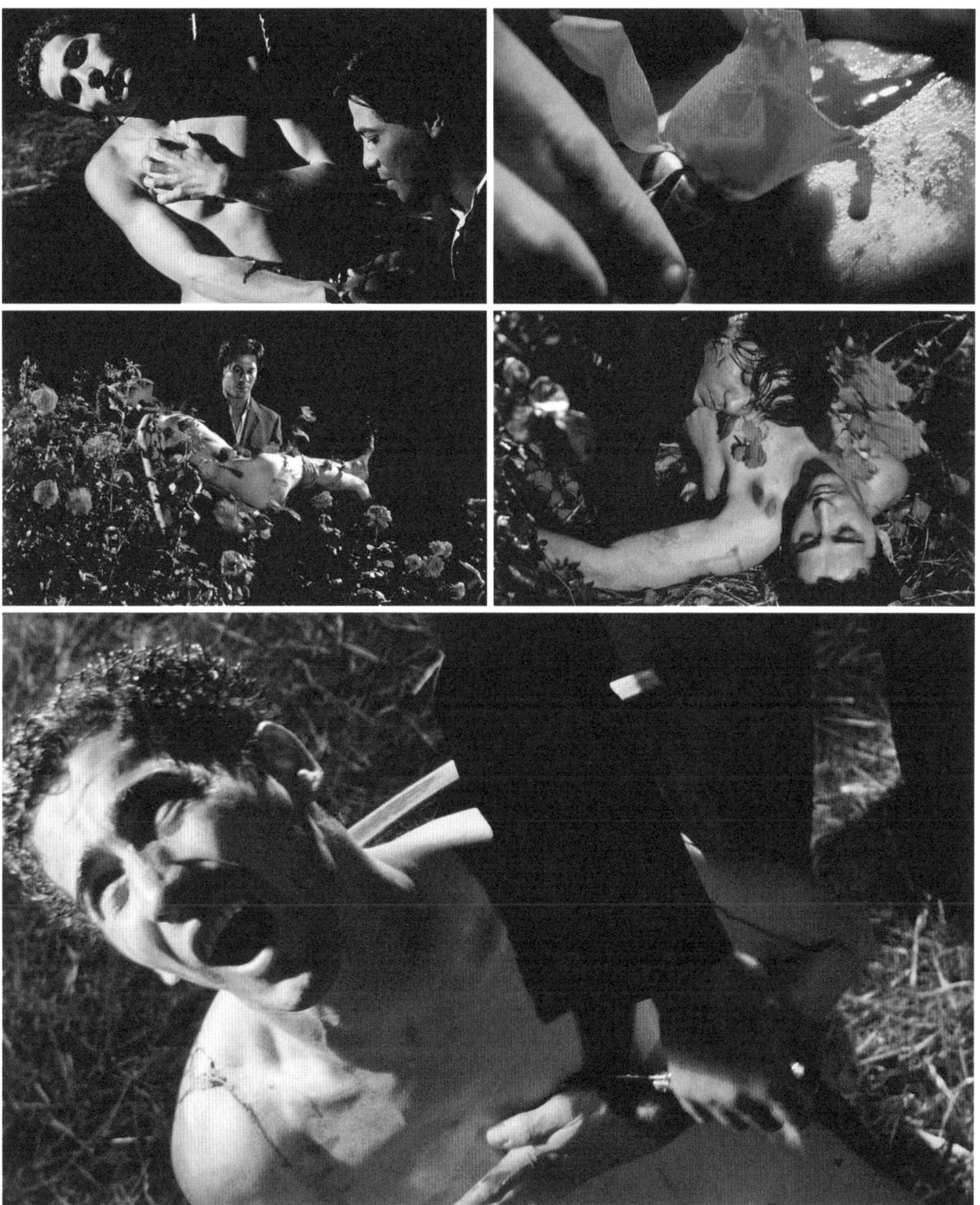

Der Rosenkönig (1986)

Fernando's deliverance), drawing instead on Foucault's concept of "limit-experience" and Bataille's notion of "inner experience" to explore *Der Rosenkönig* for alternative implications regarding the limits of coherent subjectivity.[98] While Pendleton's untimely death did not permit him to develop this argument, it is my hope that others may be inspired by his approach to explore new directions for discussing the film.

That a film so centrally revolving around cutting would also come to constitute a *caesura* in Schroeter's personal and artistic trajectory is a poignant coincidence. *Der Rosenkönig* was the last film of Schroeter's close friend and collaborator Magdalena Montezuma, who died shortly after filming was completed in 1984. Montezuma's death left Schroeter devastated and unable to touch the footage for over a year. The film did not get released until 1986, and it would take Schroeter five more years to make his next theatrical feature, *Malina*. External circumstances—some of which, such as his growing reputation as a stage director, were far from negative—played their part in preventing Schroeter from making more films in the second half of the 1980s (he did release one documentary, *Auf der Suche nach der Sonne*, in 1987). It is hard to deny, however, that with Montezuma's death, personal loss at least indirectly influenced Schroeter's creative path, as it had in 1977, after his idol Maria Callas passed away (his mother had died the previous year), and Schroeter decided to end his career as an underground filmmaker.

It would be reductive and misleading to describe Schroeter's last three feature films as a trilogy. The intervals between these films are too long and the respective subjects and the circumstances of their production are too different. Yet, some links and similarities are undeniable. All three are easily among Schroeter's densest, most complex films, demanding that viewers jettison expectations of coherent plot lines and part with even elastically conceived notions of character psychology. Although Schroeter's late films are not devoid of markers that have made art-house cinema palatable to the mainstream—the use of literary source material in the case of *Malina* and *Nuit de chien*, and of art-cinema stars like Isabelle Huppert in the case of *Malina* and *Deux*—these films did not use their relatively high budgets and production values (*Malina* cost 8 million Marks) for the purpose of turning the films into mere eye candy. The attractive locations, elaborate sets, and well-known actors Schroeter assembles become at once disassembled, relentlessly fragmented through his associative montage, the *lingua franca* Schroeter deploys to articulate his worldview. In *Malina*, it is the search for a life of sensual fulfillment, the question of how to find that life with another person, how to find oneself in the other without incurring mutual disappearance, that haunts the central figure, Huppert's writer, who is torn between her libidinal and intellectual attachment to the story's eponymous male protagonist and an-

98 On the topic of extreme, quasi-ecstatic experience in Foucault and Bataille, see Martin Jay, "The Limits of Limit-Experience: Bataille and Foucault," in *Constellations* (New York), vol. 2 no. 2 (1995), pp. 155–174.

Deux (2002)

other man. The film also deals with the question of how life and art in very different ways figure into processes of self-finding and self-expression.[99]

Related concerns course through *Deux*, which centers on a pair of identical twins (both played by Huppert) who were exchanged at birth, one living in Paris, the other in Portugal. Not based on a literary source, but filled with Schroeter's personal memories and autobiographical elements, the film, in Schroeter's own description, charts each sibling's search for beauty, poetry, sex, music—and, ultimately, self-fulfillment—as a "surreal *tour d'horizon*" across a series of friendships and romances. *Deux* is conceptually similar to *Tag der Idioten* in that it sets up a binary that it then undermines. In *Deux*, the siblings do not symbolize the split between good and evil. Their existence as doubles signifies a more profound split that Schroeter sees running through the human personality, an internal incommensurability that yearns for unity but fails to achieve it.[100]

In her contribution to the present volume, Fatima Naqvi discusses how *Malina* and *Deux* function as studies in disorientation, whose various dimensions—mental, physical, biographical, artistic—prompt the filmmaker to formulate his own concerns on the "big" screen. Each film presents a trajectory of decline: in *Malina* disorientation leads to disappearance, while *Deux*, as Naqvi explains, may be regarded as a study of "ways of dying." However, each film presents this trajectory through visual excess. Naqvi traces the relation between form and content, images and language, to explore how these works, despite their own etiological pull, may be said to proffer formal and thematic possibilities of renewal and rebirth.

The final sentence of Schroeter's autobiography reads: "I am a hopeful person."[101] It completes the book's chapter on Schroeter's final feature film, *Nuit de chien*. Schroeter took the title from the French translation of the film's

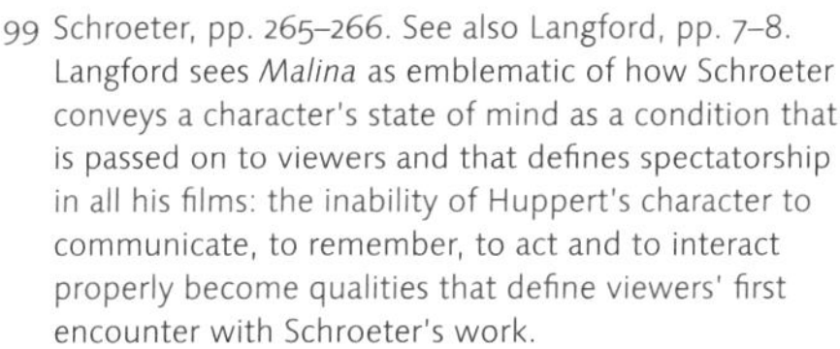

99 Schroeter, pp. 265–266. See also Langford, pp. 7–8. Langford sees *Malina* as emblematic of how Schroeter conveys a character's state of mind as a condition that is passed on to viewers and that defines spectatorship in all his films: the inability of Huppert's character to communicate, to remember, to act and to interact properly become qualities that define viewers' first encounter with Schroeter's work.

100 Schroeter, p. 299. The doubling and internal splitting of personalities and stories inevitably invite placing *Deux* in a tradition of post-World War II European cinema defined primarily by mental constellations that Gilles Deleuze has characterized as the "time image." See Langford, pp. 80–83, for a discussion of *Deux* with regard to a subcategory of Deleuze's concept, the crystal image, which, as pointed out earlier in this introduction, has been of importance to other Schroeter films, such as *Argila*.

101 Schroeter, p. 320.

Nuit de chien (2008)

source novel, *Para esta noche*. Written by Juan Carlos Onetti, who was born in Uruguay but studied and worked and wrote in Buenos Aires during the 1940s and early 1950s, the book is a terrifying analysis of the aftermath of a failed Latin American revolution during which former freedom fighters turn on each other. Schroeter describes the story's atmosphere as a kind of *Götterdämmerung*, which is suggested already in the film's establishing shots of its location, the city of Porto. It is shown in nocturnal splendor, but the sky is traversed by a plane that could serve the military. As soon as it passes, the building lights go out, the image goes nearly dark, and the increasingly disillusioning and violent events begin to unfold.

The film's production, too, had a twilight character. Schroeter was already stricken with cancer when Paolo Branco, the producer of *Der Rosenkönig*, approached him with the project. The film's subject, itself a mélange of Onetti's impressions of the Spanish Civil War and oral histories of Nazi survivors, reminded Schroeter of his own 1983 theater workshop in Argentina that was shut down by the country's military junta under the threat of death.[102] But Schroeter insists that *Nuit de chien* harbors hope amidst all the betrayals, killings, and chaos it shows. This hope resides in revolution's intangible ideal, the truthfulness that gives rise to it in the first place. But what the anarchist in Schroeter, who rejects association with any political ideology, shares with Onetti is to make this story not

102 For a more detailed discussion of the film's production, see Schroeter, pp. 313–320.

about a particular war, but about war in general, and the state of siege it lays to all of humanity.[103] In his contribution to this volume Edward Dimendberg compares the film to its source novel, analyzing the significance of the setting and illuminating the link between the story's central elements and their cultural contexts. Dimendberg also explores the relationship between the film's visual opulence and its textual density that, so he argues by referencing Susan Sontag's 1964 essay "Against Interpretation," generates an erotics of form that helps Schroeter underscore and articulate his pursuit of hope against the bleakness of the source material. To find truth and beauty in suffering is an axiom as central to Schroeter's last film as it is to his first.

NON-FICTION FILMS AND STAGE WORK

Theatrical feature filmmaking was but one of three areas Schroeter would pursue from the late 1970s to the end of his career—the other two were the making of small-scale non-fiction films and his work in the theater, which by the mid-1980s was rapidly becoming his bread-and-butter occupation. Each of these areas comprised a different facet of a kind of post-Edenic, post-1970s mode of artistic production. Admittedly, periodizing Schroeter's artistic trajectory this way seems counterintuitive on several counts. The nature of all of Schroeter's films as symptoms of a radical rupture that is already in effect lends them the status of allegories. They enable meaning to go in multiple directions rather than narrowing it into a one-directional before-and-after trajectory.[104] Further, to cite a mundane historical fact, the state-sponsored nature of Schroeter's underground films placed him on the West German cultural radar as early as 1970/71. In this sense, his voice was already marked for inclusion long before he gave up underground filmmaking. My point, however, is that this inclusion did not diminish the quasi-paradisiacal creative freedom he was afforded by the one-of-a-kind funding system from which he benefited up to and including the production

103 Schroeter selected this scenario precisely in order to pursue the question of how to maintain dignity and a sense of utopian hope in a world of chaos and violence. In an essay about the necessity for utopia published in conjunction with the DVD release of *Diese Nacht* (*Nuit de chien*), he writes: "While even an injured person still tends to have the option to resist violence, brutality, and bestiality, he, too, gives in to them all too often. And those who have given in to this violence have let go of all utopian hope—hope as the only possibility to maintain life, love, and passion and to endure death with dignity." [Author's translation] See Werner Schroeter, "On the Necessity of Utopia: Remarks by the Director Werner Schroeter," DVD liner notes, *Diese Nacht* (Filmgalerie 451, 2010), pp. 4–5.

104 This no matter whether one wants to think of them, as Kuzniar's psychoanalytic reading does, as unmoored signifiers of literalized passion, or, in Langford's critical materialist terms, as ruins proving cinema's power to implode the prison house of industrial modernity—or, considering Schroeter's anarchist tendencies, as allegorical cobblestones testifying to his ability to perceive culture as always already broken down into its smaller components that can be made available for resignification. In each of these theoretical accounts, we are presented with an image of scattered pieces or debris that hold the potential for re-formation, re-imagining and re-building. See Gary Indiana, "Scattered Pictures: The Movies of Werner Schroeter," in *Artforum* (New York), vol. 20 no. 3 (March 1982), pp. 46–48, for a characterization along similar lines.

La Répétition générale (1980): Pina Bausch

of *Les Flocons d'or*. It is really not until after he completed that film that Schroeter's creative efforts stratified into the three distinct areas outlined above. While each of these enabled him to keep working and to evolve artistically, each had a distinct character, rhythm, and set of constraints and demands signaling a departure from experimental film's liminal, organic nature and the creative freedom it afforded.

Schroeter's theatrical features prove that these constraints and demands did not hamper his creativity *per se*. Evident in all his post-1970s films, however, is an urge to reflect anew, and with increasingly retroactive character, on his long-standing ideals—particularly the notion of utopia. Since most of his industrial features were about some form of unfreedom, they did not enact a personal utopia in the manner of his underground films, but posited it only indirectly, or in abstract or refracted form. It was his small-scale non-fiction films—particularly those about opera and theater—that allowed Schroeter to continue to engage with utopia more explicitly.[105]

In 1980, in the midst of the imbroglio around his dismissal from the Augsburg staging of *Salome*, Schroeter made a film that unabashedly celebrates theater and performance in a nourishing institutional setting, the Festival Mondial du Théâtre in Nancy. *La Répétition générale* (1980) focuses on the festival's dancers, performers, and choreographers, in whose themes—the artistic exploration of love, passion, and death—Schroeter recognized his own work. The film is not a systematically structured exposé but a *collage*-like assemblage of scenes and moments that catch the performers *in medias res*. Its utopian dimension lies less in its depiction of the festival as an oasis of artistic experimentation (though the implication is there), but in tracing the performers' ability to use gesture and language to resignify meaning away from reified sociocultural traditions and contexts. It is precisely these "gestural expropriations"[106] and the freedom inherent in them—as demonstrated, for example, by Pina Bausch and her choreographies—that also characterize Schroeter's films.

105 For several of these, ZDF, which had financed many of his experimental films of the 1970s, continued to act as his main sponsor. In 1980 Schroeter made one last film in the mode of his earlier experimental works, *Weisse Reise*, which is currently unavailable. For a description of it, see Schroeter, pp. 189–192.

106 The term comes from Langford (p. 177), who uses it to characterize Pina Bausch's gestural dance theater. Langford (pp. 177–184) proffers a detailed discussion of Schroeter's coverage of Bausch and Kazuo Ohno.

Schroeter's next documentary, *Der lachende Stern* (*The Smiling Star*, 1983), was likewise occasioned by a festival—the inaugural Manila International Film Festival. In contrast to the Nancy Theater Festival, this one was a sham. Its patron was Imelda Marcos, who tried to use a cultural event to distract from the dictatorial politics of her husband and increase the cachet of the Philippines. Schroeter had accepted an official government invitation to cover the festival, but had no intention of ignoring the country's history of colonialism and whitewashing its role in U.S. expansionism. Yet his *collage* approach made any explicit editorializing against the regime unnecessary. He shot interviews with citizens willing to share how they dealt with various aspects of colonial and neocolonial oppression. The film juxtaposes these accounts with excerpts from Imelda Marcos's speeches, full of *faux* humanist platitudes, and shows the kitschy cult of Marcos worship. Schroeter also included footage of religious processions and flagellation rituals performed in rural communities to document the power of the Church; he combined these with excerpts from Hollywood war movies set in the Philippines to illustrate the sway of American pop culture in shaping the country's image. He edited his material in his characteristic *collage* style, out of which, as Langford has pointed out, "an ironic but never overtly critical attitude arises. Schroeter leaves the spectator to form their own opinion of these scattered pieces of history."[107] The film's subject is political oppression, but its tapestry of

Der lachende Stern (1983)

107 Langford, p. 126.

cultural fragments, in its attention to local knowledge and its scrambling of official cultural messages, is radically anti-propagandistic. The film's aesthetics locate utopia at the same point where it resides in gestural performance—the point of semantic juncture, marked as it is by the refusal to sync up or to close down meaning.

Schroeter's next two documentaries—*Auf der Suche nach der Sonne* (1986), about Ariane Mnouchkine and her Théâtre du Soleil, and *Poussières d'amour – Abfallprodukte der Liebe* (*Love's Debris*, 1996), about opera as a forum for exploring life's great passions and central questions—modify the *collage* structure of his previous ones only by slightly lengthening the interview segments and the excerpts of individual performances.[108] What Schroeter states in voice-over to footage of Mnouchkine's actors performing on stage is also thematized in *Poussières d'amour*, and functions as a motto for all of Schroeter's films: "Every work of art, every artistic creation, is the ever-recurring attempt to suspend unbearable reality, the attempt to unhinge reality by allowing desire to unfold."[109]

In both films, Schroeter uses a specific interview technique. The Mnouchkine film includes interviews with every member of her troupe; in *Poussières* Schroeter interviews his own troupe of sorts—a diverse group of singers and performers, all personal friends of the filmmaker, whom he invited to stay at a former abbey near Paris to sing and to muse about art as a by-product of life and love. While each interview briefly assumes the classic talking-head correspondence of voice and image, Schroeter frequently combines the voices with footage in which the interviewee sings or performs or the camera explores details of the location. This technique lends both films a fluid, elegant structure.[110] In *Auf der Suche nach der Sonne*, shots of Mnouchkine's performers in action are frequently followed by close-ups of their faces or details of their costumes, interspersed with shots of the theater, whose ornamental, festively lit decoration may be read as a signifier of utopia.[111] This porousness of film form is a correlative to Mnouchkine's insight that truth—to be found within one's performance and one's self—is achieved by opening oneself up to the world.

The gradual, processual nature of this opening of the self is facilitated in both films by the *modus operandi* of being "in residence." Schroeter's visit with Mnouchkine's troupe gave him a chance to experience its members as a kind of family. The project of *Poussières*

108 While Schroeter became a sought-after stage director in the second half of the 1980s, this period was a difficult one for him in the realm of film. In addition to his film about Mnouchkine's Théâtre du Soleil, Schroeter made only one other film, *De l'Argentine* (1985), a documentary about his ill-fated theater workshop in Buenos Aires in 1983 that is currently unavailable.

109 Schroeter voice-over, *Auf der Suche nach der Sonne* (1986). [Author's translation]

110 The influence of this interview approach is apparent in Wim Wenders' documentary *Pina* (2011), which uses footage of Bausch's *Café Müller* from Schroeter's *La Répétition générale*.

111 The play Mnouchkine's troupe was performing during the time of Schroeter's shoot was about the history of Cambodia, which links it to his earlier film, *Der lachende Stern*, with its focus on colonialism.

Poussières d'amour
Abfallprodukte der Liebe (1996):
Isabelle Huppert,
Martha Mödl,
Elisabeth Cooper,
Werner Schroeter

Die Königin (2002):
Marianne Hoppe

d'amour – Abfallprodukte der Liebe hinges on organizing the shoot as a kind of family retreat, which enabled the singers to explore the links between art and self in their rehearsals, their performances, and in conversation. This linkage, as I argue in my own essay in this volume, re-emerges in Schroeter's revisiting of an old interest of his, the tension between professionalism and amateurism. He explores the topic by showcasing his favorite opera divas, several of whom were retired by the time of filming and had largely lost their voices, but still possessed what Roland Barthes has famously termed "the grain of the voice." What do these opera legends have in common with Schroeter's underground stars? Where is the utopian nexus that links these different kinds of performance? What are the qualities that make performance whole and dignified?

Schroeter would also explore some of these questions in his last documentary, *Die Königin (The Queen,* 2002), about actress Marianne Hoppe. A prominent theater and film actress during the Third Reich, Hoppe re-emerged after the war from under the shadow of her image as a Nazi diva and her marriage to controversial theater director Gustaf Gründgens[112] to advance to something like a *grande dame* of the German stage. After casting her in a play as a substitute for opera singer Martha Mödl, whom he had known since *Poussières d'amour*, he became close to Hoppe, and their friendship resulted in the film about her. While Schroeter personally takes a propitiatory attitude towards Hoppe's past, the film extends Schroeter's earlier films' interest in performance to questions of history and memory. If Schroeter's early work explores "the diva's dialectic," to cite Marc Siegel's term, between life and death, his portrait of Hoppe posits a different conceptual tension—between personal memory and official history.

Schroeter's post-1970s work is marked by a shift in creative activities. As the subsidy and television financing structure changed, and Schroeter's filmmaking became more sporadic and bifurcated into theatrical features and small-scale documentaries, the third leg in Schroeter's *oeuvre*, his work in the theater, assumed ever greater importance. Schroeter initially did not regard the theater as an artistic medium of choice.[113] His career as a stage director was a direct result of his growing success as a filmmaker. Following the 1971 TV premiere of his film *Salome*, he was contacted by three separate heads of theater, Jean-Pierre Ponnelle,

112 The marriage was considered questionable because both she and Gründgens were known to have homosexual relationships and functioned as each other's "beard," and also because of Gründgens' ambiguous position under the Nazis—he was a careerist who, at the same time, was able to direct plays the Nazis disliked because they were deemed subversive of National Socialist ideology.

113 Sabina Dhein, "Gespräch mit Werner Schroeter: Theater—das sind umgesetzte Bilder von Schmerz," in Sabina Dhein, ed., *Regie im Theater: Werner Schroeter* (Frankfurt: Fischer Taschenbuch Verlag, 1991), pp. 32–33. In the interview, Schroeter recounts that, while he was impressed as a boy with the actress playing the mother in the 1955 Bielefeld production of *Emilia Galotti*, the theater, with the exception of his obsession with Maria Callas, captivated him only occasionally, such as in 1965, when he saw touring productions in Heidelberg of *The Maids* and *Mysteries* by the Living Theater.

Mondo Lux – Die Bilderwelten des Werner Schroeter (2011, Elfi Mikesch)

Peter Zadek, and Ivan Nagl, each offering him a directing project. In 1972 Schroeter directed *Emilia Galotti* for Nagl at the Deutsches Schauspielhaus in Hamburg, and in 1973 Oscar Wilde's *Salomé* for Zadek at the Schauspielhaus Bochum. Both were significant assignments that launched his stage career.[114] During the 1970s, his theater work would remain confined to just over a handful of productions, all of which, however, were prestigious commissions by well-known stages. The plays Schroeter took on were all classic texts about misunderstood, wronged, and suffering female protagonists. His scenography for the 1980s lists 27 productions, many of which were invitations that took him to cultural metropolises outside Germany. During the same period he also established himself more firmly at two renowned German stages, Bremen, and, from the mid-1980s onwards, Düsseldorf, where he worked under Volker Canaris. The 1990s would bring 30 engagements in Germany and abroad, and there were almost as many between 2000 and his death in 2010.

It seems that Schroeter modeled his approach to directing in the theater at least partially on the dynamics he witnessed in Ariane Mnouchkine's troupe. The guiding philosophy of this approach, as Schroeter discusses in *Mondo Lux*, is the processual aspect of theater work: the long days and weeks of developing

114 A complete list of Schroeter's stage works can be found in the appendix to Schroeter's autobiography.

the staging in close collaboration with the whole company, who become a family of sorts.[115] Working in theater gave Schroeter considerable creative freedom, which, in turn, would lead to controversial productions that reinforced his reputation as an *enfant terrible*. But that reputation was now based on the quality of the actual work rather than on scandalizing interview remarks. In Düsseldorf, to mention just one example, he followed Volker Canaris's request to direct Shakespeare's *King Lear*, but infused the staging with insinuations of incest and homosexuality, which caused a political scandal not unlike the Augsburg imbroglio a decade earlier.[116] For Schroeter, the theater remained one of the last strongholds of radical art-making, precisely because its status as a state-subsidized institution shelters it from the commercial pressures that push the cinema into conformity with the *status quo*.[117] Schroeter not only enjoyed the trust and support of famous heads of theater, but also met other artists whom he recruited for both his film and stage work—a case in point being the costume designer Alberte Barsacq, who designed the costumes of many of his films, starting with *Nel regno di Napoli*.

Schroeter's work is many-faceted and entirely too expansive to be covered adequately in a single book. This essay collection aims to explore hitherto neglected areas of Schroeter's filmography. While some essays revisit well-known works such as *Der Tod der Maria Malibran* and *Palermo oder Wolfsburg*, others cover thus-far under-researched early films, such as *Salome*, *Willow Springs*, and *Der schwarze Engel*, as well as some of Schroeter's late works, including *Malina* and *Nuit de chien*. The essay contributions benefit from the ongoing restoration of Schroeter's films by Filmmuseum München. The book includes a completely updated filmography by Stefan Drössler, who has been overseeing the restoration. Also included are some of Schroeter's own thoughts, as featured in a conversation with French philosopher Michel Foucault, which gives insight into Schroeter's central artistic and philosophical concerns. Finally, the volume includes an interview with Schroeter's longtime collaborator, the cinematographer Elfi Mikesch, who has had detailed insight into Schroeter's thinking as an artist and his work as a director, and who with *Mondo Lux* has made her own film about Schroeter. The hope is that the present volume will make Schroeter's work more accessible to English-language readers, and that it will stimulate critical discourse on Schroeter for many years to come.

115 See Dhein, p. 34. In the interview Schroeter explains that as a director he was never interested in keeping any distance from the people he worked with. He never heeded the rule that theater and private life ought to remain separate.

116 For a detailed account of this production, and also of Schroeter's artistic approach to stage directing, see Schroeter, pp. 267–273.

117 Dhein, pp. 46–47.

Gertrud Koch

Operatic and Filmic Gesture in Werner Schroeter's Films

1. ONCE UPON A TIME IN THE SIXTIES

Imagine we are back in the late 1960s in Germany—in my case, Frankfurt. Film history then spanned two-thirds of the period it covers today. The film programs in the newly opened art cinemas, student film clubs, and communal foundations, which featured important milestones of film history as well as independent and non-commercial films, were oriented towards European art cinema (including Eastern-bloc films) and American classics, and also participated in the renaissance of silent cinema. We could enjoy retrospectives of Feuillade, Stroheim, Keaton, and Lloyd, along with recent American experimental and queer underground films, as well as early stag films.

But film was only one of our preoccupations. We also followed new directions in music, theater, fine arts, and literature. What linked these diverse arts was the concept of performance. Artists like Valie Export, Rainer Werner Fassbinder, Peter Handke, Alexander Kluge, and many others worked in more than one art form across a spectrum of exhibition modes and places. The logic behind the fraying of the arts thus entailed the productive dislocation of their sites: a stag-film retrospective could be organized by the student union in the main hall of the university, framed and introduced by an art historian, while a musical performance might take place in the communal swimming pool, experimenting with the site-specific acoustics of the tiled walls and the water. The emphasis was on performative actions that generated different instances of the fraying of the arts, thus dislocating the arts from their traditional frameworks and stages.

It is against this backdrop that one has to place the use of early cinema in Kluge's films, the impact of spoken theatrical dialogue in Fassbinder's films, and the use of opera in Schroeter's—to cite just a few well-known examples representative of a multi-dimensional and multi-directional art—an art, however, that in the area of film was understood exclusively through the constricting paradigm of auteurism. In fact, at the center of this new aesthetic was not so much the author/creator, but the idea of art as *bricolage*, in the sense that Alexander Kluge attributed it to his films. When the new directors referred to themselves with the Brechtian term "filmmakers," they may have emphasized less a material notion of production and more the pragmatist idea of *doing*, articulated as the desire to "do" this or that film, piece, object, performance, and so on. It is stunning to see that many of these filmmakers had no formal education in filmmaking, only a few having attended the new film schools in Munich or Berlin. Someone like Schroeter was "doing" films in a very private setting, with the support of families, friends, and kindred spirits. One could say that the late 1960s was the hour of the amateur, in the original sense of the word: someone who is doing something out of love and passion, and not for functional, commercial, or professional reasons. I don't mean to say there was no professionalism involved. This was always a mixed *milieu*, and after a few years the amateurs, if only for social reasons, became professionals, transforming themselves from amateurs into *auteurs*.

But the figure of the amateur is crucial to the concept of high style, which is what the amateur imitates, on several levels. It contains a specific mimetic relationship to art and life insofar as the amateur is at a mimetic distance to tradition he can quote and perform without being part of. The amateur has no obligations to observe the rules of production, influence, and imitation; he can re-invent anything from the wheel to the reel or the real. This moment of infinite liberty places the amateur in the dangerous, but also glamorous, role of the bystander who sticks out and can move from the periphery to the center in a revolutionary step of inventing something that doesn't belong to the tradition. The amateur can turn the underground into a new center; he can fray and make permeable the borders between the arts and also between the different publics that convened at the sites of spectacle. The notion of the amateur that I wish to establish here is not to be understood by the binary that, as it were, juxtaposed him to the educated professional, but as an aesthetic and stylistic concept that aims at undermining the functional frames of "professional art." In a similar way, Siegfried Kracauer referred to the figure of the historian as an amateur, whose preoccupation is characterized by his social and historical distance to the object of desire and his wish to get hold of it.[1]

A typical field of playful amateurism is karaoke, the mimetic repetition of a complete object in parts. Partiality itself is initiated here as a challenge to unity, which makes karaoke into a kind of appropriation art. Appropriation art is another art style overtly mobilizing amateurism, and as such it is a central part of the context in which I want to place certain aesthetic practices in Werner Schroeter's early films.

To return to the artistic events unfolding across screens, stages, and public sites in Frankfurt in the late 1960s. Most of us were still young enough to be amateurs of film history, and one of our formative encounters was with early silent film, marked as it was by its radical split between image and sound, voice and body, and its two levels of performance—by live musicians or vocal narrators in front of the screen (theatrical), and by the projection on screen (technical). The oldest of films was the

1 Siegfried Kracauer, *History: The Last Things Before the Last* (Oxford: Oxford University Press, 1969). See Kracauer's characterization of the historian Jacob Burckhardt as an amateur in the book's last chapter, "The Anteroom," pp. 191–220.

newest. This crystallizing new viewing experience was influenced in equal parts by the works of the composer Mauricio Kagel, who projected silent films on stage accompanied by live musicians, and by the historical, sometimes mute, projections of early cinema in the Frankfurt Filmmuseum. Kagel was an Argentinian composer who lived in Cologne and became interested in "doing" film, which resulted in *Match* (1966, produced by WDR, Cologne), *Synchronstudie für Sänger, Geräuschemacher und Filmprojektionen* (1969), *Soundtrack – Ein Film-Hörspiel* (1975), *MM 51 – Ein Stück Filmmusik für Klavier* (1976), and of course the famous *Ludwig van: Hommage von Beethoven* (1969/70, WDR, Cologne). *Ludwig van* illustrates the close intertwining of the two avant-gardes, which Peter Wollen in his famous essay[2] tried to divide into the structuralist filmmakers, who worked strictly on film as material, and another camp, which sought to undermine the popular feature film by infusing it with queer, underground, and political meaning (Godard, Kluge, and others). But this division does not work with regard to the period under discussion, when the avant-garde and the underground, professionals and amateurs, were present on the same stage and screen.

The impact of all these films, old and new, and the poetics of projection and performance they initiated, were enormous, which can be illustrated with an anecdote: we happened to gather around the dinner table. There was music, and we spontaneously started to make a film out of it, without a camera, only using the movements of our bodies—a karaoke of gestures, not of voices, a trance-like practice that was neither dance, nor music, nor film, but that nonetheless resulted in a strange table movie theater, performed by passionate amateurs. In hindsight, this anecdote taught me something about the embodiment of musical experience through gestures. How this experience was enabled and what was at stake became clear only after re-watching Werner Schroeter's film *Eika Katappa* some years ago at a screening in Berlin. In *Eika Katappa* the fetishistic love for the great diva Maria Callas and the amateur's love for film and opera created an explosive piece of underground film that was in its most musical parts a compilation of classical and avant-garde compositions known from operas, concerts, and festivals, which Schroeter combined with tangos and popular songs. Schroeter's film unfolded as a mesmerizing work of art that had no forerunners in its style, even if bits and pieces from stage practices and silent film (for example, early portraits of opera singers, or a city portrait like the 1929 *Napoli che canta*) might serve as models.

The renaissance of early cinema made evident what had been forgotten or repressed in the evolution of perceptual habits built by sound (and talking) film: the radical split between body and voice, image and sound, that is one of the technical preconditions of the medium, constituted precisely by the capacity

2 Peter Wollen, "The Two Avant-Gardes," in *Studio International* (London), vol. 190 no. 978 (November/December 1975), pp. 171–175.

Eika Katappa (1969)

to mix and mount different materials into a time-based sequence, bringing them into a time grid that allowed synchronicity as well as a-synchronicity. In the beginning of *Eika Katappa* a female figure gestures in dramatic manner, like a silent film heroine, while performing an operatic aria. This makes clear how strongly the aesthetics of silent film figure in the montage and poetics of this film. In his book *Film as Subversive Art* Amos Vogel refers to *The Death of Maria Malibran*, Schroeter's most widely acknowledged film about an operatic subject, with a highly accurate description of the split between sound and image, voice and mouth, writing: "The lip-sync is off; the singing is off-pitch; mouths are frequently open while no sound issues forth, or closed, with mellifluous arias or cheap popular songs heard on scratchy renditions of old records. Neither burlesque nor slapstick, the film's intent, at least in the beginning, is nevertheless ironical and subversive, though mysteriously so."[3]

2. NEAPOLITAN AND OTHER GESTURES

It comes as a nice coincidence that Schroeter, who already during his teenage years had spent time living in Naples, and who devoted parts of *Eika Katappa* and all of *Nel regno di Napoli* to this city, staged a thoroughly performative play of gesture in his films. At issue is the so-called "Neapolitan gesture" performed by the Italian economist Paolo Sraffa in a conversation with Wittgenstein. This gesture consists of bringing the closed fingers of one hand to the chin and then abruptly opening the fingers to a wide open hand that points away from the chin. Sraffa asked Wittgenstein what he thinks this gesture "means," assuming that the meaning was not a symbolic one but that the performance was the embodied gesture itself. It caused Wittgenstein to theorize a use of gesture we can link to Schroeter, who, with good reason, rejected the frequently made assumption that his films are based on a code of operatic gestures. Sraffa's Neapolitan gesture caused Wittgenstein to change his assumptions that

3 Amos Vogel, *Film as a Subversive Art* (New York: Random House, 1974), p. 70.

there is a kind of inner resemblance between object and sign. Generally speaking, gestures are part of a practice of embodiment—in the case of Wittgenstein/Sraffa's Neapolitan gesture, they embody rejection and disavowal. Yet, the gesture Sraffa made had no inner resemblance with its meaning; it is not the representation of the emotion of rejection, but an effect of immediacy that was grounded in the body itself. It performs rejection rather than representing or symbolizing it. In this sense, the gesture is not a sign that attributes meaning to an object or a cause; it captures emotion itself through a performative embodiment. To take this one step further, the gesture is not a sign for the emotion we glean from it, but is the very expression of the emotion itself. In the following discussion I want to argue that Schroeter's operatic, musical, and filmic gestures are better described in Wittgenstein's term of gesture than through the conventional frame of reference used for gestures.

"Neapolitan Gestures" are an iconic topic in the arts, and have attracted many artists, who took it as an opportunity to paint theatrical scenes in naturalistic *milieux*. The gestures introduced an element of histrionics into the paintings, as seen in an example by the French painter Greuze from 1757, in which one sees a young beauty leaning toward an old woman and making the gesture towards a fleeing peddler, whose intentions remain unclear. In German it became customary to differentiate gesture and gesticulation (*Geste und Gebärde*), to distinguish the gesture as linguistic sign from the one functioning as expressive enactment.

Le Geste Napolitain, 1757 (oil on canvas)
by Jean Baptiste Greuze (1725–1805)

Whatever the choice of words may be, in Wittgenstein's use it is the term gesture that undergoes different definitions with regard to its relationship to language, and to language games as mundane practices. I follow the arguments that Malcolm Budd discusses in his contribution to *The Oxford Handbook on Wittgenstein*, "Wittgenstein on Aesthetics." He writes: "But it will have been noticed that Wittgenstein operates with a rather unusual notion of a gesture, for under the head of gestures he includes, not just expressive movements of the body, but all characteristics of the voice that, considered in abstraction from any thought-content that an utterance may possess, are indications of either the kind of vocal action performed or the psychological state of the speaker. Accordingly, Wittgenstein uses 'gesture' and 'expression' more or less interchange-

Eika Katappa

ably, indicating that the item referred to has, in this wide sense, an expressive character, as when, speaking of a door that is slightly too large, he is reported as saying that 'it hasn't the right expression – it doesn't make the right gesture.'"[4]

Wittgenstein's remark on the gesture as a criterion for lending cogent aesthetic expression to what is being said—in the sense that the performance and what it expresses is giving coherence to the whole utterance—comes to mind when one watches Werner Schroeter's early films, which are based on a performative cinema of gestures, gestures that include the image, the movement, the voice, the rhythm of montage, and the synchronization of movement of *objets trouvés*. We can see this holistic closure of location, action, and dubbed music score in a scene from *Eika Katappa*: in the foreground is a wall that belongs to a factory whose chimneys are producing steam; on top of the wall lies a man on his belly, dressed in a white shirt, his right arm hanging down and moving rhythmically with the music, and at times even with the steam that is periodically emitted from the chimney. The metronomic gesture of the arm—itself performing a gesture of mimetic affinity with the world around him—creates the hypnotizing effect of placing the spectator at the center of a universe that is entirely fictional, while at the same time referencing the real in the form of the body and its surroundings. In this context, consider a comment by Wittgenstein on the illusionistic qualities of art: "The same strange illusion which we are under when we seem to seek the something which a face expresses, whereas, in reality, we are giving ourselves up to the features before us—that same illusion possesses us even more strongly if repeating a tune to ourselves and letting it make its full impression on us, we say 'This tune says something,' and it is as though I had to find what it says. And yet I know that it doesn't say anything such that I might express in words or pictures what it says. And if, recognizing this, I resign myself to saying 'It just

4 Malcolm Budd, "Wittgenstein on Aesthetics," in Oskari Kuusin, Marie McGinn, eds., *The Oxford Handbook on Wittgenstein* (Oxford/New York: Oxford University Press, 2011), p. 786. The Wittgenstein quote is in Ludwig Wittgenstein, *Lectures and Conversations on Aesthetics, Psychology and Religious Belief* (Oxford University Press, 1966), p. 31.

expresses a musical thought,' this would mean no more than saying 'It expresses itself.'"[5]

Self-expression takes on a second sense, which is distant from psychological subjectivism in the sense that, with regard to aesthetic matters, it references the expressive qualities of an object and not a person—or, one might say, it ascribes qualities of a person to an object. This may account for the strong animistic quality Wittgenstein attributes to the strange feeling that non-verbal things seem to "speak" in a way we understand without being able to respond or refer to the utterance as a part of our language games. This is not the place to delve further into Wittgenstein's theory of gesture as a medium of speaking without words. Aesthetic gestures are apophantic utterances that do not merely accompany language but are the full communication.

In an essay dealing with Wittgenstein's use of the terms gesture and picture, Karlheinz Lüdeking points to the status of the gesture as the embodied capacity for language. He writes: "This is also the reason why gestures display a vigor that distinguishes them from more abstract signs. A certain 'wild' bodily force animates a gesture, even though this force has already been formed into a meaningful shape. The corporeal energy of the gesture never entirely gives way to pure symbolism."[6]

Of course, a physical action becomes a gesture only by fulfilling a semantic function; but the meaning of a gesture is still not reducible to a fixed propositional content. Whereas a written sentence always represents the same proposition regardless of its calligraphic execution, a gesture can acquire a completely different meaning even by minimally varying its performance. Therefore, gestures can "surprise" us again and again, even if they are well known and well expected.[7] The "wildness" of the gesture makes it into a medium that takes possession of the body as its origin. In Schroeter's film gesture plays a similar role, as in the anecdote about us performing the silent film gestures while listening to music. The anecdote underscores a further argument derived from Wittgenstein: namely, that the gesture that is not a symbol reaches back into a life-world, where it is part of a communicative net. In Lüdeking's words: "Gestures do derive their communicative force from their connection to the body, but they attain to meaning only in the moulding contexts of particular 'forms of life.' This peculiarity of gestures secures them a place on the borderline of the realm of signs, where they shift in an area 'between wilderness and civilization.' This ambivalence of gestures is entirely in accordance with a note that Wittgenstein wrote down (probably shortly after his aforementioned exchange with Sraffa) about Frazer's interpretation of archaic rituals, in which he declares that 'what we have in the ancient rites is the practice of a highly cultivated gesture-language.'"[8]

In other films by Schroeter, such as *Der schwarze Engel* (1974), we find the conversion of

5 Ludwig Wittgenstein, *The Blue and Brown Books* (New York: Harper & Row, 1965), p. 166.
6 Karlheinz Lüdeking, "Pictures and Gestures," in *British Journal of Aesthetics*, vol. 30 no. 3 (July 1990), pp. 218–232 (especially p. 231).
7 Lüdeking, "Pictures and Gestures," p. 223.
8 Lüdeking, "Pictures and Gestures," p. 224.

different modes of gestures wrapped up in a mythical setting of accidental events related to death. The mixture of ethnological contexts and mundane social interaction leads into fictions of a peculiar kind—stories found at the intersections of mythical determinism and aleatory encounters in the streets. We find this constellation also in the work of Ulrike Ottinger, and certainly in Werner Herzog, were travelers are driven to seek adventure and passion in the encounters with cultures whose language is not shared and thus cannot be used—which then leads back to the gesture as expressive medium. The Nietzschean, Dionysian appeal of this aesthetic and its focus on practices of embodiment were acknowledged in the few remarks Michel Foucault made about *The Death of Maria Malibran* in a conversation with Gérard Dupont: "[...] escape itself is of a completely different type. The goal is to dismantle this organicity: this is no longer a tongue, but something completely different that comes out of the mouth. It's not the organ of a mouth that has been soiled and meant for someone else's pleasure. It's an 'unnameable,' 'unusual' thing, outside of all programs of desire. It's the body made entirely malleable by pleasure: something that opens itself, tightens, palpitates, beats, gapes. In *The Death of Maria Malibran*, the way in which the two women kiss each other, what is it? Sand dunes? A desert caravan, a voracious flower that advances, insect mandibles, a grassy crevice. All that is anti-sadism."[9]

This, as Foucault put it, "anarchizing of the body, in which hierarchies, localizations and designations [...] are being undone,"[10] refers to the body that is overwritten by gestures that are performing the body into a new play.

3. THE PERFORMANCE OF THINGS

The framing culture of gestures in which Schroeter's films established a new pictorial aesthetic of a theater of gestures stems from an entirely new mix of early cinema, opera, avant-garde music theater, and neorealism with its emphasis on urban landscape, objects, and location shots. The human body is becoming a filmic body, a filmic gesture. To perform the film as gesture in the sense Wittgenstein spoke about architecture and music as gestures goes beyond the body performance—it brings the filmic body itself forward as gesture in the same way as Wittgenstein speaks of music as gesture. In order to achieve this effect, film makes things perform—and I take this quality of performance as the precondition, the material foundation, for any film.[11] Films differ from other images in that they have a kind of show before the show; before we see them on the screen as moving images, something happens in front of the camera: objects will be staged so as to be

9 Michel Foucault, "Sade: Sergeant of Sex", in Paul Rabinow, James D. Faubion, eds., trans. Robert Hurley, *Aesthetics, Method, and Epistemology: Essential Works of Michel Foucault (1954–1984)*, Vol. 2 (New York: The New Press, 1994), p. 224. Originally published as "Sade sergent du sexe / Michel Foucault; propos recueillis par Gérard Dupont," in *Cinématographe* (Paris), no. 16 (1975), pp. 3–5.

10 Foucault, "Sade: Sergeant of Sex," p. 224.

11 With the exception of all those films that bypass the dispositive of the camera and work directly on the filmstrip, as in some animation techniques.

recorded by the camera, or the camera is framing things and objects in a way that they can be seen as gestures and be displaced from their functional and practical environments and life-worlds.

Lesley Stern, in an impressive essay, draws attention to the cinematic combination of histrionic play and everyday references in which lies the performative power of film.[12] To a far greater extent than stage theater, cinema lives by the combination of gestures and objects—in the words of Bresson, "those things that provoke gestures and words."[13] Bresson points to the role things play in film as they provoke actions—actions that are not exclusively performed through the gesture of actors. Films combine gestures and objects in image-acts that may or may not include speech-acts, but that, even in the absence of speech-acts, will resemble the latter. This is on display in a scene in *Eika Katappa*, in which two men who will be lovers are crossing a street side by side, while during their crossing two gigantic cranes start to move and bring their beaks together as if they would start to bill and coo. This poetics of the objects creates a world full of unforeseen correspondences that don't exist beyond the filmic body. In this sense, one could expand Foucault's description of the anarchizing tendency of gestures to the general relationship Schroeter constitutes between the pre-filmic and the filmic world.

Eika Katappa

12 Lesley Stern, "Paths That Wind through the Thicket of Things," in *Critical Inquiry* (Chicago), vol. 28 no. 1 (Autumn 2001), p. 327.

13 Robert Bresson comments: "Les gestes et les paroles ne peuvent pas former la substance d'un film comme ils forment la substance d'une pièce de théâtre. Mais la substance d'un film peut être cette ... chose ou ces choses que *provoquent* les gestes et les paroles [...]." Robert Bresson, *Notes sur le cinématographe*, (Paris: Gallimard, 1975), p. 69.

Marc Siegel

Longing Is Your Own Affair (I Always Remained Underground)

The mesmerizing opening 15 minutes of Werner Schroeter's *Der Tod der Maria Malibran* (*The Death of Maria Malibran*, 1972) consists predominantly of two-shots of various combinations of women, one of whom gravitates longingly towards the other. Blue title cards introduce Heinrich Heine's poem "Der Asra" ("The Asra"), the final lines of which are repeated like a mantra in a later title card: "Und mein Stamm sind jene Asra, welche sterben wenn sie lieben." ("And my clan is that of Asra, who must die whenever they love.")[1] Strong frontal lighting singles out heavily made-up and whitened faces against an indifferent black background. The women's gestures, wide-eyed stares, and hesitant dry kisses communicate both intense longing and studied disinterest. They emote individually, yet in close proximity, seemingly unable to affect the other with the experience of extreme emotion. This yearning fosters an intimate atmosphere of melancholy, which is furthered by the musical accompaniment of excerpts from Brahms' *Alto Rhapsody* on the soundtrack.[2] As the sequence comes to a close and the music shifts to the brisk, driving opening movement of Beethoven's *Triple Concerto*, a slightly low-angle medium shot introduces two women. A shorter one with reddish curls, shown in profile on the left, moves her hands slowly and deliberately towards the neck of a tall blonde woman to her side. In keeping with the display of unrequited emotions depicted thus far, the blonde feigns ignorance of the other's impassioned gestures, staring off expressionless into the darkness. Dramatic tension builds over the long static shot, as it remains unclear whether one woman will kiss or strangle the other. Before this passion can be conclusively tied to single action, a cut interrupts and we are presented with the same setting once again, reframed in a medium close-up with even more extreme lighting that lends the faces a peach-colored, angelic glow. The redheaded

1 See Heinrich Heine, "The Asra," in Heinrich Heine, trans. Edgar Alfred Bowring, *The Poems of Heine: Complete* (Palala Press, 2018; first ed. London: George Bell and Sons, 1884), pp. 406–407. First published in German in 1851, the poem was part of Heine's "History" cycle, initially published in his third poetry volume, *Romancero*. It is about the passion of a slave for a sultan's daughter, whom he observes every night at the fountain. When one night she sees him and asks him for his name and about his country and kin, he replies: "My name is / Mahomet, I came from Yemmen / And my race is of those Asras, / Who, whene'er they love, must perish." My own quote of the final lines is taken from the translation used on the title card in Schroeter's film, which differs slightly from Bowring's translation.

2 The deeply moving Brahms work would have been of interest to Schroeter not only for its setting of verses from Goethe's *Sturm und Drang* poem "Harzreise in Winter" (A Winter Journey through the Harz Mountains), which

woman, now mouthing words to herself, is visibly awestruck as she comes finally to place her lips on the other's cheeks while the music increases in tempo. A final cut to a close-up of her alone, as she slowly turns her head, opens her glistening eyes, and looks out yearningly, helplessly—a martyr to the cause of passion.

Whenever I watch this scene, I am fascinated by Schroeter's pairing of two icons from seemingly different cinematic worlds: Ingrid Caven and Candy Darling. Through her work with Rainer Werner Fassbinder, Daniel Schmid, and Schroeter, the redhead Caven became a mainstay of the New German Cinema and European art-film melodrama. Darling, on the other hand, was one of the key transgender figures in Andy Warhol's social world and films, and was memorialized in Lou Reed's epochal 1972 song "Walk on the Wild Side" ("Candy came from out on the island / In the backroom she was everybody's darling"). If Caven stands for mannered acting and Marlene Dietrich-esque distinction, Darling is New York street-savvy posing and underground glamour.[3] It's not that the juxtaposition of such performance styles and modes of appearance are unexpected in Schroeter's cinema. To the contrary, throughout *Maria Malibran*, for instance, the legend of the eponymous opera diva is recounted in the gestures, movements, and performances of a variety of performers, including Schroeter's muse Magdalena Montezuma, model and actress Christine Kaufmann, and transgender nightclub star Manuela Riva. By uniting Caven

Der Tod der Maria Malibran (1972)

attend to the rehabilitation of a man who rejected humanity after having suffered in love. Equally as significant, the soloist who performed the work at its premiere in Jena on March 3, 1870 was none other than the mezzo-soprano Pauline Viardot, Maria Malibran's younger sister.

3 Darling and the other transgender performers in the Warhol scene were acutely aware of the cultural gap between their underground movies and so-called legitimate European films. As Darling's longtime friend, Jeremiah Newton, recalls: "In 1972, after she appeared in *The Death of Maria Malibran*, Holly [Woodlawn] and Jackie [Curtis] made merciless fun of her serious attitude. It just drove them crazy that Candy aspired to be a working actress and a legitimate movie star. 'Get real! Get off your trapeze and down into the sawdust! Jackie would tell her.'" Quoted in Craig B. Highberger, *Superstar in a Housedress: The Life and Legend of Jackie Curtis* (New York: Chamberlain Bros./Penguin, 2005), p. 156.

and Darling within the frame, however, it's as if Schroeter collages together pages torn from different film-history books. This image depicts not only distinct embodiments of gender performance and emotional longing. It also figures Schroeter's own longing for the aesthetic innovations and sexual and gender transgressions of Warhol's cinema, and that of a broader American and international underground scene. Before I pursue these connections further, allow me to elaborate on the diva's dialectic that characterizes *Maria Malibran* and fuels Schroeter's aesthetic vision.

The 19th-century opera singer Maria Malibran died tragically at the age of 28, months after a horse-riding accident. Her determination to continue performing, despite serious injuries, contributed to the legend of the opera diva who dies on stage.[4] Although some of Malibran's biographical details are referenced in the film (including singing, her relationship with her father, and her death), Schroeter does not present a realistic, linear narrative, but rather a series of dramatic scenes and sequences that highlight emotional states of longing, passion, and despair, and that stage and re-stage the diva's death. Malibran serves as the model for all subsequent divas, including Schroeter's beloved Maria Callas: the female singer whose exceptional talent and emotional intensity release her from the banality of daily life and whose work interrupts a steady progression towards death. The diva's performances of longing, love, and other extreme emotions may bring *her* closer to death, but they provide her enraptured listeners opportunities for putting it off—at least for the duration of an aria. In his fascinating obituary of Callas, "The Prima Donna's Sudden Cardiac Death," originally published in *Der Spiegel* in 1977, Schroeter zeroes in on this romantic dialectic that drives his work and, as he sees it, characterizes our existence: "Those moments of artistic expression driven to excess, whether captured architecturally, musically, or otherwise, demonstrate nothing other than the need to halt the march of time. That is, to ignore the finiteness of human needs and to bestow upon them their tenability, and thereby also their pride, as an exceptional case."[5] He adds: "The unconditionality of emotion is anything but foolishness, for unconditionality already means two possibilities: death or love."[6]

Female opera singers do not have sole purchase on intense moments of artistic excess. Indeed, it was not Malibran's death alone that motivated Schroeter's film. "*The Death of Maria*

4 After suffering head injuries and refusing medical assistance, the strong-willed Malibran collapsed but did not actually die on stage. Malibran's legend, however, links her dramatic intensity and vocal prowess with death. This includes the account of an early stage appearance as Desdemona in Rossini's *Otello* opposite her father in the title role, tenor Manuel García, who is said to have threatened to kill her on stage if she didn't deliver a perfect performance. See Catherine Clément, *Opera, or the Undoing of Women*, trans. Betsy Wing (Minneapolis: University of Minnesota Press, 1988), pp. 29–33.

5 Werner Schroeter, "The Prima Donna's Sudden Cardiac Death," in DVD booklet notes for *Eika Katappa & Der Tod der Maria Malibran*, Edition Filmmuseum 51 (Filmmuseum München, 2010). Schroeter's article was originally published in *Der Spiegel*, September 26, 1977, pp. 261–267.

6 Schroeter, "The Prima Donna's Sudden Cardiac Death."

Malibran [...] came into existence as a result of reading a Spanish book on Maria Malibran, a text on Janis Joplin's death, and another on Jimi Hendrix's death—people I admired tremendously."[7] Along with Jim Morrison, Malibran, Joplin, and Hendrix all belonged to the "club of the twenty-seven year olds, who at the peak of their artistic expression, as sparkling mythical idols, irrevocably lost their lives."[8] Schroeter's much-discussed love of opera should therefore be contextualized within a broader interest in a range of classical and pop singers and film stars, each of whom differently embodies the diva's dialectic linking extreme emotion and death. It was, for instance, the voice of the versatile popular singer Caterina Valente, with her multiple language hits of the 1950s and 60s, that led Schroeter to opera in the first place.[9] Most Schroeter film soundtracks attest to this diversity of musical tastes, and the soundtrack for *Maria Malibran* is in this respect exemplary, bringing together such composers as Brahms, Beethoven, Cherubini, Händel, Mozart, and Stravinsky with singers Marlene Dietrich ("Die Mundharmonika"), Judy Rogers ("Love of a Boy"), Valente ("Spiel noch einmal für mich, Habanero"), and Candy Darling (renditions of "Ramona" and "St. Louis Woman").

Candy Darling died of leukemia at the age of 29, less than three years after the shooting of *Maria Malibran*, and could therefore be added to Schroeter's list of "sparkling, mythical idols" who tragically lost their lives at the "peak of their artistic expression." Schroeter was fascinated by Darling because of the radicality with which she lived her life as a transgender person in the repressive period of the late 1960s and early '70s in New York City. Androgynous and transgender performance indeed permeate Schroeter's work, from Magdalena Montezuma's appearances in male clothing in *Eika Katappa* (1969) and *Maria Malibran* to the dual-gendered egos of *Malina* (1991). The opening sequence of *Maria Malibran*, for instance, establishes a circuit of unspecified, if predominantly lesbian, desire and longing across close-ups of transgender, female, and male faces.[10] This foregrounding of non-normative desire across genders attests both to Schroeter's interest in the operatic and theatrical tradition of the *Hosenrolle* (trouser role) and to his queer subcultural investments in expressions of gender and sexual variety. But his specific interest in

7 Michel Foucault, "Passion According to Werner Schroeter," in Sylvère Lotringer, ed., *Foucault Live: Collected Interviews, 1961–1984*, trans. Lysa Hochroth and John Johnston (New York: Semiotext[e], 1996), p. 320.

8 Werner Schroeter, *Tage im Dämmer, Nächte im Rausch* (Berlin: Aufbau Verlag, 2011), p. 101. (All translations from this source are my own.) In his Callas obituary, Schroeter mentions James Dean and Marilyn Monroe as further examples of stars whose untimely deaths resulted not only from the intensity of their lives and the excesses of their artistic expression, but also from a destructive consumer society.

9 "I listened to radio and records as often as I could. The incomparable Caterina Valente was the star of my childhood years. I also listened to Hertha Töpper on the radio as a self-conscious Amneris in Verdi's opera *Aida*. At the time, I found her singing similar to that of Caterina Valente. And because I held Caterina Valente in such high regard, I also began to appreciate opera." (Schroeter, *Tage im Dämmer*, p. 28.)

10 For an extensive analysis of the film that emphasizes the queer aspects of these "sapphic desires," see Alice A. Kuzniar, *The Queer German Cinema* (Stanford, CA: Stanford University Press, 2000), pp. 118–131.

Der Tod der Maria Malibran

Candy Darling was certainly tied to an affinity for Warhol and American underground film culture more broadly.

Scholarship on Schroeter typically refers to the "underground" as a phase in his career, a period of experimental filmmaking with 8mm and 16mm film formats that lasted from 1968 until 1978, when he made his first feature that was released on 35mm, *Nel regno di Napoli*.[11] Rainer Werner Fassbinder's oft-quoted praise of Schroeter in a 1979 article in the *Frankfurter Rundschau* has become the touchstone for this critical perspective that—to my mind—provides limited understanding of underground film and neglects its genuine significance for Schroeter's work. "For more than a decade, which is a long time, almost too long, Werner Schroeter was the most important, exciting, decisive, as well as decided, director of alternative films, films generally referred to as *underground films*, a term that well-meaningly limits and prettifies this sort of film, eventually suffocating it in a tender embrace."[12] Fassbinder contends that there is in reality "no such thing as *underground* film." It is simply a divisive term that allows for the easy dismissal of those aesthetically appealing, yet commercially non-viable cinematic experiments, "beautiful but exotic plants that bloomed so unusually and so far away that

11 Michelle Langford suggests that Schroeter's underground phase lasted only a year, 1967–68, ending with his first feature, *Eika Katappa*, which was purchased by Zweite Deutsche Fernsehen (ZDF). In her account, the second phase includes the more narratively complex works made for television up until 1978, while the third phase incorporates all the documentaries and surrealist-tinged narrative films made thereafter. As a heuristic, such a rough division can be useful. It risks, however, obscuring essential connections across the filmmaking phases in terms of aesthetics, thematics, narrative technique, and production context. For instance, Schroeter worked with 16mm and incorporated underground thematics and aesthetics in all three of Langford's phases. See Langford, *Allegorical Images: Tableaux, Time and Gesture in Werner Schroeter's Cinema* (Bristol, UK: Intellect, 2006), pp. 19–30.

12 Rainer Werner Fassbinder, "Chin-up, Handstand, Salto Mortale—Firm Footing: On the Film Director Werner Schroeter, Who Achieved What Few Achieve, with *Kingdom of Naples*," in Michael Töteberg and Leo A. Lensing, eds., *The Anarchy of the Imagination: Interviews, Essays, Notes*, trans. Krishna Winston (Baltimore/London: Johns Hopkins University Press, 1992), p. 100. Fassbinder's article was first published in *Frankfurter Rundschau*, February 24, 1979.

basically one couldn't be bothered with them."[13] Schroeter's work was "beautiful but not exotic," and, with *Nel regno di Napoli*, Fassbinder hoped that his cultural significance would finally be widely acknowledged.

Fassbinder's venom was primarily directed at a film industry, funding system, and critical establishment that pigeonholes filmmakers (underground/amateur vs. mainstream/professional) and thereby restricts their mobility, creative license, and access to funds and audiences.[14] Despite the legitimacy of this critique, his argument ignores the existence of a self-defined and self-conscious underground film scene, whereby it obscures the very dynamic institutional context that enabled and sustained Schroeter's work in the first place. Foregrounding Fassbinder's perspective only risks furthering a misunderstanding about the extent to which Schroeter participated in, drew inspiration from, and was accepted by this developing world of German and international underground film. Admittedly, Schroeter himself regularly expressed ambivalence about the category of the underground as affixed to his work and tended as well to relegate it to a phase in his film production. However, while retrospectively dubbing his 1980 16mm gay sailor love story, *Weisse Reise* (White Journey) the definitive, "final spasms of the 'Queen of the Underground,'" he also defiantly insisted: "I always remained underground."[15] I suggest we take this claim of "always remaining underground" as both an assertion of Schroeter's commitment to punk, sexual, and aesthetic provocation and as an invitation to explore further the links between his work and underground film more generally.

13 Fassbinder, "Chin-up, Handstand, Salto Mortale," p. 101.

14 Fassbinder's article was not motivated simply out of admiration for Schroeter, however, but also out of anger over Rosa von Praunheim's nasty attack on the filmmaker in an article published that same month in the journal *Filmkritik*. See von Praunheim, "Mit herzlichen Gruss an Champagner-Schroeter," *Filmkritik* (Munich), no. 265 (January 1979), pp. 2–5. For an English translation, see Rosa von Praunheim, "With Fond Greetings to Champagne Schroeter," in Eric Rentschler, ed., *West German Filmmakers on Film: Visions and Voices* (New York: Holmes & Meier, 1988), pp. 191–195. Fassbinder apparently called up Schroeter to read him his counterattack—initially titled, "Betrayal of My Best Friend"—over the telephone in order to get his approval before publishing it. (See Schroeter, *Tage im Dämmer*, pp. 187–188.)

15 With "Queen of the Underground," Schroeter refers to an Italian-language book on German cinema in which he was so characterized. He plays off this reference in his statement "'*Untergründig*' *blieb ich immer*," which I am translating literally as "I always remained underground." My translation makes explicit Schroeter's connection to actual existing underground film, a connection he solicits by placing the word "*untergründig*" in quotation marks, thereby tying it back to the Italian publication. However, the word "*untergründig*" in German, as Caryl Flinn points out in her contribution to this volume, also carries with it a more general implication of "under the surface" or "profound." See Schroeter, *Tage im Dämmer*, p. 192. In an interview with Gérard Courant, Schroeter claims that his films up until *Nel regno di Napoli* were the work of a "very young person." See Courant, "Entretien avec Werner Schroeter," 1978, www.gerardcourant.com/index.php?t=ecrits&e=159. See also Timothy Corrigan, "Werner Schroeter's Operatic Cinema," in *Discourse* (Los Angeles) no. 3 (Spring 1981), pp. 46–59, particularly p. 55. Corrigan argues that with *Nel regno di Napoli*, Schroeter did not abandon his earlier aesthetic radicality; he simply "translated it" into a more accessible form.

Schroeter's entry into filmmaking coincided with the emergence of a broad interconnected European underground film scene. With a sole silent 8mm black & white 10-minute film to his name, he joined many other aspiring young filmmakers in December 1967 at EXPRMNTL, the 4th Experimental Film Festival in Knokke-le-Zoute, Belgium. The festival was "the door to another world, to American underground cinema, to Gregory Markopoulos, Andy Warhol, Jackie Curtis. Fantastic! It was a glance at something completely unknown, a different film form and an expression of my longing."[16] Schroeter was not alone in his longing for underground film. The 1967 Knokke festival marked the beginning of a newfound sense of cooperation, communication, and collaboration among previously isolated filmmakers throughout Europe. Soon after the festival, numerous film institutions were established, including screening venues, co-ops, magazines, and distribution outlets, all of which facilitated the establishment of European underground film culture.[17]

At Knokke, Schroeter met Rosa von Praunheim and his star Carla Aulaulu, with whom he began an intensive collaboration. Together with Magdalena Montezuma and photographer and cinematographer Elfi Mikesch, the five young artists formed the core of a germinating queer faction within the German underground. Over the next few years, von Praunheim and Schroeter made numerous short and medium-length films with and for each other, including the jointly authored *Grotesk-Burlesk-Pittoresk* (1968) and von Praunheim's *Schwestern der Revolution* (Sisters of the Revolution, 1969).[18] These performance-driven films, predominantly episodic in structure, with asynchronous sound and—like the American underground films that inspired them—featuring a gender transgressive cast of characters, were screened in underground venues alongside the more stringently formal or material works of the contemporary avant-garde. Von Praunheim's *Rosa Arbeiter auf goldener Straße* (1968) and Schroeter's *Argila* and *Neurasia* (both 1968) premiered in 1969 at the Hamburg Filmschau. Their films were featured in programs at XSCREEN, Birgit and Wilhelm Hein's radical underground screening venue in Cologne, and information on both filmmakers was included

16 Schroeter, *Tage in Dämmer*, p. 51. Schroeter's first film, alternately known as *Verona* or *Zwei Katzen*, consists of footage he shot in Verona, Venice, and Milan during a trip through Italy with his mother in 1967: "I wanted to show it in a side section [of the Knokke festival], but I was too shy at the time."

17 For the specifics about these institutional developments, see Birgit Hein, "Film in the Underground," in *Film als Idee. Birgit Heins Texte zu Film/Kunst*, Nanna Heidenreich, Heike Klippel, and Florian Krautkrämer, eds., trans. Daniel Hendrickson (Berlin: Vorwerk 8, 2016), pp. 261–270, and Xavier García Bardón, "EXPRMNTL. An Expanded Festival. Programming and Polemics at EXPRMNTL 4, Knokke-le-Zoute, 1967," *Cinema Comparat/ive Cinema* 1.2 (2013): 57–58. Available at: www.ocec.eu/cinemacomparativecinema/pdf/ccc02_eng_article_garciabardon.pdf.

18 The intimate exchange and jovial competition expressed through their joint filmmaking practices perhaps reached a peak with their versions of *Macbeth* produced for German television in 1971, each starring Magdalena Montezuma. Von Praunheim's film was shot on 16mm, while Schroeter used an early video format. The films were broadcast, one after the other, on Hessischer Rundfunk and Westdeutscher Rundfunk in December of that year.

in XSCREEN's 1971 publication of materials related to underground film.[19] Carla Aulaulu, star of most of von Praunheim and Schroeter's films between 1968 and 1970, was crowned the "first Superstar of the German underground."[20] In sync with the movement of underground and avant-garde films into the art world, von Praunheim's *Nicht der Homosexuelle ist pervers, sondern die Situation in der er lebt* (It Is Not the Homosexual Who Is Perverse But the Situation in Which He Lives, 1971) and Schroeter's *Maria Malibran* were included in the screening program of the Documenta 5 in Kassel in 1972.

Critics even tended to review von Praunheim and Schroeter's work together, recognizing a shared sensibility despite their distinctive aesthetic and thematic concerns. Birgit Hein situates their films in the subcategory of the underground narrative film, along with work by the British Stephen Dwoskin, German F.A. Kracht, and the Dutch Frans Zwartjes. While praising improvisational and anti-illusionistic qualities of their films, Hein takes issue with what she considers a lack of precision in von Praunheim and Schroeter's approach to the formal properties of the medium.[21] Hans Scheugl and Ernst Schmidt Jr. go even further than Hein in their hierarchy of innovation within the broad international underground and avant-garde film movements when they link the two filmmakers to a "pseudo-underground" that imitates American "camp" predecessors and uses pop music to gloss over "a lack of formal inventiveness."[22] Although Schroeter certainly took inspiration from the narrative experiments of an American underground that often recreated Hollywood glamour and spectacle on an artisanal scale, his work departed significantly from these predecessors through his studied, obsessive interest in the aesthetics and emotional states of opera. Call it camp, if you will, but only if camp is recognized as the very site of formal inventiveness and intermedial experimentation. In other words, Schroeter's early cinematic experiments combine an interest in female performance with a reflection on the materiality and intermedial relations of fandom.

In 1968, Schroeter made a series of short 8mm films exploring the mediated nature of his interest in Maria Callas, including the 13-minute *Maria Callas Porträt* (Maria Callas

19 Schroeter's *Eika Katappa* was screened twice, in January and December 1970, while von Praunheim's *Rosa Arbeiter* and *Schwestern* were included in a program with George and Mike Kuchar shorts in November of that same year. See W & B Hein, Christian Michelis, and Rolf Wiest, eds., *XSCREEN. Materialien über den Underground-Film* (Cologne: Phaidon, 1971), pp. 95–97, 122–125. Schroeter's *Neurasia* was listed in the 1970 distribution catalogue of the Hamburg Film Cooperative. More research into the distribution and exhibition history of Schroeter's early films is needed. These select references are meant simply to sketch his involvement in the evolving underground.

20 By Birgit Hein. See Hein, *Film im Underground. Von seinen Anfängen bis zum unabhängigen Kino* (Frankfurt am Main/Berlin/Vienna: Verlag Ullstein, 1971), p. 162.

21 Hein, *Film im Underground*, pp. 160–164, particularly p. 163.

22 Hein, Scheugl, and Schmidt Jr. were all filmmakers focusing almost exclusively on cinematic form and the materiality of film, so their critiques and hierarchies are not exactly impartial. See Scheugl/Schmidt Jr., *Eine Subgeschichte des Films. Lexikon des Avantgarde-, Experimental-, and Undergroundfilms, 1.Band* (Frankfurt/Main: Suhrkamp, 1974), p. 216.

Maria Callas Porträt (1968)

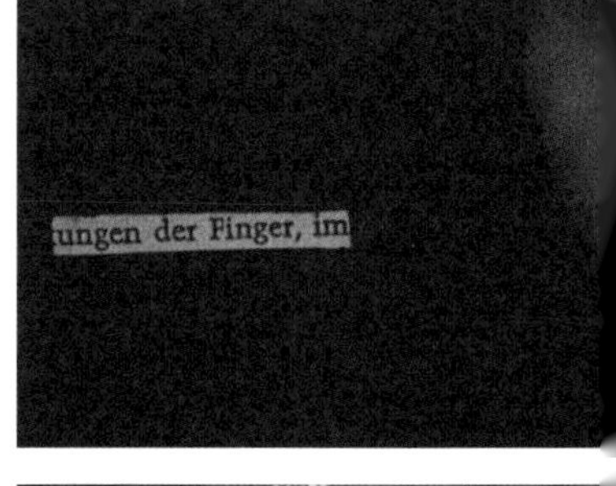

Portrait).[23] The silent, opening minute-and-a-half of the film introduces repeated shots, reframings, and slow pans of a static color image of the diva with a long mane of red hair casting a sideways glance back at the camera. A precisely looped excerpt of Callas in the second act of Verdi's *Un ballo in maschera* soon takes over on the soundtrack as the montage of still images acquires dynamism and variation. This almost 7-minute section of the film features details from select color and black & white photographic reproductions of Callas on stage and in private settings from newspapers, magazines, television guides, and record album covers. Through close-ups and the use of handmade vertical masks, Schroeter highlights the diva's gestures, posture, costuming, facial expressions, and intense stare. The masks create split-screen effects that momentarily isolate Callas against a black background, before alternating between vertical images that appear unexpectedly like slices through the frame. There are moments in which a quick editing rhythm syncs up with the music so as to animate the static images, particularly during the striking sequence of grainy black & white stills from the

23 Sebastian Feldmann's extensive commented filmography lists four Callas films: *Maria Callas Porträt*, *Mona Lisa*, *Maria Callas singt 1957 Rezitativ und Arie der Elvira aus Ernani 1844 von Giuseppe Verdi*, and *Callas Walking Lucia*. In Schroeter's autobiography, the last film is listed as a "Testfilm, Fragment, or Unfinished Project." See Feldmann, in Sebastian Feldmann, et al., eds., *Werner Schroeter* (Munich/Vienna: Hanser Verlag, 1980), pp. 86–93; and Schroeter, *Tage in Dämmer*, pp. 348, 357. As of this date, *Maria Callas Porträt* is the only one of these films that has been made available on DVD. See Schroeter, *Eika Katappa & Der Tod der Maria Malibran*, DVD.

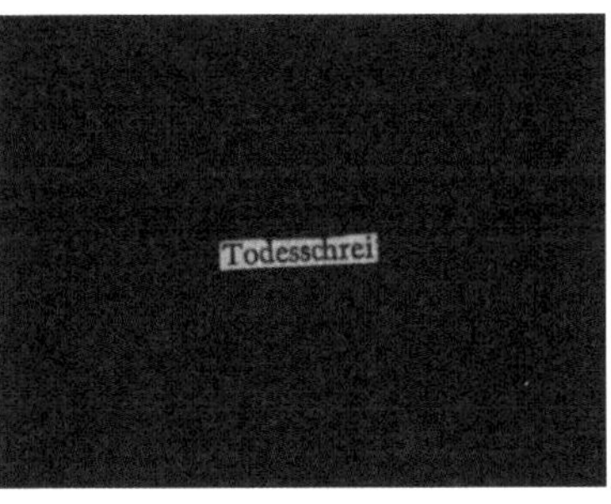

Scarpia murder scene from Puccini's *Tosca*. For the most part, however, the editing reflects a strict adherence less to the rhythms of the music than to the shifts in attention that characterize the act of listening, or rather, the act of flipping through images while listening to records or the radio.[24] Callas's heart-wrenching rendition of the aria "Qui la voce... Vien, diletto" from Bellini's *I Puritani* opens the film's final, 4-minute section, which features an almost word-by-word rendering of a euphoric critique of the diva's performance in Donizetti's *Lucia di Lammermoor*. Moving a small handmade horizontal mask across the black & white text, Schroeter reveals only a few words at a time, thereby compelling viewers to join him in savoring praise about his beloved diva. Callas's voice on the soundtrack proclaiming, "Ah rendetemi la speme / O lasciate, lasciatemi morir" ("Oh, return my hope, or let me die"), syncs up with the final words of the on-screen critique—the only words Schroeter repeats—which single out the singer's brilliance at the moment of her character's cries of death. The complex intermedial relations throughout the film culminate in this final link between the audiovisual image and the written word, as if bearing out Roland Barthes's observation, "I listen the way I read."[25]

At a few points in the final section of *Maria Callas Porträt*, Schroeter's fingers are visible, sliding the mask across the image. These moments obviously make evident the film's handmade quality, but they also figure the filmmaker's body as mediator of its depiction of obsessive fandom. In his other underground films as well, Schroeter staged his fandom through the mediation of performance, not just that of his own fingers, but of the bodies of others, foremost among them his female stars Aulaulu and Montezuma. Here, too, Schroeter's interest in female performance is tied to an investigation of film's formal properties. In his perhaps most radical formal experiment, the 16mm double-screen film *Argila*, for instance,

24 Speaking of his teenage years in Heidelberg, Schroeter notes, "[t]hat was the time when I started a scrapbook (*ein Album*) about Maria Callas and began to collect images and newspaper reports of her appearances. [...] Back then I heard music for many hours at a time.... I owned a tape recorder and began to record everything that was broadcast with or about Maria Callas." (Schroeter, *Tage in Dämmer*, p. 31.) The soundtracks to Schroeter's films often index the mediality of this home-listening experience by including the sounds of scratches and pops from old records.

25 Roland Barthes, "Listening," in *The Responsibility of Forms: Critical Essays on Music, Art and Representation*, trans. Richard Howard (New York: Hill & Wang, 1985), p. 245.

short scenes with three alternating female performers (Aulaulu, Montezuma, and Gisela Trowe), who each yearn for the same silent and placid man (Sigurd Salto), dramatize familiar Schroeter themes of longing, unrequited love, and forebodings of death. Throughout the medium-length film, the performer's repetitions of expressions of dramatic intensity—with such lines as, "You want me to die. You don't have any compassion for me. You have no mercy for me who adores you. What else should I do?"—echo the doubling of the cinematic image in an expanded cinema that extends the time and space of action, only to fold it back upon itself. *Argila*'s two images present the same scene, side by side, first in black & white on the left and then, after an approximately 30-second delay, inverted and in color on the right (see p. 17). The right image therefore both mirrors the one on the left, and, being the only image with sound, retrospectively lends it voice and presence. It's as if Schroeter's characters cannot keep up with the images of their own emotional disarray. This "aesthetic-structural experiment," as Schroeter referred to it, recalls Warhol's 16mm double-screen films, particularly *The Chelsea Girls* (1966), which also depicts scenes of emotional turmoil across side-by-side, black & white and color images that are slightly out of sync with each other.[26] Douglas Crimp aptly characterizes Warhol's film as a "misfitting together" and links the disjunctions between the two images with the social and sexual mismatchings depicted within and across them.[27] Like this seminal underground predecessor, Schroeter's film, with its performances of repeated desire and despair presented alongside their delayed mirror images, similarly binds innovation at the level of content to a radical experimentation with film form.

As a means of returning to *Maria Malibran*, I'd like to conclude by recalling Wim Wenders' perceptive early review of Schroeter's short and medium-length films.[28] After emphasizing the various repetitions in the films—dialogue lines, female performers, and themes—and the opportunities they present for an extended moment of reflection about the cinematic image, Wenders refers to two underground publications: Alfred von Meysenbug's comic book *Glamour Girl* (1968) and Mikesch and von Praunheim's photo-novel *Oh Muvie* (1969).[29] Like Schroeter's early films, these books each feature Carla Aulaulu, but it is not her appearance alone that interests Wenders. Instead, he singles out a line from *Oh Muvie* to characterize

26 This was not the only time Schroeter gestured toward Warhol with an aesthetic-structural experiment. In 1972, as a follow-up to *Maria Malibran*, he planned a film essay about Marilyn Monroe, "a kind of structural work about Warhol's Monroe images with Elvis Presley music and Allen Ginsberg and everything possible." He eventually lost interest in the idea and made the existential Los Angeles melodrama *Willow Springs* instead. See Schroeter, *Tage in Dämmer*, pp. 62–64, 113.

27 Douglas Crimp, *"Our Kind of Movie": The Films of Andy Warhol* (Cambridge, MA: MIT Press, 2012), pp. 96–109.

28 Wim Wenders, "Filme von Werner Schroeter," *Filmkritik* (Munich), no. 149 (May 1969), pp. 318–319.

29 Wenders, "Filme," p. 319. *Oh Muvie* is both the title of the photo-novel and the pseudonym of photographer Elfi Mikesch. The book was published in the same series as Meysenbug's underground comics. As if cementing von Praunheim and Mikesch—and by extension Schroeter, Aulaulu, and Montezuma—to the history of underground film, an image from *Oh Muvie* is used for the cover design for Birgit Hein's book *Film im Under-*

the experience of watching Schroeter's early films: "She could commit so completely to a single expression that her screams transformed the image into waves."[30] Like Wenders, I too am suggesting that Schroeter's depiction of female performances of extreme emotion transforms our experience of the image. This may be perfectly obvious when considering such film experiments as *Maria Callas Porträt* and *Argila*, which, through the use of either handmade masks and filmed photographs or double-screen projection, foreground the materiality and temporality of the film image. Even in a performance-driven film like *Maria Malibran*, however, Schroeter's depiction of emotional states lends them a temporal density and material presence such that they emerge out of the dramatic scenes as, in Dietrich Kuhlbrodt's words, "a sensual contact with joyful duration."[31] Removed from the forward movement

Der Tod der Maria Malibran

of narrative causality, the performers' communication of emotion through repeated gestures and expressions functions as a kind of "emotional superimposition."[32] The close-up of Ingrid Caven's face that concludes the brief sequence with Candy Darling, for instance, does not present us with the narrative result of the actions in the previous shots. Caven is not weeping because Darling rejected her. Her longing is her own affair. Schroeter's images of that longing, however, his temporally dense images that call attention to their own plasticity, are clues to his affair with the underground.

ground. See Alfred von Meysenbug, *Glamour Girl* (Frankfurt/Main: Heinrich Heine Verlag, 1969), Streit-Zeit Bücher 2, Oh Muvie; *Oh Muvie* (Frankfurt/Main: Heinrich Heine Verlag, 1969), Streit-Zeit Bücher 5.

30 Wenders, "Filme," p. 319. Author's translation. The original reads: "Sie konnte sich so intensiv auf einen einzigen Ausdruck festlegen, dass ihre Schreie das Bild in Wellen verwandelten."

31 Dietrich Kuhlbrodt, "Erfahrene Erfahrung. Über den Umgang mit Werner Schroeter, will sagen seinen Filmen," in Feldmann, et al., eds., *Werner Schroeter*, p. 35. [Author's translation] The sensuality of the images derives in no small part from Schroeter's care in lighting the low-sensitive color film stock. "This illusory impression of physicality arose from the experimentation with the material. It was important for me to achieve such a plasticity, let's say, a false three-dimensionality with the coloration." (Schroeter, *Tage in Dämmer*, p. 126.)

32 This is Kuhlbrodt's term (Kuhlbrodt, "Erfahrene Erfahrung," p. 34).

Michelle Langford

Werner Schroeter's *Salome* (1971)

Writing of Werner Schroeter's *Salome* some ten years after it was produced, American film critic Gary Indiana described it as "one of the most beautiful adaptations of [Wilde's] text to film ever made."[1] As with so many of Werner Schroeter's films, such high praise was a long time coming. Indeed, in an impassioned article published in the *Frankfurter Rundschau* in 1979, fellow New German Cinema director Rainer Werner Fassbinder bemoaned the lack of appreciation for Schroeter's talent. He wrote: "Werner Schroeter's grand cinematic scheme of the world was confined, repressed, and at the same time ruthlessly exploited. His films were given the convenient label of "underground," which transforms them in a flash into beautiful but exotic plants that bloomed so unusually and so far away that basically one couldn't be bothered with them, and therefore wasn't supposed to bother with them. And that's precisely as wrong as it is stupid. For Werner Schroeter's films are not far away; they're beautiful but not exotic. On the contrary."[2]

Indeed, as Fassbinder highlights in more general terms, Schroeter's *Salome* barely garnered anything by way of critical attention at the time of its release, and may rightly have appeared to critics and audiences alike to be one of those "beautiful but exotic plants" that bloomed so "unusually and so far away." Looking back from the vantage point of the 21st century, and with a complete view of Schroeter's vibrant career as a filmmaker and a theatre and opera director, it might be easy to relegate *Salome* to the domain of a minor work "made for television." However, as I want to show in this chapter, *Salome* was a pivotal film for numerous reasons, not least because it was made at a crucial juncture in Schroeter's career as he branched out into theatre and opera, but also because it is emblematic of the productive relationship between film and television in Germany in the 1970s. Before moving on to look at the distinctive aesthetics of the film and at Schroeter's unique approach to the adaptation of Oscar Wilde's play, I will first provide some background and context for the production.

1 Gary Indiana, "Scattered Pictures: The Movies of Werner Schroeter," in *Artforum* (New York), vol. 20 no. 3 (March 1982), p. 49.

2 Rainer Werner Fassbinder, "Chin-up, Handstand, Salto Mortale—Firm Footing: On the Film Director Werner Schroeter, Who Achieved What Few Achieve, with *Kingdom of Naples*," in Michael Töteberg and Leo A. Lensing, eds., *The Anarchy of the Imagination: Interviews, Essays, Notes*, trans. Krishna Winston (Baltimore/London: Johns Hopkins University Press, 1992), p. 101. Fassbinder's article was first published in the *Frankfurter Rundschau*, February 24, 1979.

SALOME IN BAALBEK

In January 1971, Schroeter set out for Lebanon with a small production team and a retinue of actors, many of whom were also close friends and collaborators on previous films. Among them were the cinematographer Robert van Ackeren, who had already worked with Schroeter on *Eika Katappa* (1969) and *Nicaragua* (1969; now lost), and the actress Magdalena Montezuma, one of Schroeter's closest friends. This statuesque and somewhat androgynous woman would embody the character of King Herod with grace, *gravitas*, and a touch of camp. The year before, Mascha Elm-Rabben, who plays Salome, had appeared alongside Montezuma in Schroeter's *Der Bomberpilot* (The Bomber Pilot). Together with Carla Aulaulu they formed a trio of former Nazi showgirls trying to figure out what to do with their lives after the fall of the Third Reich. For Ellen Umlauf, who plays Herodias, *Salome* would be the first of four important collaborations with the director. She was the only actor in the troupe with formal training, having studied at the Max Reinhardt Seminar at the University of Music and Performing Arts in Vienna. In typical Schroeter style, he also engaged numerous locals to play minor roles, even incorporating a troupe of Lebanese folk musicians into the film. Elfi Mikesch, who would later become one of Schroeter's most trusted cinematographers, accompanied the team to work on costume and make-up. As Schroeter recalls, Elfi "turned Magdalena's surreal face into an abstract mask," and transformed Ellen Umlauf "into a poisonous, gloomy Liz-Taylor-Cleopatra figure."[3]

Aside from the human players, who helped Schroeter realize his vision, it was the ancient ruins of Baalbek that provided an ideal setting for the film. Situated in present-day Lebanon, approximately 90 kilometers from Beirut, the complex of Roman temples was built over a period of about two centuries, commencing around the 1st century BC on the site of a Phoenician agricultural village in what was then part of Syria. Throughout the 19th century, when the city was part of the Ottoman Empire, Baalbek had been a favourite stop for European tourists in search of adventure in the Orient. According to Mary Bergstein, the ruins at Baalbek were "one of the most photographed of all archaeological sites in the nineteenth century," and among its more famous visitors was none other than Charles Baudelaire, who marveled at Baalbek's architectural beauty.[4] Indeed, German Emperor Wilhelm II even made a fleeting but highly significant visit to Baalbek on his way home from Jerusalem in 1898, and it seems that the ruins made quite an impression. According to Thomas Scheffler, the Kaiser and his wife arrived shortly before sunset on November 10, and departed around 8 a.m. the following morning; just enough time to view the famous sunrise and for the inauguration of a commemorative marble tablet—a gift from

3 Werner Schroeter, *Tage im Dämmer, Nächte im Rausch* (Berlin: Aufbau Verlag, 2011), p. 93. [All translations are by the author.]

4 Mary Bergstein, *In Looking Back One Learns to See: Marcel Proust and Photography* (Amsterdam/New York: Rodopi, 2014), pp. 80–81.

the Ottoman Sultan. Miraculously, within little more than a month after the Kaiser's visit, a team of German archaeologists were dispatched to the site to commence excavations.[5]

I mention the Kaiser's visit not because there is any explicit reference to this by Schroeter, but because it sits at the heart of one of the many competing interpretations of the site, and to which Schroeter's production necessarily contributes. According to Dell Upton, as a symbol of Imperial Rome, for Wilhelm II the visit to Baalbek may be considered a form of "political theater," as "it represented European culture implanted autocratically in the East through imperial might, and so stood as a rebuke to the many late-nineteenth century Europeans who derived democratic or republican lessons from the Classical past."[6] But, as Upton has eloquently argued, this is only one of several interpretations of Baalbek that have circulated over time. Another, which he calls "Oriental Baalbek," was derived from local stories that "identified the ruins at Baalbek as a palace built by King Solomon for the Queen of Sheba." Central to this perspective were local Quranic stories that attributed the construction to fabled *jinn* (genies) who, according to local legend, were sent to aid Solomon. It was thus that 19th-century visitors used local "practice to confirm biblical narratives."[7]

Rather than attempting to decide which story is to claim authenticity over another, according to Upton, we need to acknowledge that these various interpretations produce multiple, reified Baalbeks: Roman Baalbek, Oriental Baalbek, Byzantine Baalbek, Arab Baalbek, and Ottoman, Syrian, or Lebanese Baalbek, each of which "is rooted in the fantasy of the stability of authentic cultural forms." Upton says that "Baalbek teaches us to value fluidity on a variety of scales."[8] On many levels, Schroeter's production of *Salome* amidst the ruins of Baalbek also reminds us of this fluidity, and of the cultural and historical contingencies that lead rulers and historians alike to impose one interpretation over another onto a cultural text. As I have argued elsewhere, Schroeter's films frequently resist reified interpretations and do not fit neatly into any single theoretical model. *Salome* is no exception.[9] In many ways, Schroeter's production sits at the opposite end of the spectrum from the Kaiser's autocratic "political theater," and even though the biblical origins of the Salome story might tie it back to "Oriental Baalbek," as we shall see the scandalous nature of Wilde's play and Schroeter's treatment of it tends to preclude such a reading.

If the ruins of Baalbek provided the ideal multilayered *mise-en-scène* for Schroeter's vision, it was German television that made it all

5 Thomas Scheffler, "The Kaiser in Baalbek: Tourism, Archaeology, and the Politics of Imagination," in Hélène S. Sader, Thomas Scheffler, and Angelika Neuwirth, eds., *Baalbek: Image and Monument, 1898–1998* (Stuttgart: Franz Steiner Verlag, 1998), pp. 27–28.

6 Dell Upton, "Starting from Baalbek: Noah, Solomon, Saladin, and the Fluidity of Architectural History," in *Journal of the Society of Architectural Historians* (Berkeley: University of California Press), vol. 68 no. 4 (December 2009), pp. 459–460.

7 Upton, pp. 460–461.

8 Upton, p. 464.

9 Michelle Langford, *Allegorical Images: Tableau, Time and Gesture in the Cinema of Werner Schroeter* (Bristol, UK: Intellect, 2006).

possible. The film was produced on a shoestring by state-sponsored German television network Zweites Deutsches Fernsehen (ZDF) in collaboration with the Wiesbaden-based company Ifage Filmproduktion. By German television standards, however, the location shoot must have made it a relatively expensive production. When the cast and crew arrived in Baalbek, they discovered that the production manager from Ifage had prepared virtually nothing: equipment sent ahead had gone missing and electrical cables at the site were not yet connected.[10] Recalling the experience to Schroeter later, ZDF producer Christoph Holch, who accompanied Schroeter and his motley crew to Baalbek, wondered whether the mysteriously depleted production account might have had something to do with the production manager's prolonged visits to the casino.[11] Despite these setbacks, cast and crew worked around the clock for two and a half weeks to complete the shoot on schedule and just before the winter snows set in.[12] Both Christoph Holch and ZDF would be instrumental to Schroeter's developing career, and the *Salome* production certainly set the scene for future collaborations. It is just one example of the crucial role that West German television played not only in Schroeter's career, but in that of other New German filmmakers as well.

Indeed, the role of television in the rise of New German Cinema cannot be underestimated. Sheila Johnston once wrote that "the New German Cinema owes its existence to the munificence of television."[13] This statement sums up the unique and rather peculiar interdependence that developed between the establishment of a new, often radical cinema in West Germany in the 1960s and 1970s and public service broadcasting. As early as 1962, young filmmakers, frustrated with the declining quality and social irrelevance of the post-war German film industry, called for major changes to the intellectual, economic, and formal parameters of West German national film culture.[14] By the late 1960s, fierce lobbying by this younger generation of filmmakers, led by the likes of Alexander Kluge, had managed to bring about some reform to the national and regional systems of film subsidy allocation. However, many first-time and less mainstream directors were marginalized by the subsidy guidelines, which still favored established directors. At this time, Germany's free-to-air television stations were faced with a mandate inscribed in Article 5 of the *Grundgesetz* (West Germany's preliminary constitution) to "provide a forum for a range of different 'socially relevant groups.'"[15]

10 Schroeter, p. 92.
11 Christoph Holch, quoted in Schroeter, p. 92.
12 Schroeter, pp. 93–95.
13 Sheila Johnston, "The Radical Film Funding of ZDF. Introduction to an interview with Eckhart Stein of ZDF German Television," in *Screen* (London), vol. 23 no. 1 (May/June 1982), p. 60.
14 Their demands were formally articulated in the Oberhausen Manifesto, which was signed by a group of filmmakers and writers at the annual Oberhausen Short Film Festival. For an English translation of the document, see Eric Rentschler, ed., *West German Filmmakers on Film: Visions and Voices* (New York/London: Holmes & Meier, 1988), p. 2.
15 Richard Collins and Vincent Porter, *WDR and the Arbeiterfilm: Fassbinder, Ziewer and Others* (London: British Film Institute, 1981), pp. 21–22.

With their links to and interest in a variety of social issues, from women's rights to workers' organizations, the gay liberation movement and the rights of guest workers, the New German filmmakers were in an ideal position to fulfill this mandate at relatively low cost to the broadcasters. In turn, apart from some of the more conservative regional stations such as Bayerischer Rundfunk, television commissions enabled young filmmakers like Schroeter to work in relative freedom from editorial constraints and commercial considerations.

It is in this context that Werner Schroeter began producing work for the second national station ZDF's weekly late-night program *Das kleine Fernsehspiel* in 1970, with his production of *Der Bomberpilot*—a relationship that lasted some fifteen years. One of the unique aspects of *Das kleine Fernsehspiel* was its commitment to promoting aesthetic experiment while allowing filmmakers to maintain full artistic control. This enabled Schroeter to forge an alternate path into the German cinema scene during the 1970s and largely allowed him to bypass the various social and cultural obligations that came with state funding. *Salome* was one of two "theatrical" projects that Schroeter made for ZDF in 1971. The second was a studio-filmed adaptation of Shakespeare's *Macbeth* (1971) with Magdalena Montezuma in the title role. In retrospect, they may be seen as pivotal not only to the development of his peculiar cinematic aesthetic, but also to the development of his parallel career as a theater and opera director. This began a year after the TV production of *Salome*, with his production of Lessing's *Emilia Galotti* at the Deutsches Schauspielhaus in Hamburg in 1972. The film also predates his stage production of Wilde's play at the Schauspielhaus Bochum by two years. Reflecting his preference for what film critic Gary Indiana has described as "radically expressionistic, dramatically extreme works that lend themselves readily to a hyperventilated notion of drama,"[16] Schroeter was drawn once again to *Salome* in 1986, directing Richard Strauss's opera for the Teatro de Bellas Artes in Mexico City. In many ways, Schroeter's *Salome* film might be seen as the first installment of a complex intermedial fascination not just with the Salome story, but with its many and various cultural artifacts.

For his 1971 film, Schroeter worked from Hedwig Lachmann's German translation of Oscar Wilde's play, which retells the famous story of Salome, King Herod's stepdaughter who asked for the head of John the Baptist in return for performing the Dance of the Seven Veils. Lachmann's translation of the play from the original French helped to facilitate its wide circulation through the German-speaking world. In England, public performances of the play had been banned until 1931, because the Lord Chamberlain considered its treatment of biblical content blasphemous, but in Germany the ban only lasted until 1903. In both countries, a number of private performances were staged prior to the lifting of the ban. In Germany, Max Reinhardt directed a private performance in November 1902, followed by a series of public performances the following year. According

16 Indiana, "Scattered Pictures," p. 49.

to Petra Dierkes-Thrun, composer Richard Strauss attended one of Reinhardt's productions in 1903, inspiring him to create his operatic adaptation, also basing his libretto on the Lachmann translation.[17] This premiered just two years later, in 1905 in Dresden. Despite several excerpts of Strauss's opera making it onto the soundtrack during post-production, in his autobiography Schroeter states emphatically that he did not take inspiration from the Strauss opera.[18] Rather, he recalls that his inspiration came primarily from the musicality of Wilde's original French text, with the Lachmann translation serving a much more practical purpose. Schroeter recalls that for the first time in his career he had a "proper script [*Drehbuch*], a plot, a story,"[19] and as such the film marks a significant departure from the entirely improvisational mode he had used for his previous short films and his first feature-length film, *Eika Katappa* (1969).

Although Schroeter remains for the most part faithful to the text, he has truncated it somewhat by omitting the debate between the five Jews, the Sadducee, the Pharisee, and the Nazarenes, and by cutting many of the soldiers' lines. Those that remain are spoken in Arabic. Despite these omissions—and the obviously limited budget—Schroeter managed to turn Wilde's single-act play into a many-layered and complex cinematic work that, it could be argued, does audio-visual justice to the elaborate metaphorical imagery of Wilde's drama. Not only was Schroeter emphatic in not taking Strauss's operatic adaptation as his starting point, he was similarly adamant that the film's aesthetic should have "nothing to do with [the] Aubrey Beardsley Symbolist kitsch illustrations"[20] produced for the English version of Wilde's play.

For many, the name Salome may summon the imagery of 19th-century Orientalist and Symbolist painters such as Gustave Moreau, who surrounds his Salome in the opulent riches and elaborate drapery typical of 19th-century imaginings of the exotic East. For others, Aubrey Beardsley's Art Nouveau illustrations, which were produced to accompany Wilde's English text, served to imbue the ancient story with the spirit of the *fin de siècle* and *l'art pour l'art* philosophy of the Aesthetic Movement. In a sense, both traditions inscribe the legendary story of Salome with a spirit and an aesthetic far removed from the biblical origins of Salome, Herodias, King Herod, and John the Baptist. At the same time, a hunger for popular entertainment and the birth of cinema in the late 19th century further contributed to the emergence of "Salomania," a "Salome Craze" that straddled the worlds of high art and popular culture, stage and screen, and caused controversy no matter which strata of society it was intended for.[21] In 1907, for example, the Strauss opera made its U.S. debut at the Metropolitan Opera in New York; however, outraged board mem-

17 Petra Dierkes-Thrun, *Salome's Modernity: Oscar Wilde and the Aesthetics of Transgression* (Ann Arbor: University of Michigan Press, 2011), p. 64.

18 Schroeter, *Tage im Dämmer*, pp. 90–91.

19 Schroeter, p. 90.

20 Schroeter, p. 91.

21 Toni Bentley, *Sisters of Salome* (New Haven: Yale University Press, 2002), p. 42.

bers caused the remaining performances to be cancelled.

With the rise of film as one of the most popular forms of mass entertainment in the early 20th century, the "Salome Craze" spread to the silver screen. German film pioneer Oskar Messter was one of the first, with two films, *Tanz der Salome* (1906) and *Salome* (1910).[22] In Hollywood too, numerous film adaptations were made in the 1910s and 1920s, prior to the introduction of the Production Code. Not only do these films contribute to the first cycle of grandiose "biblical" or "oriental" epics, stylistically, the early feature films draw variously from either the Orientalist or Aesthetic artistic traditions. In the Orientalist tradition, *Salome* (1918) was directed by J. Gordon Edwards for the Fox Film Corporation. Theda Bara (*née* Theodosia Goodman), who played Salome, became known for being one of the silver screen's first "vamps." Early in her career, Hollywood publicists cultivated her "vampish" star persona. According to Eve Golden, this was suggestively amplified when someone at Fox realized that her adopted screen name was also an anagram for "Arab Death," enabling a dovetailing of her star persona with the role of the fatal Eastern princess.[23] Just a few years later, in 1923, Charles Bryant and Alla Nazimova produced a new silent film version, this time drawing heavily on Aubrey Beardsley's illustrations as a model both for the set design and costumes.

Gaylyn Studlar has pointed out that Orientalist films flourished during Hollywood's silent era, and the appeal of such films for female audiences was linked to the popularity of an Orientalist aesthetic that became widespread in both high art and mass culture. Studlar writes that "cinematic signifiers and cultural intertexts [...] targeted *female* consumers of film in the 1910s and 1920s through a visual language of Orientalism well established in fashion, design, and the arts."[24] This extended into the marketing of consumer culture through packaging and displays in department stores.[25] However, as Studlar emphasizes, dance, as a respectable art form, also served as an important reference point beyond the more vulgar realm of consumer culture, and this dovetailed closely with the rise in the early 20th century of the "New Woman."[26] In fact, Studlar credits the controversial and short-lived debut of Strauss's *Salome* in New York in 1907 with the rise of "Salomania" in the U.S.[27] It was in this sense that, like Orientalism in general, the Salome craze operated across high and low cultural domains. Later, during the 1950s with the rise of the biblical epic in widescreen and color, Hollywood would once again tap into Orientalism. It was during this period that Rita Hayworth portrayed Salome in William Dieterle's *Salome*

22 "Oskar Messter," www.filmportal.de/person/oskar-messter_95edc384ff074aaf99cd1502202a1591

23 Eve Golden, *Vamp: The Rise and Fall of Theda Bara* (Lanham, MD: Vestal Press, 1998), p. 131.

24 Gaylyn Studlar, "'Out-Salomeing Salome': Dance, the New Woman, and Fan Magazine Orientalism," in Matthew Bernstein and Gaylyn Studlar, eds., *Visions of the East: Orientalism in Film* (London: I. B. Tauris, 1997), pp. 99–100.

25 Studlar, "'Out-Salomeing Salome'," p. 103.

26 Studlar, p. 105.

27 Studlar, p. 106.

(1953), parts of which were famously filmed on location in the Holy Land.

Schroeter's production departs significantly from its cinematic forebears. His film, however, retains the convergence between high and low culture that had characterized "Salomania" earlier in the 20th century. Through his setting of the film amidst the ruins of Baalbek, Schroeter embeds the ever-present imagery of death and decay that shadows every moment of Wilde's play into the very *mise-en-scène*. Right from the opening scene, the ruinous structures of the temple buildings seem to entomb the characters and visually echo the words of Herodias's Page, who remarks of the Moon: "She is like a woman rising from a tomb. She is like a dead woman. One might fancy she was looking for dead things." This choice of location tends to literalize and concretize the moral decay of Herod's court, which bubbles to the surface of the text through Herod's increasingly long and garbled speeches. Here, the ruinous and decayed structures of the temple complex attest to the decay of all things—even those that are meant to stand the test of time. According to Walter Benjamin, this is central to the peculiarly Baroque allegorical way of looking at things. In his book on the German *Trauerspiel* (mourning play) of the 17th century, Benjamin writes that "in allegory the observer is confronted with the *facies hippocratica* of history as a petrified, primordial landscape. Everything about history that, from the very beginning, has been untimely, sorrowful, unsuccessful, is expressed in a face—or rather in a death's head."[28]

Indeed, Wilde's play is populated by many such deathly faces and littered with the fatal gazes that are exchanged between them. Salome's fatal beauty is reflected in the pallid appearance of the Moon: those who gaze too insistently upon her are doomed to a kind of death. In the case of the Young Syrian, who takes his own life, this death is quite literal. The demise of Herod (Magdalena Montezuma), on the other hand, is metaphorical; he undergoes a transformation into a living corpse as he quickly descends into madness. Even Herodias (sternly played by Ellen Umlauf), whose beauty has long faded and can no longer hold the attention of the King, evokes the image of a death's head. Finally, of course, there is Jochanan (John the Baptist) himself, the death's head toward which the entire play drives. This play of death's heads and fatal gazes is central to Schroeter's complex visual, musical, and performative interpretation of Wilde's text.

This complexity is played out through the *mise-en-scène*, performance, camerawork, editing, and most of all through Schroeter's rather idiosyncratic *collage* of music and other sounds. Interestingly, as Schroeter himself recalls, it was not until he and the film's editor Ila von Hasperg had prepared the initial edit that he decided to add the complex music mix to the film. Schroeter remarked that they tested the film without music, but he didn't like this much: "the voices had too little atmosphere," so music was added to provide another, contradictory layer to the images and dia-

28 Walter Benjamin, *The Origin of German Tragic Drama*, trans. John Osborne (London/New York: Verso, 1985), p. 166.

Salome (1971)

logue.[29] Throughout the film, Schroeter accompanies the action and dialogue with a range of eclectically compiled musical fragments. These primarily take the form of non-diegetic musical accompaniments to the images, and range from "La Paloma" by the popular Chilean singer Rosita Serrano to classical pieces from a wide range of composers, including Gaetano Donizetti, Mozart, Verdi, Gluck, Wagner, Giacomo Meyerbeer, and Vincenzo Bellini, as well as traditional Lebanese folk music. The latter accompanies Salome's dance, and is the only diegetic music in the film. Schroeter also includes some haunting experimental electronic music, the late Baroque organ music of Antonio Soler, the occasional sound of aircraft overhead, and excerpts from Richard Strauss's opera *Salome* (1905), which Sebastian Feldmann has described as functioning not so much as a "duet" with the image, but as a "duel."[30]

In fact, throughout the film, this rather haphazard *collage* of diverse musical styles often works in juxtaposition with rather than to underscore the images and the emotions conveyed by the characters. Their fragmentary and often illogical relationship to the image adds to the sense of chaotic decay that characterizes Schroeter's films and his allegorical style more generally. One of Schroeter's most persistent techniques was to collapse the distinction between high art and popular culture, rendering them as fragments. A key example of this may be seen in *Salome* through the recurrence of Rosita Seranno's rendition of the popular Spanish tune "La Paloma." This piece is initially heard approximately five minutes into the film, just after the first appearance of Salome (Mascha Elm-Raben). It cuts in abruptly as she slowly descends the worn and cracked marble staircase of the ruined temple. On the soundtrack, the gentle and melodious sounds of a Mozart string quartet give way abruptly to the sound of static from a record player before the first, rather jaunty, strains of "La Paloma" are heard.

This is a key characteristic of Schroeter's style in his early films, including *Eika Katappa* (1969) and *Der Bomberpilot* (1970), and this is by no means intended as mood music, serving merely to underscore the drama, but rather works as an ironic counterpoint to it, creating a disjunctive sonic image that rubs against the grain of the austerity of the scene. Adding to the disjunctive quality of this sound/image *montage*, Schroeter further complicates the soundtrack by overlapping Salome's voice with that of Jochanaan's off-screen prophesying and the voice of an Arab soldier, thus creating a confusing cacophony that points to the ruinous and degraded nature of Herod's court. Later, "La Paloma" returns as Herod pleads with Salome to dance for him; the rhythmic pace of the song, Seranno's melodious voice, and the kitschy lyrics of the love song striking a stark contrast with the intensity of the dialogue. The effect here is to lend something of a camp aesthetic to

29 Schroeter, *Tage im Dämmer*, pp. 95–96.

30 Sebastian Feldmann, in Sebastian Feldmann, et al., eds., *Werner Schroeter* (Munich: Carl Hanser Verlag, 1980), p. 140.

the scene, particularly as the pace of the song increases in absurd concert with Herod's crazed premonition of the angel of death, and finally gives way in hyper-melodramatic fashion to the blast of a great orchestral climax that seems to (and indeed does) emanate from another place and time. Even more absurdly, "La Paloma" returns for a third time, just as Salome asks for the head of Jochanaan, and quite literally follows Herod on his final descent into madness.

This effect is further enhanced by the sudden change in shooting style employed by Schroeter's cinematographer Robert van Ackeren. Up to this point, the action had been filmed in conspicuous long takes (the entire film consists of only 25 shots), with the camera fixed on a tripod at the bottom of the stairs of the ruined temple. Yet due to Van Ackeren's rigorous use of pans and the zoom lens to vary his framing and the careful choreography of Schroeter's performers, the film rarely seems static. However, significantly, as Herod's resolve begins to weaken, the camera begins to move, and tracks alongside the characters.

During this sequence Salome reiterates her request for the head of Jochanaan, and then begins to descend the stairs of the ruined temple in slow and graceful movements, accompanied by the now-familiar strains of "La Paloma." In contrast, Herod follows her, shoulders hunched and circling Salome like an excited dog, all the while jabbering madly. The camera adds to Herod's sense of disorientation and visually partakes in his downfall. Throughout the film, Herod has been framed in such a way (usually in low-angle shots) to emphasize the monumental and regal stature of his position. Until this point, the camera has allowed Herod to command the space of the monumental architecture that surrounds him. In this sequence, however, as Herod descends the stairs from his high podium he begins to lose his monumental presence and the architecture begins to dominate him. This creates a visual metaphor for the implosion of his power. Finally, as the figures come to rest, Schroeter affords Salome the greatest visual presence in the image as she once again reiterates her request for Jochanaan's head. Visually she is positioned in front of and above Herod, who has by this stage collapsed against a great stone pillar, visibly exhausted, stripped of his power and finally relenting to Salome's demand. Somehow the "La Paloma" musical accompaniment to this downfall is appropriate, as it at once aesthetically complements his frenzied demeanor as the song's rhythm gains pace with the clicking of the singer's heels, and also trivializes his plight, just as he had trivialized Salome's body by his grand, but ultimately disingenuous, offer to give her "anything" to dance for him. "La Paloma" ironically becomes Herod's melancholy theme song.

From a cinematic perspective, Schroeter's film displays numerous "theatrical" elements, including the way the ruins of Baalbek function as a proscenium stage, the predominant use of frontal staging, and the frozen poses of character groups at various moments to emphasize and focus attention onto the action taking place. Indeed, the majority of Schroeter's cinematic *oeuvre* exhibits these characteristics—

Salome

particularly his preference for *tableau* staging—right from the early experimental films such as *Neurasia*, which involves a group of actors performing a series of theatrical and often histrionic gestures for the camera. In his last feature *Nuit de chien* (2008), based on the allegorical novel by Uruguayan author Juan Carlos Onetti, Schroeter similarly employs a range of rather theatrically staged scenes and figures who occasionally strike a static pose while action plays out before them. In *Salome*, Schroeter pushes this to the extreme, emphasizing this theatricality, ironically through his use of cinematic techniques. One of these is his decision at several moments to drop out the dialogue track and allow a non-diegetic musical piece to play out in its entirety while the action continues. In doing so, not only does he rely on the spectator's knowledge of Wilde's play, but he foregrounds the cinema's capacity to produce these disjunctive sound/image combinations. These drop-outs re-orient the spectator away from a reliance on the text itself and shift the focus to the rather haphazard gestural performances and the crucial role played by music in the film.

All these elements combine to produce a cinematic interpretation of Wilde's play that incorporates the decadence and decay of Herod's court into the very structure of the film itself, a film which privileges the fragmentary over conventions of narrative continuity. In this sense the filmic techniques play a destructive, allegorizing role, much like that described by Walter Benjamin in his famous "Work of Art" essay. For him, the invention of film in the late 19th century provided a way out of the industrializing, reifying, and alienating mechanisms of modernity, which "have us locked up hopelessly." Along came film, and "burst this prison-world asunder [...] so that now, in the midst of its far-flung ruins and debris, we calmly and adventurously go travelling."[31] It is to the haphazard techniques of "primitive" or early cinema, *tableau* staging, histrionic gesture, episodic narrative, and non-continuous editing that Schroeter returns, to imbue his films with an adventurous quality that resists the convention-laden structures of classical narrative cinema. Films like *Salome* mount a protest against the reification of culture in late 20th century capitalist society not unlike young women's adoption of the Salome persona as an escape from the constraints of bourgeois domesticity in the early 20th century.[32] In Schroeter's film the commodity-value of music, for example, is at once laid bare and destroyed through the eclectic and dissonant *montage*, which collapses all distinctions between high and low culture. We can locate here a similar impetus in the irreverent Wilde, for whom "nothing which has ever interested men or women [could] cease to be a fit subject for culture."[33]

He was also the proverbial Benjaminian *flâneur*, a modern city wanderer who "protests with his ostentatious languor (*Gelassenheit*)

31 Walter Benjamin, "The Work of Art in the Age of Mechanical Reproduction," trans. Harry Zohn, in *Illuminations* (London: Fontana Press, 1992), p. 229.

32 Studlar, p. 106.

33 Oscar Wilde, "The English Renaissance of Art," in Robert Ross, ed., *Essays and Lectures by Oscar Wilde*, Project Gutenberg eBook, 2013, www.gutenberg.org/files/774/774-h/774-h.htm.

against the process of production."[34] In his writings, Benjamin often compared this moment of modernity (exemplified for him by the work of French poet and Baalbek visitor Charles Baudelaire) in the second half of the 19th century with certain tendencies he identified in the literature and theater of the Baroque age. The film camera and its attendant techniques of framing and editing the image reactivate the "disjunctive, atomizing principle of the allegorical approach"[35] that he found in the *Trauerspiel* (literally "mourning play") of the 17th century. The decaying ruins of Baalbek used as the setting for Schroeter's *Salome* evoke Benjamin's understanding of allegory, which, he once wrote, "attaches itself to the rubble."[36] In doing so, the fragments of culture are freed of their conventional signifying function, so that "any person, any object, any relationship can mean absolutely anything else."[37] It is not so much that Schroeter's screen adaptation of Wilde's *Salomé* becomes an allegory *of* something else, but that it subjects the text to a process of allegorization, calling on his viewers to interpret the gap opened up between image and sound, word and meaning. Just as the moon in Wilde's play is contradictorily beautiful and deathly, so too Schroeter's film treads a fine line between drama and *pastiche*. If this is a *Trauerspiel*, what we mourn is our ability to distinguish between the two and our ability to know whether to take the film seriously or not: it is both earnest and camp at the same time.

With this film, Schroeter certainly displays a desire to rub against the grain of conservative German society, just as Wilde himself had provided a keen-eyed affront to the even more conservative values of Victorian English society. Unlike Wilde, however, whose play was banned in England by the Lord Chamberlain due to its biblical content, the support of the New German Cinema by the German television networks enabled Schroeter's peculiar way of looking at the world into the nation's living rooms. Although, viewing this film almost fifty years later, it may strike some viewers as rather haphazard and amateurish, it still remains a key and pivotal work in the *oeuvre* of one of Germany's most important, radical, and creative directors.

34 Walter Benjamin, "Central Park," trans. Lloyd Spencer, in *New German Critique* (Durham, NC: Duke University Press), no. 34 (Winter 1985), p. 47.
35 Benjamin *The Origin of German Tragic Drama*, p. 208.
36 Benjamin, "Central Park," p. 38.
37 Benjamin, *The Origin of German Tragic Drama*, p. 175.

Christine N. Brinckmann

"Leaping and Lingering"

Narrative Structure in Werner Schroeter's Willow Springs *(1973)*

Willow Springs came out in 1973, following *Eika Katappa* (1969), *Der Bomberpilot* (The Bomber Pilot, 1970), *Salome* (1971), and *Der Tod der Maria Malibran* (*The Death of Maria Malibran*, 1972). In order to cope with the debts he had accumulated by going way over budget with the Malibran film, Schroeter was supposed to make a *collage* film about Marilyn Monroe for the German Television network ZDF.[1] He had already received some funding and had traveled to Los Angeles in preparation for the project. But he lost interest and decided to make *Willow Springs* instead.[2] ZDF was shocked at first, but then graciously accepted the replacement, even though it was not the film they had originally commissioned (an act of generosity unthinkable today).

Given the circumstances, *Willow Springs* had to be made on a minimal budget with a very small crew. Schroeter produced the film himself, operated the camera, and supervised the sound and the editing. It was an improvised family enterprise—Schroeter considered his actresses, actors, and other collaborators his "family," with whom he sought to work again and again (like Fassbinder or Cassavetes, who also assembled temporary "families" to work with). In the case of *Willow Springs*, the members of the family are co-creators, co-filmmakers, as the credits expressly state. Schroeter had been traveling with an entourage of actresses, consisting of Magdalena Montezuma, his muse and favorite performer in many films, Ila von Hasperg, who served also as editor, and former child star Christine Kaufmann, who had already appeared in *Maria Malibran*. They stayed in Los Angeles for a while, taking drugs, developing ideas, creating characters and story lines together, collecting costumes for the film-to-be, and driving around location-hunting. The part of the male protagonist had been reserved for Rosa von Praunheim, who was replaced by Michael O'Daniels, a young man from Los Angeles. The female trio confronted with a single man mirrored the situation of the group itself—a constellation that usually means gender trouble.

1 ZDF regularly showcased the work by Schroeter and other artistically ambitious filmmakers of the New German Cinema in its series *Das kleine Fernsehspiel* (The Little Teleplay).

2 For the production history of *Willow Springs*, see Werner Schroeter's autobiography (written with the help of Claudia Lenssen), *Tage im Dämmer, Nächte im Rausch* (Berlin: Aufbau Verlag, 2011), pp. 112–123; and Paul B. Kleiser, "*Willow Springs*: Gespräch mit Magdalena Montezuma und Werner Schroeter," in *Filmkritik* (Munich), no. 201 (September 1973), pp. 408–415. For the part German TV played during the heyday of the New German Cinema, see Michelle Langford, *Allegorical Images: Tableau, Time and Gesture in the Cinema of Werner Schroeter* (Bristol, UK: Intellect, 2006), pp. 33–37.

Willow Springs developed out of the lifestyle of the group, expressing their personal counterculture. In spite of its artificiality and theatrical or even operatic staging, the film represents an actual episode in their lives, a document of the (musical and other) tastes of the group at the time, their dreams and images of themselves, and their desire for role-playing. *Willow Springs* can thus be considered a collective daydream acted out for the camera—partly fact and partly fiction.

The personal nature of the film is underlined by the fact that the actresses import their own first names into the fiction, the characters they play being called Magdalena, Christina, and Ila. We are thus reminded of the double nature of film characters, their combined or split identities between the actor or actress on the one hand and their fictional roles on the other, both being conflated in the case of *Willow Springs*. To pay attention to both aspects simultaneously or consecutively is one of the pleasures the cinema grants, as opposed to the novel. In mainstream film, our awareness of the actors *as* actors usually develops sporadically and is left to viewers' preferences and dispositions, and it is only by including cameo appearances of specific actors and well-known personalities that some films capitalize on the effect. In the case of Schroeter's films, however, a kind of extended cameo appearance unfolds. And as the names of the actresses are listed in the opening credits not as performers but as collaborators in the filmmaking, their creative contribution will also be realized by viewers not familiar with Schroeter's "family." The making of the film is thus overtly inscribed in its images and its structure. The actresses draw attention to their acting, posing, interpreting, creating the scenes together, foregrounding their awareness of being filmed. The result is a weakening of the fiction as fiction, and a shift of the viewer's attention to the performers and their performances, away from the parts they play: naming the characters after the actresses is one way of defictionalizing a film.

Schroeter saw no reason to conceal the fact that he had to make *Willow Springs* on a shoestring budget—reversing the way Hollywood films display the opulence of their production values. He deliberately exhibits a certain amateurism, as if he were proud of the imagination and intensity he could master in spite of the situation: the pride of *arte povera*, but also the expression of a desire to keep the spirit of spontaneity. As in his earlier work, Schroeter included slightly out-of-focus images or images with end flares that could easily have been edited out, thus linking his work to the period's experimental films that self-reflexively include traces of the technical process of filmmaking and of the idiosyncrasies of the medium—baring the device, as it were. Parts of the dialogue are rather stilted, reeled off perfunctorily,[3] and there are sounds on the soundtrack that do not belong to the fictional story. There are no expensive crane shots, no stunts, no crowds, very few extras (and the two policemen who appear on the set may have dropped in coincidentally).

3 The *dilettantish* touch is, however, partly intentional, adding to the artificiality of Schroeter's style. Schroeter's characters often speak as if quoting from an unknown source.

A number of stray dogs keep running to and fro; elements of the landscape, of a freight train or the deserted buildings close by, serve to set the mood. The film also suggests that the location was used as found, full of authentic cobwebs and mold (a fact confirmed by Schroeter in his autobiography). In keeping with this, and in memory of the abandoned Marilyn Monroe project, there is a crumpled and soiled poster with her famous centerfold photograph pinned on a door. But there are also Schroeter's elegant anthropomorphic camera movements and his selection of striking angles and beautiful frame compositions, which constantly keep us aware of his creative decisions as camera person, and there is the masterly, poetical editing of the film—and much more.

We feel that we are watching a film in the process of being made, but watching it after it has been edited. This may sound like a paradox, but it makes sense if we take Schroeter's self-conscious style into account. We experience the film one or even two steps removed from the story, imagining simultaneously how it was made during production and how it came together in the editing room. Post-production can be considered a kind of second creation of *Willow Springs*: out of the fragmentary and willful footage, Schroeter and Ila von Hasperg constructed a film with a modicum of narrative organization, adding synchronized sound and music to give coherence to the footage. Thus the film has a highly elliptical, non-sequential and fragmentary character without being a fragment. *Willow Springs* is a work more of performance than of story, more of texture, color, music, and gesture than of rigorous structure. It holds the spectator in what Michelle Langford calls "haptic fascination," addressing us not so much intellectually as somatically.[4]

The title of the film refers to a California small town whose name suggests a totally different landscape from the one we will actually see: Willow Springs is not a village surrounded by lakes and lush farming country. It is located in the Mojave Desert, and has, according to Schroeter's images, an abandoned ghost town quality that would befit a Western; the buildings look like an outpost of civilization. It is a very male location, complete with a saloon with swinging doors, but the collective daydream of the filmmakers has populated it otherwise.

The story of *Willow Springs* can be told in a few sentences. Three women have decided to live in the middle of nowhere, depending exclusively on each other in their secluded *huis-clos* universe. Their relationships are, however, complicated. Magdalena is a self-installed evil stepmother, an insane lesbian madame, a man-hating sectarian and irrational sorceress who sadistically dominates her two companions. She demands that the neurotic Christina—a somewhat conventional beauty like Snow White from the fairy tale—make herself up glamorously and display herself. And she forces the less-glamorous Ila to provide breakfast or to fetch water from the well, like a servant-girl Cinderella. Christina and Ila stand in fear of Magdalena, and comply with her wishes masochistically.

4 Langford, *Allegorical Images*, p. 69.

One day, when Magdalena is alone in the house, she is assaulted by a stranger. Thereafter, the three women make a living out of luring men into their saloon in order to rob and murder them and mysteriously dispose of their bodies. Eventually, this claustrophobic hothouse situation is interrupted by Daniel, a gentle young man—a kind of fairy-tale prince to Cinderella—who requests permission to stay with the women. Ila falls in love with him, much to the anger and disgust of Magdalena, who watches their lovemaking voyeuristically through an open door. Daniel and Ila try to get away, but Magdalena shoots them during their attempt to escape. Magdalena also kills Christina and remains alone on the porch in the desert, dressed in black, looking like a veritable angel of death.

This summary is, however, incomplete and misleading, as it does not account for the music or the exquisite framing, color scheme, and lighting of the film. "Both the exterior desert and the interior rooms glow with a surreal light and color that overwhelm the naturalistic setting," as Timothy Corrigan remarks.[5] Nor does it account for a number of strange and unusual narrative features. Several images and scenes do not seem to belong in the story—they could be outtakes from another film the group tried to make, or just images that occurred to Schroeter when he had his camera in hand. Moreover, there is some confusion as Magdalena Montezuma seems to portray two different characters simultaneously, the other one being the mother of the young man who comes to visit.[6] And there is the fact that Schroeter is not interested in the psychology of the characters or their backstories—sometimes the characters refer to their pasts, but the information we get is always fragmentary and explains little of what is going on.[7] There are hints, implications, and suggestions, but the audience can take them or leave them. Sometimes it is not even clear whether the scenes are to be taken for real or are meant to be dreams,[8] fantasies, or hallucinations.

Thus a better way of understanding *Willow Springs* than in terms of the events is to take the film as a sketchy, deliberately campy *collage* or accretion of sensual images, operatic moments, and theatrical posing in autonomous shots or *tableau*-like scenes,[9] held together by a tenuous, ambiguous story that allows for all kinds of diversion. Told in jumps and starts, it shifts in and out of realistic plausibility.

5 Timothy Corrigan, "Schroeter's *Willow Springs* and the Excesses of History," in: Timothy Corrigan, *New German Cinema. The Displaced Image* (Bloomington/Indianapolis: Indiana University Press, 1994), p. 176.

6 This kind of confusion is typical of Schroeter's style, again drawing attention to the actress instead of the character portrayed. See Ulrike Sieglohr, *Imaginary Identities in Werner Schroeter's Cinema. An Institutional, Theoretical, and Cultural Investigation*. PhD Dissertation, University of East Anglia, Sept. 1994, p. 191.

7 This applies particularly to Daniel's long-winded, ultimately tedious voice-over diary about his boyhood.

8 In the interview with Paul B. Kleiser (in *Filmkritik*, no. 201, September 1973) p. 410, Schroeter comments on a scene in the desert with Magdalena and Christina, holding a huge red Japanese fan, as "Magdalena's dream," but there is no clear indication in the film to mark it as such.

9 For Schroeter's use of the *tableau*, see Michelle Langford, *Allegorical Images*, pp. 89–132. It is, however, to be noted that *Willow Springs* displays fewer *tableaux* than most of Schroeter's films.

Willow Springs (1973)

The beginning of *Willow Springs* provides an initiation to its style and narrative structure, displaying how story elements, atmosphere, imagery, and music interrelate. The film opens with a pre-title sequence. We are taken through an arid California landscape by a motorcycle via an extended subjective shot with lens flares and the rattling sound of the engine. After a moment sweet music starts softly; it is Mignon's aria "Connais-tu le pays" from Ambroise Thomas' eponymous opera. A cut takes us to Magdalena, standing in a long white dress in front of her solitary house, looking longingly into the distance. Simultaneously, the music gains volume as if it were "her song" we hear. A motorcyclist approaches the building, steps through the swinging doors, and, after a short altercation, forcefully pulls Magdalena into the house and out of view. The music has stopped. When the stage is empty, a stray dog saunters leisurely across the street and enters the house. Images of dilapidated architecture follow, a train passes by from right to left in the distance, lens flares dance across the screen and explode in silence as the camera travels gently from left to right. The man and Magdalena, now in disarray, reappear after what must have been a rape. He threatens to strangle her with his leather belt, but departs without doing so. The music resumes over the sobs of Magdalena. Unexpectedly, a mysterious image appears on the screen: a ship lying motionless in the emerald sea. After a moment, a shot of the dilapidated architecture takes us back to the location. It is now that the credits unfold.

The following sequence opens at another time, but in the same location. We hear loud and insistent music in a style that is very different from Thomas' opera: it is the well-known Andrew Sisters' hit "Rum and Coca Cola" from 1944, about a mother and her daughter working in Trinidad as prostitutes for American GIs. A traveling shot along the façade of the building reveals first a blue pickup truck, then another woman: Ila, holding an unruly cat, standing by the swinging doors, delivering a strange little monologue to the camera about moral integrity and sexual persecution. Soon the music stops, and a third woman, Christina, flamboyantly dressed in red, the same white cat in her arms, rushes, or rather floats, towards the house and takes up a position at another corner, while Ila has disappeared. The surrounding environment, in its stark, dry grays and browns with a sprinkling of dusty greens, serves as a backdrop for and contrast to the theatrically opulent, immaculate costumes and the eccentric and mannerist behavior of the women: beauty and perfection in a world of decay and wilderness, the liveliness of primary, pristine color against the muted color of the land.

Are the women waiting for customers? Is this a roadside brothel? The answer is given right away: a car arrives, and Christina asks the driver in. After a moment, we hear him scream. Ila hides his car behind the house, then helps Christina to drag his lifeless body out on a rug. Throughout this action, Camille Saint-Saëns' *Havanaise* starts gently, almost inaudibly, stops, and resumes again, violins playing harmoniously as if to contradict the violence unfolding on the screen. Following the disposal of the body, there are a number of shots of the building and its environment, with the sequence ending on another mysterious shot of the ship,

Willow Springs

almost identical to the one included in the pretitle sequence. These "pillow shots" will come up now and then in the film—like Ozu's enigmatic images of interior still lifes, landscapes, and cityscapes,[10] they are interspersed throughout the film with no clear relevance to the scenes next to them. They all show the same

10 For an explanation of the term "pillow shot" and the function of pillow shots in Ozu's films, see Martin Schneider, http://dangerousminds.net/comments/yasujiro_ozu_and_the_enigmatic_art_of_the_pillow_shot.

Willow Springs

ship lying in the sea, the image slightly varied from instance to instance, displaying vivid greens and yellows absent from the chromatic scheme of the rest of the film. The frame is structured in horizontal layers, barriers, as it were, to the progress of the narrative. Several cables, presumably telegraph lines, intersect the frame, and may serve as a clue to the meaning of the image: the ship as a means of transport across the limitless sea, the cables as a means of communication—suggesting the desire to get away from the isolation of *Willow Springs* and to connect with the outer world. It is the theme of *Sehnsucht*, of ineffable desire, that also informs Mignon's aria, "Connais-tu le pays," in the beginning of the film, a theme persistently present in Schroeter's *oeuvre*.[11]

The dogs and cats could or could not serve as symbols for masculinity and femininity respectively. The cats are always close to the women, the dogs will appear now and then like jackals out of the wilderness, echoing the arrival of the male visitors. However, there is no need to emphasize masculinity and femininity in a film where the sexes are in mortal conflict with each other. Rather, the artificiality of the women's gestures and speech is contrasted and heightened by the uncontrollability of the cats. Schroeter's universe is characterized by the tension between the indomitable and the totally controlled. But the animals also serve other functions, adding to the atmosphere of the house and the desert, the texture of their fur contrasting with the thorny vegetation, the stony surface of the buildings, and the smoothness of the women's garments.

Another element is the music. Next to Mignon's romantic aria we hear the Andrew Sisters' calypso song with its irresistible and catchy, erotic rhythm. As usual in Schroeter's films, it is source music, not score music, and it is neither supportive nor subtle or subdued, but always meant to be heard. Both pieces have only oblique connections to their respective scenes, their main function being to set the mood. Perhaps Mignon's aria, full of solitary desire, explains one side of Magdalena's character. "Rum and Coca Cola" stands in contrast to Ila's dire and philosophical little speech, while at the same time emphasizing her sensuality—and the song will serve as a *leitmotif* for her that comes up repeatedly in the film, accumulating more and more meaning in its repetition.

The function of music in Schroeter's films is manifold, and always crucial to the emotive im-

11 Sieglohr (pp. 154–159), describes "Romantic *Sehnsucht*" as a "striving for merging," never to be fulfilled.

pact of the scenes. It is mostly an expression of desire and obsession, and an enhancement of pathos. But it also serves a number of structural purposes, providing *leitmotifs* and commentary, providing contrast, counterpoint, or tension, easing transitions between scenes, or creating a sense of formal circularity and repetition that halts the flow of time or renders it irrelevant. Sometimes the music fades out gently; sometimes it stops abruptly. Sometimes Schroeter's music is non-diegetic, sometimes diegetic—at one point we see Christina listening to a record on her record player (and Schroeter's often abrupt truncations of the music recall her interrupting her records in the middle of a piece). But it does not seem particularly important which is which. Blurring the boundaries is one of Schroeter's pleasures, and his choice of music ranges eclectically from high culture to low: classical and modern, folk and pop, *bel canto* opera, Viennese operetta.

A later scene is dedicated to Magdalena and Christina. It is a lyrical moment, and it is one of the most strikingly beautiful and mysterious images Schroeter ever composed. Christina has been sitting by the window alone, when Magdalena appears outside like a ghost, slightly overexposed in the eerie white light of dusk. The camera moves closer and cuts to an extreme close-up of Magdalena's face. A jubilant waltz is to be heard, but stops abruptly before the end of the scene. There is no dialogue.

The image is framed by the window—a composition Schroeter is particularly partial to. It occurs in numerous variations throughout this film, as well as in many other instances of his *oeuvre*. Placing figures into a frame—be it a window or a mirror—tends to arrest the action: time becomes unmeasurable. Magdalena's face is contained within the frame, singled out, beautified and rarefied. It is a painterly composition, layered in depth by the dusty pane of glass, but at the same time flattened thanks to the rectangular shape of the frame within the frame. An image of a centripetal rather than a centrifugal nature (to use André Bazin's famous distinction), centering in itself, ignoring off-camera space. Framing an image in such a way suggests that it contains the essence of what is depicted: the essence of a character or the essence of a situation, a constellation, or a space.

Willow Springs

At first Christina seems to be the main subject of what is to come. The music is of the type associated with her—it is the overture to Johann Strauss's operetta *Die Fledermaus*, recalling the scene where Christina is playing her records. But soon Magdalena takes over and attracts all our attention. Her uncanny appearance is further stressed by the effect that her head seems closer to the camera than Christina's, an impression not based on fact but owing to Montezuma's personal anatomy. She approaches the window slowly, and Schroeter's camera welcomes her and moves towards her, until Christina is obliterated and the visual pyramid they formed has metamorphosed into a close-up.

By now it has become clear that Magdalena not only dominates Christina and Ila, but also has the most prominent role in the film. Montezuma was Schroeter's favorite actress, and had been a close friend for a long time. Her strange and strangely expressive, larger-than-life face never ceased to fascinate him. Compared to the other actresses, she seems to be a breed apart, a kind of alien with a touch of the transvestite. She comes across as being more than the part she is playing, always in excess of the fictional character she portrays. Each role of hers is an exaggeration of herself. So one almost waits for the film to implode around her. Magdalena's face invites contemplation, as it changes with every angle chosen by the camera, sometimes expressing vulnerability and grief, sometimes arrogance, sometimes cruelty, sometimes concern and care—a volatile instability that makes her alluring as well as intriguing and threatening.[12] One way of reading *Willow Springs* (within a number of ways) is to see the film as a portrait of Montezuma.

Emotions keep streaming in this powerful image, which seems to express the essence of the relationship between the characters, if not between the actresses, and it is typical of the structure of the film (and many other Schroeter films) in that the moment is stretched out, prolonged out of proportion for the development of the plot. A moment of pure emotive sentiment, lyrical and haunting, in which the meaning of the film is achieved and deepened in a magical way. Narrative flow is replaced by the flow of atmosphere and sentiment.

Maya Deren called this type of scene "vertical"—as opposed to "horizontal"—scenes that develop in a dramatic, linear way, based on causality according to the concept of *post hoc ergo propter hoc*: what comes after an event must be the result of the event. As Deren explains: "The distinction of poetry is its construction, and the poetic construct arises from the fact [...] that it is a 'vertical' investigation of a situation, in that it probes the ramifications of the moment, and is concerned with its qualities and its depth, so that you have poetry concerned, in a sense, not with what is occurring but with what it feels like or what it means. A poem [...] creates visible or auditory forms for something that is invisible, which is the feeling, or the emotion, or the metaphysical content of the movement. Now it also may include action, but its attack is what I would call the 'vertical' attack, and this may be a little bit clearer if you

12 On Montezuma's unfathomable face, see Katharina Sykora, "Kino-Ikon. Magdalena Montezumas Amalgam aus Leinwand und Maske," in Katharina Sykora, *Figurenspiele. Texte zum Film* (Marburg: Schüren, 2013), pp. 90–94; and Dietrich Kuhlbrodt, "Magdalena Montezuma," in *Cinegraph. Das Lexikon zum deutschsprachigen Film*, pp. E1–E4.

will contrast it to what I would call the 'horizontal' attack of drama, which is concerned with the development, let's say, within a very small situation from feeling to feeling."[13]

Willow Springs unfolds its narrative between intervals of non-narrative images, revealing emotionally charged situations instead of telling a story in a linear progression of detail. It is thus a highly "vertical" film. The story is at the service of the aesthetic moment, reversing the usual narrative hierarchy where atmospheric images or music are at the service of the action, accompanying or underlining it without drawing attention to them. And as the vertical moments of the film are so numerous and rich in texture and tissue, the brief horizontal moments of action that occur elliptically between them seem all the more fragmentary, the film leaping from one event to another without preparation or explication, and with a number of scenes or images in between that may or may not belong to the plot, possibly being fantasies or dreams of the characters. It is, in Timothy Corrigan's words, a narrative "stripped of any distracting realism."[14]

It would be wrong, however, to take this focus on moments of affect and mood as proof of Schroeter's interest in character. As mentioned before, there is next to no character development in *Willow Springs*. Thus, the protagonists are stuck in situations full of conflicts that are unresolved and seemingly unresolvable. And there is no attempt to make the audience empathize with the characters or to consider the characters realistic entities.[15] We do not feel pity for the stranger who is murdered, nor empathy with Christina or Ila when Magdalena bosses them around and finally kills them. As in a fairy tale, a comic strip, or a B-Western, the characters have little psychological depth.

The ending of *Willow Springs* takes up and heightens the narrative style of the film. It moves fluently from one mode into another, intermingling subjective and objective moments, leaping from one phase of the events to another and back again. And it prioritizes Magdalena Montezuma once more over what is actually taking place. At the same time, it mirrors the way the film was made—as a fantasy acted out for the camera.

The love affair between Ila and Daniel is under way; they are fervently making love, accompanied by Ila's audio *leitmotif* "Rum and Coca Cola." The sexual act is, however, soon overshadowed by Magdalena, who voyeuristically watches the lovers through the open door. We see her beautiful face, intensely focused on the spectacle, expressing fascination as well as disgust, foreboding catastrophe. It is an image we have seen before, much earlier in the film, when she was stalking Christina. The repetition heightens the impact of the image, but also serves to blur the chronology of the story, harking back to a previous scene that in turn becomes a prefiguration of the present moment. But there is more to come. The scene shifts to what turns out to be a fantasy of Magdalena's—

13 Maya Deren: contribution to the Symposium *Poetry and the Film* (New York: Gotham, 1972; first printed in *Film Culture* [New York], no. 29, Summer 1963).

14 Corrigan, p. 171.

15 Cf. Sieglohr, p. 143.

Willow Springs

a narrative device not used before in the film. Magdalena envisions Ila and Daniel on the verge of an attempt to escape, and she sees herself shooting them to death with her revolver. The fantasy is coded as unreal by the suddenly decreasing volume of the music as well as the return to the lovemaking, with the lovers still unaware of Magdalena's presence. What makes this scene of lust, violence, anger, and revenge even more shocking in retrospect is the fact that it will be re-enacted for real shortly before the very end of the film, with only slight changes to mark the difference between fantasy and reality: an incremental repetition of momentous effect. The killing has become inevitable, or so it seems, because we have seen it already. That the story will now be brought to completion by killing Christina as well appears, for no intelligible reason, to be just as inevitable.

But let us return to Maya Deren's distinction between horizontal and vertical attacks. Adding to *Willow Springs'* vertical, poetical nature is Schroeter's penchant for symmetries and reversals of symmetry, situational echoes, repetitions, re-enactments, similarities and contrasts that give unity and a sense of inevitability to the film. There are the mysterious pillow shots; there are repetitions of music; architectural and landscape shots that are almost identical; there is the recurring motif of characters behind misty windows; there are the comparable introductions of the three women, all standing in front of the building, and the comparable arrivals of men, their cars coming and going; there are the stray dogs and cats, reappearing again and again; there are identical or slightly varied shots of Magdalena's voyeuristic stalking; and, last but not least, the re-enactment of the murder.[16]

As for the temporal structure of *Willow Springs*, the chronology of events seems of minor importance, and may have been further obfuscated in the editing room. For one thing, many events could have happened at any time during the story, and some of the scenes have a generic, iterative character, showing events that could happen again and again: Magdalena bossing the women around, Ila hating to fetch water, Christina listening to her records, the women murdering a visitor. So it does not matter (in terms of narrative logic) whether the scenes are presented sooner or later. For another thing, most scenes foreground the *mise-en-scène* against the action—color composition, music, props, costumes, the atmosphere of the moment are of prime importance. Transitions from scene to scene are mostly straight cuts, without taking account of the leaps in time and situation. Moreover, it does not seem to matter whether a scene or an image is a flashback, an apparition, or a dream, as their narrative status is much less important than their emotional valence.

But the function of the plot is not minimal. It gives the scenes a backbone, however slender and tenuous, and a modicum of coherence. And it also supplies a trajectory, an arc of emotional development and escalation that reaches a point of finality in deadly silence. *Willow*

16 Sieglohr as well as Langford comment extensively on repetition as a characteristic of Schroeter's films.

Springs is considered the most accessible of Schroeter's early films, presumably because of its subdued narrative structure that softens its "vertical attack." It is perhaps also for this reason that it was awarded the Grand Prix of the Hyères festival in 1973.

"Leaping and lingering"—the title of this essay—is a phrase coined in 1907 by the ballad scholar Francis B. Gummere that refers to the narrative style of the Scottish traditional ballad: "[T]he story [...] keeps lingering, still lingering, and then leaps to a new part somewhat like those clocks whose hands point only to the five-minute intervals on the dial. A great deal has been made of this leaping, springing movement of ballads, the omission of details, the ignoring of connective and explanatory facts, the seven-league stride over stretches of time and place which in [a] regular epic would claim pages of elaborate narrative. Far too little, on the other hand, has been made of the lingering, of the succession of stanzas or of verses, mainly in triads, which are identical save for one or two pivotal words, delaying and almost pausing on the action, and marking a new phase in the grouping of persons and events. And practically nothing at all has been made of the combination of these two features as a formula of the situation-ballad [...]."[17]

There are many similarities between the traditional ballad and Schroeter's way of constructing his film: to tell a story in terms of its crucial elements, but not necessarily following causality or linearity; to leap to these crucial moments without preparation, elliptically and suggestively; to focus and linger on lyrical, vertical moments, giving priority to sentiment over action; and to rely on repetitions and echoes in order to render additional coherence and weight to the texture. Throughout the work, stasis and progress develop in constant tension.

Although the ballad is only one pre-existing form the film evokes—the comic strip, the fairy tale, and the Hollywood Western have been mentioned earlier, and the melodrama could be added—the ballad structure can shed light on many characteristics of *Willow Springs*, especially those that make it the beautiful achievement it is. "Leaping and lingering" is a formula which may have pleased Werner Schroeter, although he probably never intended to create a ballad. But similar to many traditional ballads, the film is as violent as it is gentle, and it is as poetical as it is sensuous and musical.

17 Francis B. Gummere, *The Popular Ballad* (Boston: Houghton Mifflin, 1907; reprinted New York: Dover, 1959), p. 91.

Willow Springs

Caryl Flinn

Werner Schroeter's Exotic Music and Margins

No one familiar with Werner Schroeter's work could reasonably object to the musical references often used to describe its exaggerated artifice and heightened emotionality. For Wolfram Schütte, *Tag der Idioten* (*Day of the Idiots*, 1981) was "An Imagined Symphony on Madness,"[1] Timothy Corrigan wrote of the director's "operatic cinema,"[2] and, Ulrike Sieglohr explored his magnificent obsession with divas.[3] Schroeter himself scarcely differed, referring to himself as a "musically-inclined director,"[4] and told one film festival audience that "My films are a form of opera."[5] His 2011 autobiography opened with an account of meeting Maria Callas for the first time, at a dinner party. Schroeter referred to La Callas as his "spiritual mother" and the wellspring of innumerable passions and creative work. Her recordings anchor early shorts—all made in 1968—such as *Maria Callas Portrait*, *Callas Walking Lucia*, and *Maria Callas Sings 1957*; they culminate four years later in *Der Tod der Maria Malibran* (*The Death of Maria Malibran*, 1972), a personal favorite of the director. In the latter, Callas's voice underscores a profusion of stagey scenarios inspired by her predecessor, Maria Malibran, the radiant but temperamental 19th-century mezzo widely considered modern opera's first diva. Obsessing fans across the continent, Malibran cemented her diva cult by dying young—at 28—and tragically, after a horse-riding accident. (Schroeter thought Malibran should have been in the "27 Club," along with Janis Joplin, another diva whose voice he used.) For *Poussières d'amour—Abfallprodukte der Liebe* (*Love's Debris*, 1996), Schroeter invited several opera singers, and three retired ones in particular—Martha Mödl, Rita Gorr, and Anita Cerquetti—to reflect on how they brought emotions into their voices. He asked them to bring along their loved ones as well. "The title of the film," he said, "is based on my very personal conviction that everything we express with our voice is the product of our

1 Wolfram Schütte, "Kopfsymphonie über Wahnsinn," *Frankfurter Rundschau*, April 1, 1982.

2 Taken from the title of Timothy Corrigan's article, "Werner Schroeter's Operatic Cinema," *Discourse* (Los Angeles), no. 3 (Spring 1981), pp. 46–59.

3 Ulrike Sieglohr. *Imaginary Identities in Werner Schroeter's Cinema: An Institutional, Theoretical, and Cultural Investigation* (PhD Dissertation, University of East Anglia, Sept. 1994).

4 The term was Schroeter's response to being called an "operatic" director, which, he maintained for critics, "was […] more like a curse word, as if everything I did was just kitschy and colorful." Werner Schroeter, *Tage im Dämmer, Nächte im Rausch* (Berlin: Aufbau Verlag, 2011), pp. 275–276. This and subsequent translations are courtesy of Charly Mostert.

5 Notebook for Locarno Film Festival, 1973. Courtesy of the Cinémathèque Suisse.

Maria Callas Porträt (1968)

Der Tod der Maria Malibran (1972): Christine Kaufmann, Magdalena Montezuma, Candy Darling

search for coming closer to the other, for love and all imaginable abilities to love."[6] In song, the human voice is at once a precious container waiting to be filled *and* the vibrant emotions poured into it.

For all things Schroeter, "music" involves much more than descriptive vocabulary. As a conduit "for coming closer to the other," the director replicates the aim through non-musical means, such as his frequent use of doubles—the twin protagonists of *Deux* (2002), or the variously coupled actors in *Maria Malibran*. In fact, the first portion of *Malibran* is effectively a series of *tableaux* of paired women, usually in two shots. Presented against blackness, they are impossible to locate or psychologize, in keeping with the director's strict anti-realism; audiences can do nothing but absorb their saturated sounds and images. Typically, one figure will seem to reach or lean towards her unmoving, unmoved partner. The second section features wider shots, with women staged in *plans américains*, appearing now to "perform" against theatrical backgrounds, usually a simple curtain or painted screen, still pushing against three-dimensional space. The film's third and final portion, entitled "Maria Malibran," features scenarios inspired by the Malibran myth, which Schroeter now presents with unrestricted visual movement, depth of field, and variety. And here, finally, La Malibran appears as an identifiable figure, depicted by Schroeter's personal diva and muse, Magdalena Montezuma.[7] It's as

6 Quoted in "Worlds of Longing: The Cinema of Werner Schroeter," program notes [unsigned], Arsenal Cinema, Berlin, May 2011. https://www.arsenal-berlin.de/en/arsenal-cinema/past-programs/single/article/1564/2804/archive/2009/may.html.

7 This was the stage name Schroeter gave his artistic companion, Erika Kluge. His inspiration was twofold. Most directly, Schroeter took the name from Patrick Dennis's popular campy novel, *Little Me*, which he was reading at the time. More obliquely, Schroeter would state that Kluge was like "the Mexican goddess and ruler." (Schroeter, *Tage im Dämmer*, p. 45). In actuality, no such goddess existed, although two Aztec Kings bore the name Moctezuma. It is worth noting how quickly Schroeter Latinized his close friend, colleague, and muse.

if the director structured the film to his statement about music enabling a "coming closer to the other," its first two sections of paired women brought to life in the third. With its tight framing and the directed gazes of one character to another within the frames, it seems to suggest that if one yearns for the diva—however impassive or impervious she may be to that longing—she can be activated. In this universe, it scarcely seems to matter whether that "one" is an onscreen figure or an enraptured audience member, or perhaps, even the director himself.

It would not be altogether wrong to claim that Schroeter prioritizes music's expressive and affective attributes over functional ones. Instead of enhancing the narrative or visual realities of a film (which are rarely straightforward in Schroeter to begin with), music often beckons overwhelming emotionality. Scholars are correct to point out the director's debt to Romanticism in this regard, with music seemingly operating beyond the edges of language, a transcendent force that can convey sublime, remote conditions to which we might aspire but could scarcely hope to attain—a sort of directionless desire. Indeed, no Schroeter film I am aware of is without at least *one* overpowering acoustic moment, and this need not come from music. His characters will often bypass words with wails, screams, or sobs; sound effects equally discombobulate listeners, dashing across temporal contexts, spatial logic, and emotional situations. Indeed, the director's soundtracks are packed with obstreperous but unstated yearnings for new ways of living and of feeling (*Malina*; *Day of the Idiots*). In such uncharted territory critics locate some of Schroeter's most compelling effects, finding in them points of *entrée* into alternative realms of subjectivity, passion, and *jouissance*.

Aligning this aspect of Schroeter's work with the tradition of German Romanticism, Ulrike Sieglohr considers a second, equally important but far more earthbound one: camp.[8] Musically, camp is especially present in the director's early and mid-career films, such as *Der Bomberpilot* (1970) and *Maria Callas Portrait*. In the former, Carla Aulaulu sings art-music classics (Strauss, Donizetti) ecstatically and firmly off-key, but her performance, like so much of camp, shows a committed physicality whose depth arguably matches that of Callas. Camp may not induce many ecstatic moments of sublimity, but its pleasures nonetheless derive from items that somehow exceed or circumvent conventional, expected representation, playfully skirting the edges of taste and category, finding joy in imperfection and banality, and enjoying the dust and debris of everyday life.

Romanticism could hardly account for the presence of Elvis doing *Napolitani* numbers; camp addresses the offbeat choices and fragments of popular music that permeate Schroeter's scores. For our purposes here, camp does less to oppose the sublimity of opera so much as to ground its own aesthetic and personal experience in all aspects of life, and, like

8 See Sieglohr's insightful thesis (1994) for this dual formulation of influences.

Schroeter's soundtracks, takes delight in the blurring of musical styles, origins, and cultural value. For Schroeter, "The trivial takes on an emotive dimension. [...] You have to be open to all sounds, music and language in film, since it's through combination that they take on new forms."[9]

Cultural theorists whose work was influential during Schroeter's career—from Jacques Attali's influential "political economic history" of music to the equally influential material culture scholars Peter Stallybrass and Allon White—maintain that music plays a significant role in providing breaks from routine, whether in dance halls, concerts, or listening to recordings privately.[10] This perspective has been shared throughout millennia; in the West, music is claimed to offer an escape into more rarified experiences, however transient and however calculated. As ethnomusicologist Martin Stokes puts it, "The association of pleasure, licence [sic], and a festival atmosphere with music and dance makes experiences which are distinctly 'out of the ordinary.'"[11] Schroeter's cinema provides no shortage of examples to illustrate that ability to take us out of the ordinary, not altogether different from the sublime, but with other kinds of extraordinary places to land. That said, his work also demonstrates music's ability to pour itself into *all* strands of life, all parts and activities of the day. Whether arias of famous operas or long-forgotten *Schlager* (mainstream German pop hits), the music in Schroeter's films is always conspicuous—playing for too long, appearing too briefly, damaged, incongruent, ludic. In achieving this effect, the director brings music into the everyday, despite its seeming to come from outside, from beyond the characters' voices, beyond the storyline, time, or image, on the margins where weirdness might roam.[12]

Schroeter's *oeuvre*, and its music particularly, entice many viewers and commentators to reflect on realms beyond the norm, beyond lived experience or feeling, beyond realism. I wish to take a slightly different cue from our "musically-inclined director" to consider how his film music simultaneously works to ground and materialize these ostensibly otherworldly spaces.

9 Schroeter, *Tage im Dämmer*, p. 138.

10 Jacques Attali, *Noise: The Political Economy of Music* (Minneapolis: University of Minnesota Press, 1995), trans. Brian Massumi; Allon White and Peter Stallybrass, *The Politics and Poetics of Transgression* (Ithaca, NY: Cornell University Press, 1986).

11 Martin Stokes, "Introduction: Ethnicity, Identity and Music," in Martin Stokes, ed., *Ethnicity, Identity and Music: The Musical Construction of Place* (Oxford, UK: Berg Publishers, 1994), p. 13. At the same time, it should be noted that no shortage of contemporary practices, including using music to torture, still render its experience as "exceptional."

12 The director constitutes his lead figures in a similar way. All are outsiders of some sort, be they the trios of closely knit women in *Willow Springs* (1973) and *Der Bomberpilot* (1970), the unstable novelist of *Malina* (1991), or the madwoman and what Schroeter (p. 221) calls her "inner world [...] of real lived transgression" in *Tag der Idioten*. For scholars who use queer theory (such as Sieglohr, Flinn, and many others, including authors in this volume), Schroeter's emphasis on outsiders can be read as rich displacements of queer sexualities and themes. See Sieglohr, esp. pp. 232–287, and Caryl Flinn, *The New German Cinema: Music, History and the Matter of Style* (Berkeley: University of California Press, 2004), esp. pp. 173–265.

MUSIC AND MARGINS

Even though Schroeter's sense of musical elsewhereness suggests utopian energies, desires, and communions, so too is elsewhereness imprinted by specific regional and cultural imaginaries. Liminal realms, marginal existences, and their function as sanctuaries are concepts working alongside much of Schroeter's film music, and in these pages I use them as points of departure, rather than as exegetic endpoints or goals. Consider, for example, the prominent exoticized and orientalist fantasies operating within German *clichéd* fixations on Latin and Mediterranean cultures. Whether one examines patterns of tourism (northern Italy), scoring practices (the omnipresent tangos in Fassbinder's cinema),[13] or whole films pivoting on these and similar tropes,[14] German cinema has given us plenty of examples of this obsession with the "exotic" South. How many times do we encounter tourists heading south, their middle-age crises resolved by erotic or spiritual revivals of one sort or another? (Venice, however, is not to be recommended.)

Such fantasies are not particular to films. They populate various intellectual traditions, disciplines, and histories: the emergence of musicology, ethnography, the early modern travel genre, and imperial and political conquest in general. Their operative cultural logic positions white (heterosexual, masculinized) North Atlantic societies (in this case, Germany) as the stabilizing center and bearer of normative standards. Cultural, epistemological, and political powers are also located there. At the margins are the outsiders, and especially those rendered that way by dint of ethnicity or (presumed) place of origin. To Germany this might mean Turkish guest workers, passionate Italians, or flamboyant German film directors; indeed, I return to Schroeter's own marginal status below. These myths and regionalized fantasies—and the music used to connote them—require that the margins be without complexity or heterogeneity and, of course, agency. At the same time, the same subjects are expected to possess features that North Atlantic / German cultures find lacking in their own culture: to be sexually uninhibited, exotic, impassioned, and steeped in past or lost tradition—an idyll of pre-modernity.

German films are scarcely alone in this orientalist fantasy: Sally Potter's *The Tango Lesson* (1997) and Ryan Murphy's adaptation of *Eat, Pray, Love* (2010) drown in it. Both tell stories of white, middle-aged middle-class women of the industrialized West finding spiritual and sensual rejuvenation through Southern male "others." But the logic of this fantasy is altogether mobile, and can be plugged into multiple

13 Exemplified by the song "Du schwarzer Zigeuner" (Black Gypsy), to which Emmi and Ali dance in Fassbinder's *Ali—Fear Eats the Soul* (1974) and "Die Capri Fischer," a hit of the 1950s West German "economic miracle" that exemplifies West Germans' desire to suppress memories of the war and use their new-found prosperity to escape to Southern shores. The number occurs across West German cinema of the 1970s, most notably by Peer Raben in his work for Fassbinder.

14 Dorris Dörrie's *Nobody Loves Me* (1994), *Enlightenment Guaranteed* (1998), and *Cherry Blossoms* (2008) all feature "foreign" people of color who revitalize tired white Germans.

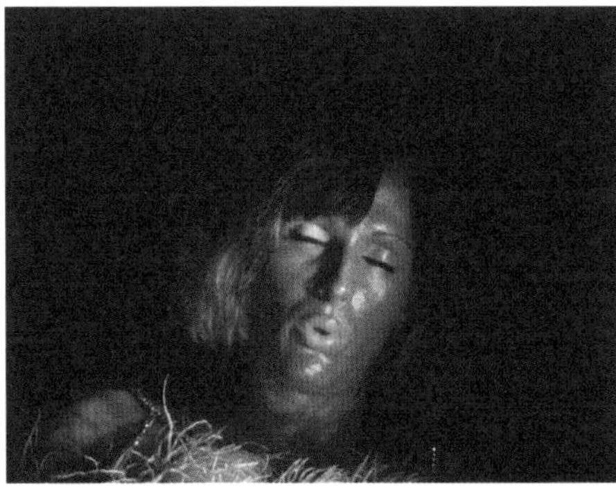

Der Tod der Maria Malibran: Candy Darling

scenarios to infuse them with hegemonic assumptions about gender, socio-economic class, sexuality, and age. Still, that fascination with a Southern exotic has a strong foothold in German-speaking cultures, and will be our primary focus here (I recall my father advising me that to learn German, I should travel to Lago Maggiore).

That cultural logic is scarcely absent from Schroeter's cinema. Indeed, his films consistently foreground it, thematically, in their narratives, their formal traits, and, especially, in Schroeter's selection and organization of music and sound. When a white American protagonist asserts that "Mexicans are passionate about their history" in *Der schwarze Engel (The Black Angel,* 1974), for instance, she imprisons a nation of rich, *multiple* peoples and histories into a single pre-industrial time cage, made charming to members of North Atlantic regions for its quaint, purported inability to move forward into the present. Not incidentally, Schroeter underscores his American character's journey to Mexico with hackneyed sounds of exotic Southern culture, such as jungle sounds, human chanting, and so on.

Schroeter's use of asynchronous sound, particularly in the early- to mid-career films considered here, may be regarded as one way he combats that Eurocentric/colonialist cultural logic, precisely *by* "othering" music to such an extent that it cannot merge seamlessly into those politically imperialist and culturally hegemonic systems of thought and fantasy. The sensual, affective appeal of music from a racialized and regionalized other is, in a word, squelched. Sound and image timing will often be off, voices will emanate from bodies perceptibly different from those visibly presented—whether by sex, age, gender, ethnicity, historical period, or setting—all heightening the discrepancy between recorded voices and the performers who might be singing them.

The effect is made uncomfortably clear in *Maria Malibran*, when white performer Candy Darling sings "St. Louis Blues" in blackface. The effect of this number and its implications are complex, especially for audiences in the U.S., whose history of slavery leaves ghosts everywhere, including white entertainment forms such as blackface. Despite the fact that Darling is *not* lip-synching to Bessie Smith, with whom the blues number is closely associated, the latter hangs heavily in the air, forty years after the 1929 short (dir. Dudley Murphy) in which she performed the number twice. Still, and, as Peter Stanfield has argued, in the 1930s and beyond, the massively popular song was performed by a wide variety of singers in an equally wide variety of styles—in 1930s "fallen women" Hollywood films, it bestowed black "shame" on sinful white women; on radios and musical stages it was performed in innumerable musical styles, including "rural and vaudeville blues, jazz, hillbilly, Hawai'ian, croon, swing, ragtime [...]"[15] Intentionally or not, Schroeter capitalizes on the fact that the song had accrued so many layers that it could never be stripped down to one meaning, even in a scene staged this way. At the same time, this scene enables Schroeter—and his viewers—to reflect on the facility with which human identity changes and mutates, accruing layers of its own.

Schroeter initially presents Darling in extreme close-up, in what Gérard Courant calls the director's "*mise-en-visage*."[16] As the camera pulls back, we note the whiteness of her short fringed dress making a stark contrast against her darkened skin, her black wig, and the indeterminate dark background Schroeter often used in staging his film *tableaux*. And as she unhurriedly stands up—affect nowhere to be found—Darling is the perfect Warhol superstar and Schroeter diva. Schroeter found plenty to admire in Candy Darling. Born James Lawrence Slattery, she was a tall, delicate person adorned in what the director called "ambisexual androgyny" and a "radical self-transformation" that Schroeter admired.[17] Katy Peplin maintains that the scene actually dramatizes how *tired* white appropriations of blackness are: on top of Darling's visible lethargy, her vocal performance is best described as weak, exuding scant sense of expression or emotional depth.[18] For the poor soul hoping to find any authenticity here, they won't. In this sense, while scarcely free of blackface's legacy of racism, Darling's casting and her performance destabilize its already contradictory theatricality. After the song is finished, the soundtrack maintains the fluidity of Darling's gender. Over the next few minutes, we hear (among many other things): a *Habañera*, snippets of pop songs by Caterina Valente, and passages from *Hamlet* relating to Ophelia's death, read in English—about the only detail anticipating the "death" of Maria Malibran in Schroeter's impassioned, ludic tribute.

For his extraordinary *Nel regno di Napoli* (*The Kingdom of Naples*, 1978), Schroeter used traditional *Napolitani* songs to establish an aura of authenticity he actually desired—unusual for

15 Peter Stanfield, "An Excursion into the Lower Depths: Hollywood, Urban Primitivism, and *St. Louis Blues*, 1929–1937," *Cinema Journal* (Society for Cinema and Media Studies), vol. 41 no. 2 (Winter 2002), p. 87.

16 Gérard Courant, "Le décor, les visages, la mort," in Gérard Courant, ed., *Werner Schroeter* (Munich: Goethe-Institut / Paris: Cinémathèque Française, 1982), p. 17.

17 Schroeter, *Tage im Dämmer*, p. 102.

18 Katy Peplin, remarks in a graduate seminar at the University of Michigan, Fall 2013.

the adamantly anti-realist director. Critics rightly compare *Kingdom* to Italian neorealism: shot on location; engaging local, non-professional actors who spoke in the city's various dialects; and not shying from depicting the impoverished lives and short-lived hopes of the denizens. Most songs are performed nondiegetically, but some appear via radios, turntables, and characters—one young lad is nicknamed Caruso. Musicality enhances the life-affirming features of the people there, who are given motifs gently played on flute, whereas threats to these uncorrupt, good people are signaled by harsher motifs and instrumentation. (Roberto Pregadio composed music for *Kingdom*, one of a small handful of films for which Schroeter includes original scoring.)

That same soundtrack structure, marked as it is by textual and aural heterogeneity, anchors most of Schroeter's film *Palermo oder Wolfsburg* (1980), made just after *Kingdom*. Here too, traditional folk songs (in this case, of Sicily and nearby regions) establish a grounded sense of place whose authenticity is magnified by the simplicity of the songs. Hearing the crackling sound of a 45-rpm record played back on a cheap phonograph or the tinny sound of a cassette recording reinforces the sense of simplicity and authenticity, as does the orchestration, which is kept to a minimum. Most songs, whether transmitted technologically or through human voice, are performed *a cappella* or with a lone acoustic guitar, further highlighting the song's unadorned reality. Still, *Palermo,* in contrast to other Schroeter films like *Kingdom*, uses music sparingly, and for viewers aware of the difference between the films' soundtracks, have solid cues that anticipate *Palermo*'s narrative's sense of dehumanization and futility.

Nicola Zarb is the film's Sicilian protagonist, whom the soundtrack introduces accompanied by traditional folk songs in Palermo, where his journey begins. He moves, as the title suggests, to Wolfsburg, Germany, to find work. When he arrives, instead of songs, Schroeter uses musicalized *sounds* to convey impressions of that place. Most conspicuous is a sound pattern that evokes the percussion of military marches, along with the thudding regularity of industrial machinery. Unsettling and relentless, it plays alongside the city's automobile plant where Nicola secures work. (Wolfsburg is home to Volkswagen's main office and factory; the town came into being during the Nazi era to house its workers. An interviewer once remarked to Schroeter that his depiction of the plant resembled a concentration camp, and the director did not disagree.) The sounds organizing our perception of Germany—and of Wolfsburg in particular—seem to originate from this one overbearing source, usually heard during interior scenes of the VW plant. Yet in a stunning exterior scene in which Nicola and his friend walk *away* from the plant, the camera zooms out to reveal the microscopic size (and power) of the two guest workers in relation to the looming scale of the factory. Visually, the scene is composed in cold, calculated symmetry, and matching it are the unabated industrial sounds, their dynamics failing to diminish as the characters move farther away from the plant. Its message is obvious, and the two characters certainly un-

Palermo oder Wolfsburg (1980): "Is that the East German Border?" – "No, that's Volkswagen." – "I don't want to work there." – "Once you're in there, you no longer think."

derstand what is happening, noting that they are "prisoners" there.

Until we get to the final courtroom act discussed below, one of the few other "Wolfsburg" sounds we hear is when the guest workers hum portions of the Bee Gees' songs from *Saturday Night Fever* (1977), the U.S. musical popular at the time of *Palermo*'s release. Despite its brevity, the choice hints at the commercial, cultural, and economic hold that the U.S. has had on both Palermo and Wolfsburg. This is something that Nicola and his colleagues already know. Audiences learn about it directly, when at the conclusion of the film the director's voice-over tells us that a U.S. chemical plant will be coming to Palermo, hiring locals while it kills their city with its toxins. Palermo and Wolfsburg are thus not so disconnected, and the South can hardly offer a real escape from/for the North, because both are embedded within one another, and within the global movement of capital.

At the same time it exposes the illusion of separation, *Palermo oder Wolfsburg* maintains the split between German and Mediterranean cultures and people, as if to keep the Northern fiction alive. During the courtroom scene (the music of which will be discussed below), char-

Palermo oder Wolfsburg: Nicola Zarbo

acters representing Sicily and Germany hurl *clichéd* insults at one other. (It must be noted that Schroeter never tried to disguise his own love for various Southern regions in which he worked and lived, preferring them to a homeland he found barren, cold, and incapable of understanding his work or way of life.) The very title of the film indicates commitment to and anchorage within two regions, and hence a sense of belonging rather than a merger: Palermo *or* Wolfsburg. Along with the irreconcilability of Schroeter's heterogeneous musical choices, other details suggest that such either/or thinking trumps all possibilities for amelioration or even a happy ending. Throughout the film the director intercuts shots of elaborate funeral corteges with enormous black carriages he encountered in Palermo, and ends the film with a trio of performers wearing centuries-old costumes and whose precise, measured gestures Schroeter could never decipher. He found the illegibility of those traditions appealing, much as he enjoyed chance musical discoveries that he might not otherwise have used. But even when using music with which he was deeply familiar, such as Italian and German opera, Schroeter seldom explains or predicts its direction, its impact, or even its connotations.

Schroeter claimed to have structured the film like a tragic opera in three acts, each with a distinct style. First is the warm realism of Nicola's life in Palermo; second the aseptic landscape he encounters in Wolfsburg; and finally, the escalating absurdity of the German courtroom, where Nicola stands trial for killing two young Germans whom he believed had taunted him. As the deliberations draw to a close, we hear portions of Alban Berg's beautiful Violin Concerto "To the Memory of an Angel." Despite being upright and alive, Nico is the angel and martyr the music clearly evokes, and whose death Schroeter's entire film has made inexorable. The effect is intensified by a series of cross-cut shots of an unidentified production of the Passion Play, the scenes of which appear throughout the film and culminate now with its crucifixion scene: the making of an angel.

Berg's Violin Concerto was commissioned to commemorate the death of the daughter of Alma Mahler and Walter Gropius. The Concerto has become one of his more frequently performed works, but its part in keeping him from ever finishing his opera *Lulu* amplifies the sense of loss, and lost potential, of Schroeter's young angel here. The Concerto is also renowned for combining tonal and atonal features, such as twelve-tone rows and conventional chord structures, mimicking the antagonisms announced by the film's title and dramatized in its plot.

Both the German legal prosecution and defense teams are adamant here about the irreconcilability of their two cultures, something Schroeter presents with humor but with evident sympathies for the (Italian) defense, as if to shed his own German-ness in the process. Says one defense witness, "[i]n this land without light, without sun, without songs, and without chatter. [...] there is nothing for us here but work, [...] we are two different worlds, as different as day and night" (closing on the improbable sound of birds). A male member of the prosecution states, "We have failed to find the difference between North and South, the difference in mentality between the two cultures," cultivating the myth *of* that difference while then chiding a witness for the "commonplaces" of her own testimony: "You see Germany only as a sad land, interested only in work. Yet we all know that in Sicily, economic and social conditions are poor. Don't you think that [...] there could be a build-up of aggression, such as in the defendant here who comes from these not-so-idyllic surroundings?"

She responds: "The sun and the sea aren't fantasies, but facts. And the Germans like to work, right. And since you want to mention culture and aggression, we never started a war. We've often been attacked, but we remain the same: human beings." Mirroring Schroeter's own contradictory position *vis-à-vis* this fantasy, both sides readily identify the *clichés* they use in characterizing themselves, yet still cling to them. Especially striking is the Sicilian woman's remark, "We remain the same: human beings," embracing the same universalizing, physical essentialism that the Germans impose on her homeland.

Condescending, liberal pity sways the prosecution towards a not-guilty verdict, until

Nicola, in a dramatic outburst, admits his guilt and his lack of remorse for the murders. His confession works only to idealize himself further, as now the character is prepared to sacrifice himself for the truth of his crimes, for his political beliefs, his sexual desires, and his heartfelt emotions. Moreover, Nicola refuses to relinquish his regional attachments, despite their utter inability to help him in the courtroom. His outburst articulates the realities of German racism, institutionalized here in the legal theater and in the earlier labor conditions for nonnationals. If it seems odd for Schroeter to create an angel in standard Christian, religious, and (German) legal terms, it must be noted that he bypasses both religion and nationalism in making a murderer that "angel," extending a beatification of Nicola's *integrity* rather than an act of Christian or legal forgiveness.

Der schwarze Engel—a film based on a 1954 song title, as will be discussed below—starts in silence. Then we are introduced to an 18-year-old deaf-mute Mexican man named Carlos, who, like Nicola, is a local whom Schroeter found interesting—doubly othered for his lack of speech. Images of the gesticulating Carlos are accompanied by the kind of dry voice-over one might expect in an ethnographic documentary. Schroeter's voice explains that Carlos is recounting a dream about the imminent visit of "McGregor" and "Magdalena," as the soundtrack hums with jungle sounds, birds, insects, and wind. Quickly changing gears, Schroeter moves on to urban images of ambulances and hospitals, his voice now rattling off figures concerning the number of people hospitalized annually for a long list of health problems, data on the overcrowded living conditions in Mexico City, and other geopolitical details. He then films McGregor, a "nutty blonde American woman with kitschy ideas and kitschy pink suits,"[19] while she reads a tourist brochure that immediately compels her to "leave everything behind to find fulfillment in the land of Mexico" (she is seduced by the Mexicans' "deep love for history"). Arriving in Mexico, McGregor encounters the intriguing Magdalena, a German woman who relocated to Mexico to sacrifice herself in order to renew ancient Mayan rituals.

McGregor's rant begins: "All that most people know about Mexico is that it's in Central America and they speak Spanish." "But there is so much more!" she gushes. "Mayan cities!" and "Mariachi everywhere!" and "The Mexicans are best known for celebrating like there's no tomorrow," making it once more impossible for the people of Mexico to move forward. Here and throughout the film, Schroeter injects small slices of Mexican music—traditional music, jazz, pop songs, and art music. With no shortage of hurdy-gurdies, acoustic guitars, and brass, it isn't hard to experience the film as a jukebox. Significantly, Schroeter includes European popular music about Mexico as well. Watching McGregor, we hear portions of Valente's "Am Golf von Mexiko"—a Mexico unequivocally produced through Western eyes and ears—with dashes of mariachi music for good measure. All salve for the woman who says, "I've come from a land that's lost its soul."

19 Schroeter, p. 137.

As played by Magdalena Montezuma, Magdalena resembles an outdoors Morticia Addams. Reading Heinrich Heine had prepared the character for her journey to Mexico, where she quickly begins her vague rituals, weaving in and out of ruins to sounds of carnival music, wind, and snare drums evoking the sound of rainfall. She promises to "replace your [American] heart of stone with a heart of flesh," as McGregor brings offerings to the dark-haired goddess. Though entranced, McGregor is beginning to complain of the heat, heard alongside an acoustic *collage* of jungle noises, crickets, bird calls, and a 1940 tune, "Lovely Hula Hands," performed by "Johnny Pineapple and His Islanders," no less. Clinging to her Northern fantasy, McGregor states, "I must live here to the point of ultimate fulfillment." The underscoring for this remark includes snippets of "Aloha Oe" (*de rigueur* for tourists in Hawai'i) and Jacques Offenbach's *Barcarolle* from *The Tales of Hoffmann*, in which romantic masquerades meet fatal endings—in Venice, not Mexico. Schroeter also cuts in Bruch's Violin Concerto, Bizet's "Agnus Dei," and selections of other Western art music. By weaving such canonical pieces into his ridiculous, campy depiction of Mexico, Schroeter undercuts their aesthetic authority while also acknowledging their role as part of an enduring cultural, colonial presence. For attentive audiences, the reverie of McGregor for an ancient, mythical Mexico splits wide open when Schroeter intercuts contemporary statistics and images addressing the catastrophic effects of sustained U.S. political and economic policy there.

While *Palermo oder Wolfsburg* and *Der schwarze Engel* adapt the model of center and margins that underpin German fantasies about Latin culture, both films render the putatively "centering" perspectives (of Germany and the U.S.) ridiculous, their institutions ominous, their citizens drama-seeking naïves—a reversal of the usual polarities, but that nonetheless reminds viewers that only those who have the upper hand can play with *not* having it. The damning statistics concluding *Der schwarze Engel* dramatize this power differential: "73 percent of the tourist dollars that are so important to Mexico return to the U.S., which owns the Hilton, Sheraton, et al. [...] Mexico is [...] a colony of the U.S."

"Schwarze Engel" (Black Angel) was an early song hit for Caterina Valente, a well-known versatile performer who enjoyed widespread success in Europe and the U.S. during the 1950s and 1960s. Singing in German, Spanish, and English, as well as her native French and Italian—not unlike Malibran—Valente's repertoire of light pop songs was predisposed to the Latin styles in vogue during the time, such as calypso, *boleros*, and *bossa nova*. Her albums had titles such as *Olé Caterina!*, *Arriba!*, and *South of the Border*. Despite her considerable talents (she was an accomplished jazz vocalist), Valente's early association with low-brow German *Schlager* has led to her remaining somewhat misunderstood and underrated. For Schroeter, however, her ability to span both the "highest art and the trivial," amplifying both in the process, was essential to his cinema, and she was one of his beloved divas. Nearly every film

Der schwarze Engel (1974)

of his from this period features snippets of her recordings, and at the end of his life he said that she "still held a strong magic for me."[20]

Valente's popularity was greatest in Germany, where she remained a household name through the 1970s and 80s; Schroeter's original audiences would certainly have been familiar with her. Decades earlier, the initial release of "Black Angel" coincided with the dawn of colonial fights against Europe for sovereignty (as in Algeria, Angola, Mozambique) and the cusp of the civil rights movement in the U.S. In addition to Valente's passionate rendering of it, its lyrics ask (with great liberal ardor) why painters

20 Schroeter, p. 138.

never depict black angels, since we are all the same, we will all die, will all stand before heaven's door, *et cetera*. Hardly apolitical, the lyrics offer a personal, acoustic correlative of Schroeter's own fascination with African-Americans and black men, dramatized cinematically through characters with brief but hugely consequential actions in *Kingdom* and *Der Bomberpilot*, films which also use portions of the song. In *Der Bomberpilot,* its declarative finale—"Schwarze Engel!"—appears as a stinger after one of the Nazi-era singers tries to kill herself. Afterwards, she and her equally naïve colleagues travel to the U.S with plans to "improve" tensions between African-Americans and whites, a mission that quickly backfires. That the song "Schwarze Engel" does not appear in the film bearing its name remains a puzzle—but then, not much of Richard Strauss's music for *Salome* appears in Schroeter's 1971 film *Salome*.

Schroeter's desires for and fantasies of Latin and Mediterranean culture are fiercely evident in his autobiography, where the director rhapsodizes about time spent in Portugal, Italy, and Latin America. Though displeased with the outcome of *Der schwarze Engel* ("my Mexican catastrophe," he calls it), he adds, "Mexico had already been one of the dream countries I longed to visit."[21] Filming in Naples "enabled me to rediscover the city's cordiality and openness [...] the people in Naples affirmed my world-feeling."[22] That "world-feeling," Schroeter writes, enabled him to "displace my tragic [German] world view," making of himself a less maligned counterpart of his kitschy American tourist in *Der schwarze Engel*.[23] None too subtle is the romanticism in his comments about being a global subject whose passions know no borders, and although Schroeter takes the odd step of establishing that sense of world citizenry through sensation and emotion rather than geopolitics, it hardly dispels the Northern fantasy of the South that his films can otherwise interrupt. In this regard, Schroeter was an active participant of the enduring, often *clichéd* German fantasies about Latin life and culture.

MUSIC MADE TO MOVE

The director's treatment of music unfailingly severed it from its roots. To keep it from slipping into billowy abstraction, though, Schroeter insisted on the importance of language and lyrics to its impact. (Elsewhere, he would qualify, if not contradict, the remark: "There isn't a single bit of music in my films whose lyrics directly line up with the image.")[24] It is not just that Callas might be singing: *what* she sings matters. Small consequence if the music skirts campy *cliché*, as in *Der Tod der Maria Malibran* when the director uses Schubert's *Winterreise* as a woman trudges through the snow. But *Winterreise* introduces another important feature of Schroeter's musical mania.

21 Schroeter, pp. 137, 138.
22 Schroeter, pp. 180, second part of quote p. 185.
23 Schroeter, p. 141. The book dedicates an entire section to "World-Feeling: Travels in South America," pp. 141–146.
24 Quoted in "La Musique," in Gérard Courant, *Werner Schroeter*, p. 21; originally in *Süddeutsche Zeitung* (Munich), 1974 [no further details supplied], translated from the German by Hilmar Rafalovitch. The translation from French is my own.

Despite maintaining that Germans were unable to appreciate innovative, good art (or understand his films), Schroeter doesn't eschew German music to convey pleasure and passions, as is clear in his moving use of Berg in *Palermo,* and will be evident in his remarks below on Wagner. Put differently, his film music denies the "purer" romantic mentality on which it otherwise insists, distilling beauty and passion from sources he also criticizes, and using ragged musical *clichés* to depict emotions and endeavors he clearly appreciates. The center and margin structure begins to weaken. And sometimes the director uses music without actually presenting it. In a scene in *Maria Malibran,* a despairing female character calls out, "Alfred, don't leave me," to a man who walks away from her and whose name the film doesn't provide. In the film's context, the line is patently absurd and seems to come from nowhere. But "Alfred," of course, emerges from *La Traviata*, where he is Violetta's lover, who, in the end, will leave her. However inorganic the connection, it enables Violetta's desperate passion to wash over Maria Malibran.

In addition to infusing his contemporary scenarios with libretti and lyrics from the canon of Western art music, Schroeter dedicates himself to the physical, material features of music, recalling the work of Roland Barthes and Julia Kristeva, who both stressed that physicality through concepts such as the "grain of the voice" and the "chora" of the pre-linguistic child/maternal womb.[25] (Schroeter's own obsession with the mezzo voice over other vocal ranges is illustrative of his focus on music's physical nature; this is the voice that he habitually calls upon to move us.) That physicality is also highlighted by his emphasis on recording and playback technologies, with his soundtracks (particularly from his early work) including music from outmoded equipment, hailing from before the advent of digital or even stereo technologies, presented as-is. Certain factions would label such techniques as "failed/inexpert" or "experimental/underground," along with his predisposition to shooting without sound, keeping sound and image out of sync, or again, playing recordings with discernable signs of wear and tear, scratches, and pops. Of the busy acoustic *collage* that is *Eika Katappa* (1969), he wrote, "Every record [used in the film] maintained its character, from the tinny sound of the *Volksempfänger*[26] to the Callas sound of the 50s."[27] For Schroeter, whatever passions any grand aria could conjure were part and parcel of the same machinery that churned out popular *Schlager*, supporting Alexander Kluge's wry 1983 description of the opera house as a "power plant of emotions."[28] Indeed, Kluge's soundtracks, like Schroeter's, consist of a *collagistic* mix of offbeat tunes and canonical musical

25 Roland Barthes, "The Grain of the Voice," in *Image, music, text*, trans. Stephen Heath (New York: Hill & Wang, 1977), pp. 179–189. Julia Kristeva modified Plato's idea of the *chora* for psychoanalytic semiotics and discusses it throughout *La révolution du langage poétique* (Paris: Editions du Seuil, 1985).
26 A mass-produced radio popularized during the Nazi era.
27 Schroeter, p. 70.
28 From Alexander Kluge's masterful *Die Macht der Gefühle* (1983). See also Flinn, *The New German Cinema*, pp. 138–169.

sources with minimal regard for their compatibility.

That grab bag of musical genres is one of Schroeter's chief trademarks. Whether from stage or screen musicals, such as *Carmen Jones*, Neapolitan ballads and other regional folk songs, arias from *La Traviata*, pop songs by Elvis Presley or Caterina Valente, or 45-rpm records that he literally pulled out of a trash can,[29] Schroeter gave his musical quotations equal footing. Even the most casual listener can apprehend Schroeter's refusal to prioritize one type of music over another. For Schroeter, he maintained that it was necessary to have a world where "one could look at the *Mona Lisa* at the Louvre while listening to a song by Sylvie Vartan."[30] And while it may be more difficult for Presley's odd Neapolitan song covers in *Der Bomberpilot* to unleash the rhapsodic bliss of a Bellini aria by Maria Callas, Presley's work, like that of his esteemed brethren, evokes the image of romantic escape through an ethnically coded "other" and a world of more intense emotion. For Schroeter—unlike many a non-mainstream filmmaker—even the quirky, mass-produced treasures he uses generate pleasure, even beauty, however defiled highbrow critics (as opposed to camp enthusiasts) might consider them.

29 While filming the courtroom scenes of *Palermo* in Berlin, Schroeter found a recording of "Padre, Padre" in a garbage can. After cleaning it up, he used it where "It consciously contrasts to the harshness with which people are deliberated over in the scene." (Schroeter, p. 41)

30 Schroeter, quoted in Cédric Anger, "Werner Schroeter: Les belles manières," *Cahiers du Cinéma* (Paris), numéro hors-série 23, "Cinéma 68" (1998), p. 98.

One of music's great joys for the director is its ability to lend itself to multiple associations. In one of his few disagreements with Michel Foucault in their lively 1981 conversation on passion, Schroeter voiced his objections to Patrice Chéreau's 1976 staging of *The Ring*. Chéreau had controversially set Wagner's opera not in a great mythical past but in an industrialized world full of greed and incipient fascism—Wotan, for instance, is a banker. Despite having had no particular admiration for Wagner *per se*, Schroeter nonetheless felt that Chéreau's staging had done the composer's *music* a disservice. To contrast his own recent production of *Lohengrin* to Chéreau's work, Schroeter deliberately foregrounded the beauty of the romantic composer's music. Needless to say, such a position was monstrously unpopular at the time, when debates over Wagner inflamed critics and performers in Germany and around the world. Few were willing to bypass the damning connotative hold that the Third Reich still had on all things Wagnerian, including artists as innovative as Chéreau. Even fewer would dare focus on its attractiveness.

THE MARGINS AND THE UNDERGROUND

Schroeter's commentators have tended to gravitate around the idea of his status as eccentric outsider. In cinematic parlance, he was an "underground" director, and to be sure, formal aspects of his early work support such a label. But over the rest of his career, those underground/marginal labels stuck, and Schroeter mischievously punned that, even after moving well beyond his phase of experimental shorts, "I always stayed *'untergründig'*."[31] When Hans-Jürgen Syberberg released *Our Hitler: A Film from Germany* to international acclaim, Fassbinder wrote a polemically charged piece in which he accused its director of filching techniques associated with the less-acknowledged Schroeter, noting the problems directors faced when painted with words like "marginal."

Infamously nomadic, Schroeter moved from place to place as spirits, projects, and finances dictated, making him difficult to reach. Nor did he concern himself with marketing his work, or even keeping track of it—much of that business he left to Montezuma. His lifelong trouble securing funding reveals the role that economic forces played in his marginalization. ZDF, the state-run TV channel that supported other New German Cinema directors, was a reliable benefactor, and certainly imposed fewer restraints than big-budget theatrical films would have. But it also deprived him of international, big-screen releases and audiences.

Nonetheless, Schroeter inhabits the self-other fantasy in various ways: in his oft-cited disdain for "Germany's cultural shit," in his complaint of being misunderstood in his own country, and in his coinage of the term "world-feeling" to describe how working in Italy, Portugal, and Latin American countries transformed his outlook. It's noteworthy that "world-feeling" abstracts a sense of place while at the same time it requires one, preferring an expansive, vague world to a specific country, but experiencing that "worldliness" only in specific locales.

When confronting the German fantasy of Mediterranean culture, Schroeter often ridicules the normative power of the ostensible centre, as in *Palermo oder Wolfsburg*—in which white German trial lawyers end up cackling like so many geese. Yet he does so from a position of (disavowed) power that enables him to endow the cultural margins with "noble" attributes—another form of exoticization. He presents the Sicilian guest workers of *Palermo* as decent people, with fluid sensualities, moral fortitude, and earthy authenticity, who are keenly aware of the unfavorable power structures and material conditions surrounding them. Yet if the director seems to be gridding non-normative non-compliance onto these people, he knows that outright resistance cannot be. *Wolfsburg* and *Kingdom* both dramatize that things will not change: the institutional machinery, whose power we hear, is set in place, and whose outcasts are left to plow through this structural hopelessness in their own meager ways. It is no small feat that Schroeter can convey such complex thoughts musically, especially given his uprooting and mixing of so many genres, canons, and places of origin. There is nothing organic about the juxtapositions he brings to his musical pairings, such as *La Traviata* and Janis Joplin in *Maria Malibran*. To an inattentive listener, his sound-

31 Schroeter, 192. Schroeter uses the English "*underground*" to refer to filmmaking. The German *untergründig* is more literal, referring to being under the surface of the ground. Using it enables Schroeter to preserve his commitment to being on the outside or edges of mainstream filmmaking, and even the norms of everyday life. My thanks to Charly Mostet for these insights.

tracks might well appear to be random musical babble.

Indeed, for all of Werner Schroeter's tangents away from the mainstream and into so many undergrounds and margins, his music most effectively articulates how limited, untenable, and simplistic the structures of center and margins are. After all, *Palermo,* which does more than its fair share of romanticizing Italian people and cultures over "heartless" German ones, nonetheless relies on German-Austrian music, such as Berg's Violin Concerto, to convey the angelic nature of the migrant, something a strict binarism would make impossible. In *Der schwarze Engel*, Schroeter's flat voice-over offers a statistics-encrusted aural critique of colonial perspective and economic domination reminiscent of Alexander Kluge. Other sounds, such as the Hawai'ian tourist tunes, the ubiquitous Mariachi, and the jungle noise, exhibit greater playfulness and depth in their criticism. "Aloha Oe," for example, has been so exhaustively exoticized by Western tourism so as to connote not simply an impossibly mythic Hawai'i, but a sense of exoticism vague and mobile enough for Westerners to attach to Mexico, as Schroeter does here. When the narrator of *Der Bomberpilot* tells us that *Nabucco* (Verdi's nationalist opera) will be performed at a concert she attends, we hear concert music by Bruckner (another composer caught in nationalist fray, due to World War II). The pairing doesn't merely send up ethnic and nationalist fantasies, but intimates how states and cultures, identities and imaginaries, are necessarily bound up in their others. In short, the fantastic, interdependent exchanges of his film music, combined with their lack of categorical purity, keep Schroeter from falling over any transcendent edge, and enable him to move onto daring ledges and declare Wagner's music "beautiful."

Der schwarze Engel: Magdalena Montezuma

Gerd Gemünden

Werner Schroeter's Italian Journeys

In his famous 1979 homage to Werner Schroeter, Rainer Werner Fassbinder defended his colleague against a facile categorization as an underground filmmaker, describing the term as a label "that well-meaningly limits and prettifies this sort of film, eventually suffocating it in a tender embrace. In reality there is no such thing as *underground* film. It only exists for people who know how to make neat distinctions between Up Here, Down There, and Way over There."[1] Already, a decade earlier, in 1969, Wim Wenders had described Schroeter as a director whose *oeuvre* defies any classification—"es spottet jeder Beschreibung."[2] Calling Schroeter's films "incredibly concentrated," Wenders marveled that "the films of Werner Schroeter are how one desires the films with Marilyn Monroe to be, how one desires everything to be, especially at the movies."[3] It is no coincidence that among Schroeter's earliest supportive critics are two notable German filmmakers. If any label can be applied to Schroeter at all, then, it would be that of "a filmmaker's filmmaker." Key directors of the New German Cinema, such as Fassbinder and Wenders, but also the Bavarian maverick Herbert Achternbusch, admire him, as do Rosa von Praunheim and Monika Treut, both documentarians and gay and transgender activists. Schroeter's influence can be detected in the films of Ulrike Ottinger, Walter Bockmayer, Frank Ripploh, Niklaus Schilling, Robert van Ackeren, or Daniel Schmid. His fascination with opera accounts for some of the affinities with Alexander Kluge and Werner Herzog, to whose *Fitzcarraldo* Schroeter contributed an important opera scene, and with Hans Jürgen Syberberg, whose relation to Schroeter Fassbinder unflatteringly described as that of a "trafficker in matters of plagiarism."[4]

Like Herzog, Schroeter is an autodidact. Schroeter was admitted to the Munich Film School, to which Fassbinder twice applied in vain, incidentally beginning in the same cohort as Wenders, only to quit after a few weeks.

1 Rainer Werner Fassbinder, "Chin-up, Handstand, Salto Mortale—Firm Footing: On the Film Director Werner Schroeter, Who Achieved What Few Achieve, With *The Kingdom of Naples*," in Michael Töteberg and Leo A. Lensing, eds., *The Anarchy of the Imagination: Interviews, Essays, Notes*, trans. Krishna Winston (Baltimore: Johns Hopkins University Press, 1992), pp. 100–103; quote from p. 100.

2 Wim Wenders, "Die phantastischen Filme von Werner Schroeter über künstliche Leute," in Michael Töteberg, ed., *Emotion Pictures: Essays und Filmkritiken, 1968–1984* (Frankfurt am Main: Verlag der Autoren, 1986), p. 15. [Unless otherwise noted, all translations are my own.]

3 Wenders, "Die phantastischen Filme von Werner Schroeter."

4 Fassbinder, "Chin-up, Handstand, Salto Mortale," p. 102.

Unlike most other directors of the New German Cinema, he has largely refrained from applying for public funding—the only exception being his co-productions with the German state television network ZDF (Zweites Deutsches Fernsehen)—fiercely protecting his independence and refusing to be used as a cultural ambassador for German national culture, or what Schroeter calls "*Kulturscheisse*" (culture shit), a yoke to which Fassbinder, Herzog, and Wenders were all tied in some ways, regardless of their critical stance towards the nation's history and its history of film.[5]

For many of the directors of the New German Cinema, the complex and idiosyncratic style of Schroeter's films served as a quarry to be mined, to build what are ultimately very diverse films and *oeuvres*. Particularly, Schroeter's various allegorical styles have had a strong influence on his German colleagues. Several also cast Schroeter's stars Magdalena Montezuma and Carla Aulaulu, and Schroeter himself frequently appeared as a guest in other directors' films. He had a small role in Wenders' early short *Alabama: 2000 Light Years from Home* (1969) and in Fassbinder's *Welt am Draht* (*World on a Wire*, 1973), where he appeared alongside his own regulars Montezuma and Christine Kaufmann, as well as in *Warnung vor einer heiligen Nutte* (*Beware of a Holy Whore*, 1971), which in itself can be considered an extended homage to Schroeter.[6] For the purpose of this essay, Schroeter's relation to Fassbinder will be the most significant creative affinity, for reasons that will become clear shortly. Theirs is arguably also one of the most complex and contradictory relationships Schroeter entertained with any colleague, both on a biographical and intertextual level.

This relationship is particularly intriguing in Schroeter's two features *Nel regno di Napoli* (*The Kingdom of Naples*, 1978) and *Palermo oder Wolfsburg* (*Palermo or Wolfsburg*, 1980), two of his most commercially successful films. As for so many German artists since the 18th century, for Werner Schroeter Italy has been a place for inspiration and contemplation. Part of his 1969 *Eika Katappa* was filmed there, and Italian musical tradition is central to his *oeuvre*. The famous Greek soprano Maria Callas, whom Schroeter cites as his most important artistic influence and who was the subject of his first shorts, built her career on the rediscovery of the *bel canto* operas of Rossini, Donizetti, and Bellini, and on her interpretations of Verdi and Puccini. But unlike other artists, from Goethe through Thomas Mann, Rolf Dieter Brinkmann, Ingo Schultze, and even Wenders, Schroeter's fascination with Italy is based not

5 See Schroeter's signature statement: "I have no intention whatsoever of playing a leading part in the New German Cinema, and submit to the expectations of producing *Kulturscheisse*, even if it may be that I carry around with me and into my films the past of this *Kulturscheisse*. I neither depend on it, nor do I admire it. The elements of this *Kultur* are the materials I play with." Quoted in Thomas Elsaesser, *New German Cinema: A History* (Brunswick, NJ: Rutgers University Press, 1989), p. 48. [The original source is Barbara Bronnen and Corinna Brocher, *Die Filmemacher* (Munich: Bertelsmann, 1973), p. 83.]

6 Werner Schroeter, with Claudia Lenssen, *Tage im Dämmer, Nächte im Rausch* (Berlin: Aufbau Verlag, 2011), p. 78.

on short-term travels but on extended stays, particularly in Southern Italy. For him, Italy is not an imaginary place or a projection screen, but one of lived experience. As such, Italy is no mere source of fantasy, no mere instrument of self-discovery and education, but at the center of a detailed study of its history and its people. Ironically, Schroeter's Italian journeys led to the creation of some of his most realist work—a term that does not come to mind readily when one discusses Werner Schroeter—and something that Schroeter in hindsight called "something fundamentally different" (*"etwas grundsätzlich Neues"*) in his *oeuvre*.[7]

At age sixteen, Schroeter went to live in Naples for one year, where he fell in love with the culture and its language, particularly its many different Southern dialects, which one can hear in his films. His command of the language allowed him to intervene as interpreter for the admired Pier Paolo Pasolini, when the famous director showed his *Accattone* in Heidelberg in 1961.[8] The films of Michelangelo Antonioni and Luchino Visconti also became sources of emulation, even if Schroeter's films are ultimately quite different. As Karsten Witte noted, "in almost all of his films, Schroeter almost obsessively depicts the contradiction between the empire of freedom (Italy) and the empire of necessity (Germany), under which he suffers."[9]

The Kingdom of Naples was released in Germany as *Neapolitanische Geschwister*, a bit of a misnomer, since the German title puts the emphasis on the two protagonists, the siblings Massimo and Vittoria Pagano, rather than the city of Naples itself. The term "Kingdom" refers, strictly speaking, to the time before Garibaldi's 1860 conquest of Sicily and Naples, while Schroeter's film chronicles the history of the port city from 1944 to the present. Yet, no matter whether a monarchy, a dictatorship, or a republic, the title indicates that time is cyclical in this city. There is no progress, no movement towards a better future, only an endless repetition of poverty, misery, and death; the throne, and more recently *Il Duce*, may have been replaced by various political parties and big companies, but to no advantage for the populace. Only the reach of the Catholic Church has remained unabated over the centuries.

Co-written with Wolf Wondratschek, *The Kingdom of Naples* marked Schroeter's first film released in 35mm, and the first with a social-realist narrative that follows a strictly chronological trajectory, providing a spatial and temporal continuity not seen before in Schroeter's work. It was also his first film to pick up distribution in Germany and thus be shown in commercial theaters; and it was the first to win a number of prestigious awards at festivals not exclusively devoted to experimental film, including the Adolf-Grimme Prize, and awards at the film festivals of Chicago and Taormina.

The film interweaves the saga of the Pagano family with the larger history of Naples from

7 Schroeter, p. 156.

8 Schroeter, p. 37. Elsewhere in his autobiography (p. 91), Schroeter notes that he was very critical of how Pasolini used Maria Callas in his *Medea* in a naturalistic way.

9 Karsten Witte, "Versteckte Zeichen und Signale: Werner Schroeters Filme," *Frankfurter Rundschau* (Frankfurt am Main), July 5, 1991.

1944 to 1977, and is divided into 16 segments, with every second new year announced by a newscaster's voice-over, garish pink numerals, and an image of a historical marker such as the poster of a political party or of a politician. At the center of this episodic narrative stand the two siblings, Vittoria and Massimo;[10] we witness Vittoria's birth on the day the German troops abandon Naples, followed by Massimo's a few years later. Their telling names embody the promise of a better future that their lives cannot deliver. Michelle Langford has called them allegorical figures, because "they embody wider social phenomena such as the conflict between politics and religion within the confines of the domestic sphere."[11] Their mother (Renata Zamengo) dies young, leaving the overworked father (Dino Melé), a shoemaker, to provide the children with a perspective for the future, a task at which he fails. Massimo follows in his father's footsteps and signs up with the Communists, who promise him an income but employ him only for menial tasks. Vittoria desires to join a convent. Ultimately, she finds work in the hotel industry, renouncing marriage in favor of keeping her independence, while Massimo is arrested during protests against the Vietnam War and serves two years in prison.

The Pagano family is surrounded by a cast of

10 Vittoria is played by Tiziana Ambretti (as a child), Maria Antoniella Riegel (as a teenager), and Cristina Donadio (as a young woman); Massimo is played by Romeo Ciro (as a child) and Antonio Orlando (as a young man).

11 Michelle Langford, *Allegorical Images: Tableau, Time and Gesture in the Cinema of Werner Schroeter* (Bristol, UK: Intellect, 2006), p. 23.

Nel regno di Napoli (1978): "You will keep the Party headquarters clean, and sell the Party paper."

Nel regno di Napoli

characters whose lives intersect with theirs. They include a French prostitute, Rosario à Frances (Margareth Clementi), who serves as midwife at Massimo's birth and much later provides him with his first sexual experience, and who finally, terminally ill, collapses in front of him at the Piazza Plebiscito during carnival season. The Pagano's neighbor, Caviola, prostitutes her daughter, Rosa (Laura Sodano), to a black GI for a bag of flour, and later kills her husband, whom she holds responsible for her daughter's death, ending her life in an insane asylum. The factory owner Pupetta Ferrante (Ida Di Benedetto) employs Vittoria to clean her apartment, but with an eye to having her service her male friends and business partners, which Vittoria refuses to do. When her factory falls on hard times and the workers demand their outstanding wages, Ferrante shoots and kills their leader and flees town. As these brief summaries indicate, violence, misery, and death shape the lives of all *Napolitani*, a fact the film underscores by repeatedly inserting scenes of a horse-drawn hearse traversing the streets.

What is new here, and what remains of the style Schroeter had established in his previous films? Most important is the film's insistence on realism, which critics saw as an extended homage to Italian neorealism, most notably through its use of lay actors and location shooting. *The Kingdom of Naples* is confined to a single neighborhood. We see the same walls (adorned by changing political slogans and posters), the same squares, the cramped interiors of the same small apartments. Thomas Mauch's camera (which frequently also served Werner Herzog) provides no establishing shots, no sweeping vistas of the many picture-postcard locations of Naples. When we glimpse the blue ocean, it is framed by a shabby window sill, curtailing its promise of a getaway.[12] As Sebastian Feldmann has noted, "Streets, squares, churches function as petrified conditions of life, as overpowering determinants of human existences. For the first time in a Schroeter film, the topography is the protagonist, the optic symbol of social pressure."[13] Furthermore, in its dissection of political history the film is analytical rather than associative, which had been the predominant mode in films such as *Der Bomberpilot* (1970). Covering some thirty years of Italian post-war history, *The Kingdom of Naples* makes larger claims about the presence of the past in contemporary Italy, reminiscent of Fassbinder's BRD trilogy, which was inaugurated that same year by *Die Ehe der Maria Braun* (*The Marriage of Maria Braun*).

Yet this analytic dimension is infused with Schroeter's well-known penchant for histrionics and melodrama. *The Kingdom of Naples* is quite literally a drama in which music plays a significant role, ranging from popular tunes and folk songs of Naples to revolutionary songs and opera. Significantly, Maria Callas, who assumes a redemptive function in Schroeter's work, is only faintly heard here in the background. Life

12 Mauch has commented in positive ways on the collaboration with Schroeter. See Gérard Courant, ed., *Werner Schroeter* (Paris: Goethe Institut/Cinémathèque Française, 1982), pp. 94–95.

13 Sebastian Feldmann, "Kommentierte Filmografie," in Feldmann, et al., eds., *Werner Schroeter* (Munich: Hanser Verlag, 1980), p. 181.

in Naples is repetitive, not redemptive. Love, death, and longing, the trademarks of Schroeter's earlier work, also structure *The Kingdom of Naples*. Frequent shots featuring blood (as a result of childbirth, various injuries, assaults, and diseases) rupture the narrative flow. Time and again, characters are assembled in theatrical *tableaux*, offsetting realism with more stylized characterizations (again reminiscent of many of Fassbinder's melodramas). Largely devoid of psychological depth, they instead represent easily recognizable types with telling names. The heavily made-up factory owner Pupetta (literally "puppet"), a witch-like creature with red hair and red lipstick, will try to corrupt the innocent, virginal Vittoria, while Palumbo, the homosexual and lecherous mama's boy and Christian Democrat, lures young boys into his parlor. The prostitute Rosario à Frances, who conducts her business behind a flaming red curtain, dies a miserable death during carnival, convulsing in the cobblestoned piazza to the drumroll of a harlequin.

When the film was released, it attracted widespread attention. Wolfram Schütte wrote that the film "counts as one of Schroeter's most accomplished and beautiful films, [a film] that unpretentiously combines epic calm with the operatic drama."[14] Writing in the *Süddeutsche Zeitung* (June 17, 1979), Martje Grohmann noted that *The Kingdom of Naples* marked a transition in Schroeter's *oeuvre* "from the grotesque to the graceful, from gesture to sensuality" (*"von der Gebärde zur Sinnlichkeit"*), and in *Le Monde* (January 20, 1980), Jacques Siclier marveled at Schroeter's *"écriture baroque."*

Yet not all reviews of the film were positive. In *Filmkritik*, Rosa von Praunheim published a polemical article whose headline translates as "With Fond Greetings to Champagne-Schroeter," in which he denounced the film as "consciously trivial and kitschy [and] sentimental masochism."[15] He was particularly taken aback by Schroeter's representation of the gay Christian Democrat, who is shown making eyes at a young boy in front of a huge aquarium, a scene that is intercut with close-ups of slithering slimy fish. As von Praunheim notes, "Why didn't Herr Schroeter play this role himself as a demonstration of his homo-sexual self-hatred?" As this quote shows, von Praunheim's attack on the film quickly shifts to one on the filmmaker: "Champagne-Schroeter, who, after wrapping up his work, lounges around with champagne and caviar, admiring the courage of the poor people." Apart from Schroeter's alleged use of *clichés* and stereotypes, what von Praunheim is really furious about is Schroeter's unwillingness to support the kind of gay activism that he himself embodies. The deeper nature of this rift clearly indicates that the two filmmakers define the political in very different ways. In contrast to von Praunheim's activism, Schroeter favors an approach in which the form itself is political—these are not films

14 Wolfram Schütte, "Cannes Bericht," *Frankfurter Rundschau* (Frankfurt am Main, May 29, 1978). [Unless noted all translations from the German are my own.]

15 Rosa von Praunheim, "Mit herzlichem Gruß an Champagner-Schroeter," *Filmkritik* (Munich), no. 265 (January 1979); English trans. in Eric Rentschler, ed., *West German Filmmakers on Film: Visions and Voices* (New York: Holmes & Meier, 1988), p. 193.

about politics, but political filmmaking. For von Praunheim, however, *The Kingdom* was simply a commercial sell-out.

Spurned by von Praunheim's *ad hominem* attack, who after all had assisted Schroeter on *Neurasia* (1969), Fassbinder (about whose *In einem Jahr mit 13 Monden* [*In a Year of 13 Moons*] von Praunheim also only had bad things to say) came to Schroeter's defense in a lengthy homage, sharply criticizing von Praunheim's "repugnant and repulsive" attack as an act of petty envy indicative of his desperation over "never having made a great film or never having had the opportunity to do so."[16]

The Kingdom of Naples was conceived as the first part of an Italian trilogy, and was followed two years later by *Palermo oder Wolfsburg*, while the third part—allegedly to be called *Italien, Hoffnung Europas* (Italy, the Hope of Europe)—was never completed.[17] As the title indicates, *Palermo or Wolfsburg* also takes place in Southern Italy, in a small Sicilian village just south of Palermo, and chronicles the experiences of the young, unemployed Nicola who comes to Wolfsburg to find employment in the VW automobile plant to better his lot. With its focus on the foreign worker in Germany, Schroeter's film is one of many of the 1970s and 1980s that deals with the *Ausländerfrage* (the foreigner question), a corpus of works focusing on so-called "guest workers" that includes Fassbinder's *Katzelmacher* (1969) and *Angst essen Seele auf* (*Ali: Fear Eats the Soul*, 1974), Helma Sanders-Brahms' *Shirins Hochzeit* (*Shirin's Wedding*, 1976), Jeanine Meerapfel's documentary *Die Kümmeltürkin geht* (1985), Tefvik Başer's *40 qm Deutschland* (1986) and *Abschied vom falschen Paradies* (1989), Hark Bohm's *Yasemin* (1988), and, more recently, Fatih Akin's *Solino* (2002). The subject matter of these films invariably revolves around the difficulties foreigners face when, having left behind the support of family structures, they try to integrate into German culture and society, an attempt that, at least in these films, is rarely crowned by success.

Schroeter's three-hour film is divided into three distinctive parts that employ starkly contrasting styles. The first part uses a neorealist aesthetic already seen in *The Kingdom of Naples*. We follow young Nicola (played by lay actor Nicola Zarbo) as he readies himself to leave Palma di Montechiaro to go to Germany, visiting one last time with his friends, seeking advice from the priest, and gathering objects that will connect him to his home while abroad. The camera assumes a largely observational stance, while episodic vignettes follow each other at a leisurely pace. In one scene, Nicola looks out over the many unfinished rooftops of houses, their completion dependent on the remission payments sent home by Sicilian workers in Germany. Again it is Thomas Mauch, who also served as producer, who captures im-

16 Fassbinder, "Hommage an Werner Schroeter," in Hans Helmut Prinzler and Eric Rentschler, eds., *Augenzeugen: 100 Texte neuer deutscher Filmemacher* (Frankfurt am Main: Verlag der Autoren, 1988), p. 417.

17 Schroeter briefly talks about this third part in his 1978 appearance at the Austrian Film Museum, a recording of which is included as a bonus feature on the DVD of *Der Bomberpilot & Nel regno di Napoli* by Edition Filmmuseum (Munich).

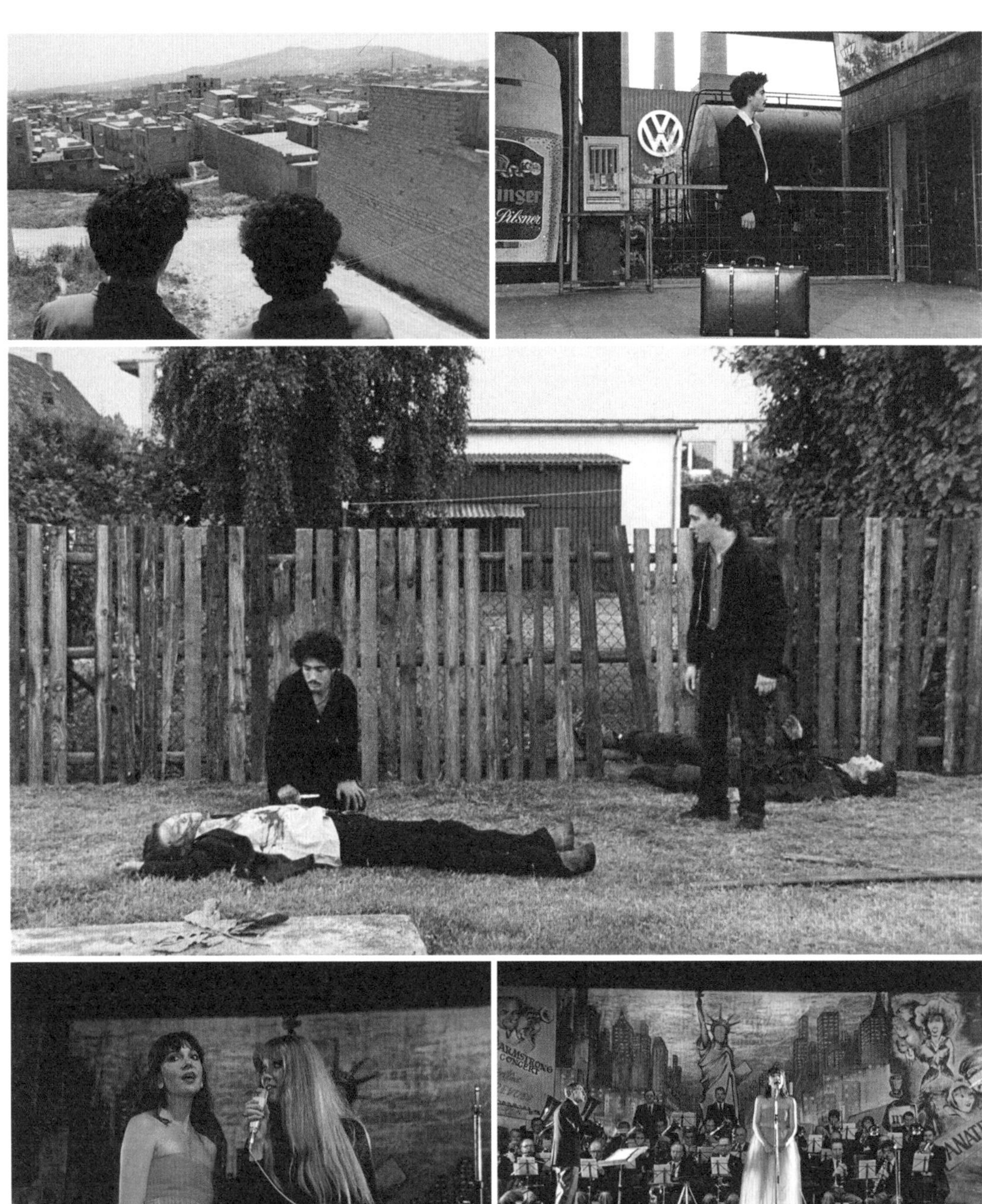

Palermo oder Wolfsburg (1980)

ages that are eloquent without dialogue or voice-over, showing us how the local agriculture can no longer sustain the peasants, a sobering fact underscored by images of garbage burning in the ravines of the hills. A landscape rich in tradition and culture is now barren and poor.

Nicola's transition to Germany is marked by a lengthy interlude on the train, symbolic of the vast geographical and cultural differences that set Northern Germany apart from Southern Italy. The town of Wolfsburg is dominated by the large neon VW-sign that illuminates the forbidding brick structure of the Volkswagen factory. The homely yellows and reds of the South are replaced by cold blue and greenish tones. As with many films in this cycle, the Germans' welcome to the foreigner is not a warm one. An Italian acquaintance refuses to let Nicola stay in his place overnight because his German wife objects to harboring strangers, and Nicola is forced to sleep in a park. Only when the bar owner Giovanna (Ida di Benedetto) takes him in does he begin to get his bearings. He meets a girl, Brigitte (Brigitte Tilg), and they seemingly forge a friendship, not realizing, however, that Brigitte's signs of sympathy are calculated to solicit more attention from her German male friends. When the two young men mock Nicola, he feels betrayed and dishonored, and he stabs them to death. The Wolfsburg episode is filmed in a style that combines stylized realism with melodrama, similar to many Fassbinder films of the period, with Giovanna recalling the Barbara Valentin character of *Ali*.

Particularly striking is the climax of the second part of the film, when Nicola understands that he has been a pawn in Brigitte's game. It is a scene fraught with discrepancies, contradictions, and cultural over-determination. The two are at a country fair, where a song contest is about to begin. The hostess is German singer-songwriter Juliane Werding, best remembered by German audiences for her early 1970s hit "Am Tag, als Conny Kramer starb," a German cover of The Band's 1969 "The Night They Drove Old Dixie Down," which describes the last days of the American Civil War and the suffering of the South, and which was also covered by Joan Baez and Johnny Cash. Werding's presence at the country fair indicates that fame is ephemeral and fortune never permanent. The contestant, a young woman from Braunschweig, choses to sing, "Zwei kleine Italiener" (Two Little Italians) by "Conny"—the Conny in question being the teenage idol and later film and television star Cornelia Froebess, who sang this song as the 1962 German entry to the Eurovision Song Contest.[18]

Providing the melody for this song about two Italian immigrants homesick for their native Naples, in what amounts to a early version of karaoke, is a German oompah band. The band performs on a stage with a decidedly American set decor. On stage left we see a poster of Louis Armstrong, and at center stage the silhouette of Manhattan, with a Statue of Liberty towering above—the symbol of the city

18 The German *Schlager* "Zwei kleine Italiener" was composed by Christian Bruhn, with lyrics by Georg Buschor.

Palermo oder Wolfsburg

and the guardian of immigrants, which historically includes a large contingent from Southern Italy who settled on the Lower East Side. Its inscription, we recall, famously reads: "Give me your tired, your poor, / Your huddled masses, yearning to breathe free, / The wretched refuse of your teeming shore, / Send these, the homeless, tempest-tossed to me, / I lift my lamp beside the golden door."

This scene, however, as well as the song, is, of course, about anything but being welcome. When Nicola confesses his love, Brigitte pushes him away, seeking the arms of the German boy she desires. Nicola's confusion and incomprehension is underscored by a cut to a whirling swing-boat at the nearby fair. He leaves the scene under the deriding eyes of the three German youths and approaches the exit. Adding insult to injury, this experience of disappointment is overlaid with the band's tune "So ein Tag, so wunderschön wie heute" (Such a Beautiful Day), an obvious moment of sarcasm. As the film insists, however, the true culprit of Nicola's deception is not Brigitte but the Volkswagen company. As Nicola exits, he approaches a huge VW sign that casts around his head a halo of materialism, until his face is caught in the giant neon letters as in the crosshairs of a rifle.

Schroeter's striking use of music recalls the opening scene of Fassbinder's *Ali*, where the female protagonist, Emmi, dances with Ali to the tune of "Du schwarzer Zigeuner" (Black Gypsy), while being stared at by the other patrons of the bar. Both Fassbinder's and Schroeter's film simultaneously emphasize ridicule and sympathy, hostility and solidarity, parody and honest empathy. We note that the song contestant comes from the provinces, like Nicola, and appears similarly insecure. At the moment when Nicola is abandoned by Brigitte, the singer's voice breaks, underscoring a fragile connection between two people, who are both targets of public ridicule. However, neither one of them registers the other's vulnerability, and they both remain isolated and abandoned.

The jarring contrasts that structure this scene reach new dimensions in the last hour of the film, which is entirely devoted to the court proceedings and filmed in a highly disorienting, surreal, and even grotesque style. We witness bizarre courtroom antics on behalf of the judge (who even falls asleep) and the district attorney, with the mothers of the killed boys at one point kissing each other. In contrast to the first two parts, in which lay actors dominate, these roles are played by professional actors, further underscoring the theatricality of the situation as well as the vulnerability of Nicola. The actors include such well-known stars as Otto Sander, who plays the DA, Schroeter's regular Magdalena Montezuma as the defense lawyer, and Schroeter's colleague Ula Stöckl as a lay assessor (Fassbinder's longtime friend Harry Baer also has a small role as the owner of a house). A character by the name of Kafka makes an appearance, her name pointing towards the obscurity of the legal system and its propensity to swallow the accused.

Distorted voices and rapid editing create a profound sense of disorientation and confusion that mimic Nicola's utter lack of comprehension of the events unfolding in front of him. He seems like a Kaspar Hauser figure, catatonic, unmoved, silent. The clash of cultures is most strongly conveyed through the simultaneously heard German and Italian translations of the proceedings, a babble that becomes increasingly difficult to follow for viewers. Called to the witness stand, Giovanna repeatedly calls Nicola "Lämmchen" (Little Lamb), an easy prey for the wolf into whose burg it has unwittingly moved. When at the end the District Attorney surprisingly pleads to acquit Nicola, Nicola finally speaks out, claiming, "I killed them and I wanted to kill them," an act of assuming responsibility not only for his deed, but also his status as a subject that speaks, rather than a mere object that is spoken about. Rather than destroying him, the confession makes him come into his own.

Intercut at various points of the three very distinct parts of the film are sequences from a lay performance of a Passion Play, creating a sense of coherence by underscoring Nicola's journey as that of a martyr (reminiscent of Pasolini's *Accattone*, 1961). As Karsten Witte commented in *Die Zeit*, "The locations are like a triptych: one hour of exposition in Sicily, one hour of conflict and action in Wolfsburg, one hour of catharsis in the courtroom. The film describes a dramatic curve that rises slowly, in almost documentary fashion, in part one; in Wolfsburg, the place of the experience of the foreign, it weaves in elements of a feature film that is directed in a very restrained and controlled fashion, leading to a steep climax of

Palermo oder Wolfsburg

a courtroom farce that vehemently approaches the grotesque."[19]

The first German film ever to win a Golden Bear at the Berlin Film Festival, *Palermo* was Schroeter's biggest critical success—a film, after all, on which he took credit not only for direction but also script, dialogue, make-up, and editing—and it received largely enthusiastic reviews. But there were also critical voices, who chided Schroeter for abandoning his more experimental forms of filmmaking or for assembling elements in one single film that had better stayed separate. Carla Rode, for example, concluded her largely positive *Tagesspiegel* review by quipping, "Unfortunately, the film has a third part."[20]

In order to adopt the perspective of the foreigner, several of the films about guest workers with which I have grouped Schroeter's film tend to foreground his or her status as the victim, the oppressed, the silenced, or the abject; and many of them were made by leftist filmmakers aiming to raise our awareness about social and gender injustice and racial prejudice. Yet as Deniz Göktürk has argued, despite their good intentions—or maybe precisely because of them—these films are often unsatisfying. For the most part they are, she writes, "informed by a social worker's perspective and haunted by residual notions of cultural purity,

19 Karsten Witte, "Ansichten eines Engels: Über *Palermo oder Wolfsburg*," *Die Zeit* (Hamburg), March 21, 1980. www.zeit.de/1980/13/zum-andenken-eines-engels.

20 Carla Rode, "Ein Sizilianer bei VW: Zu Werner Schroeters preisgekröntem Film *Palermo oder Wolfsburg*," *Der Tagesspiegel* (Berlin), April 11, 1980.

community and authenticity."[21] To be sure, Schroeter's film is not entirely immune to this criticism. Yet in contrast to Tevfik Başer's and particularly Helma Sanders-Brahms' and Hark Bohm's films, *Palermo or Wolfsburg* stands out for employing a discourse of what one might call enlightened victimology, a discourse that again places it alongside Fassbinder's *Ali*. Clearly, its sympathies lie with its protagonist.

The film opens with a sense of realist detachment, adopting an observational stance as we watch Nicola preparing for his journey to Germany. The scenes in Wolfsburg create empathy while insisting on the cultural rift between North and South. The trial, finally, is viewed through Nicola's eyes; we see his flashbacks and his dream sequences. But unlike many of the films that Göktürk criticizes, *Palermo* refuses to speak on behalf of its victim. Instead, like *Ali*, *Palermo* emphasizes the impossibility of doing so by pointing to the ubiquity of cultural misreadings: Nicola cannot see that Brigitte is an insecure young girl who does not know what she wants. She, in turn, overlooks that her flirtations can easily be misunderstood by someone from a different culture. Nicola kills the two German youths at exactly the moment when they do not want to ridicule him but seek to be his buddies. And the DA thinks he is doing Nicola a favor when he lets him get off lightly, overlooking that he once again undermines Nicola's own definition of agency and dignity.

In contrast to the other Italians whom Nicola meets, and who are at various stages of unhappy assimilation and complete isolation, Nicola's admission of guilt is a refusal of the victim role, a refusal of letting others determine what one is or is not—a rare position in German films from this period. Through its theatricality and mixing of disparate styles, *Palermo* preserves a dimension that differs from the social worker's perspective alluded to before, and that ultimately may be more rigorous and more analytical precisely because it questions dominant modes of rationality. Schroeter's film insists on the incommensurability of Wolfsburg and Palermo—it is not a comfy postmodern "*sowohl als auch*" ("as well as"), but a decisive "*entweder oder*" ("either or"). In this it approximates Michel Foucault's disavowal of the hermeneutics of interpretation, replacing the various disciplines that seek to interpret the speechless subject with an analysis of the discourses that produce the subject in the first place. Indeed, as Wenders aptly put it, Schroeter's films defy accepted classifications, challenging viewers to meet them on their own terms, even today.

21 Deniz Göktürk, "Turkish Delight—German Fright: Migrant Identities in Transnational Cinema," in *Transnational Communities—Working Paper Series* (An Economic and Social Council Research Programme, University of Oxford, January 1999), pp. 1–14; quote from p. 1.

Fatima Naqvi

"Psycho" Biography: *Malina* (1991)

When a film proves recalcitrant to interpretation, the tendency is to ignore or disavow the challenge it presents. Werner Schroeter's complex *Malina* (1991) has not found the place in post-war film history it deserves.[1] What makes it so difficult to "read"? Flowing transformations suddenly give way to the stasis of death,[2] but mortification becomes the precondition for rebirth. The metamorphoses intrinsic to gender performance are arrested abruptly, only to suddenly begin anew. Horrific nightmares segue into opalescent daydreams, and daytime phantasmagorias become iridescent nighttime sequences. The dissemination of the woman's image comes to a halt only in the emptiness of the final frame—or not. Fire and water shift shape, follow one another, and follow from one another: "for across fire, they send water" ("*denn über das Feuer schicken sie das Wasser*").[3] Perhaps this film is too much firewater: *Malina*'s rich visuals make one drunk; the careening camera causes light-headedness; the fragmentary narrative leaves one unsteady.

The translation from book to screenplay to film only augments this sense of having had too much of a good thing. Ingeborg Bachmann's original 1971 novel mixes genres and media—from music to lyric poetry to drama, from literature to interview to film—to heighten the protagonist's disorientation in a post-war culture built on fascist ruins, under which latent fires smolder. These fires become the condition for the possibility of murder *and* of renascence.[4] Elfriede Jelinek's screenplay turns the novel into another book (a "*Filmbuch*"), stressing the utopian landscapes *and* dystopian psychopathology, the war between the genders, and the cinematic aspects of the novel.[5] In turn, Schroeter recounts in his autobiography how he both incorporates and discards elements of Jelinek's *Filmbuch*.[6]

Drawing on his love for opera singer Maria

1 On the difficulty of interpreting Schroeter's film, see John Gianvito, "Against Moderation ('It's Always War') / Notes on MALINA," *VISIONS* (Boston, MA), no. 11 (Fall 1993), pp. 32–35, or Michelle Langford, *Allegorical Images: Tableau, Time and Gesture in the Cinema of Werner Schroeter* (Bristol, UK: Intellect, 2006), pp. 8–11.

2 Grafe, Frieda. "Schauplatz für Sprache: *Neurasia*," in *Filmkritik* (Munich), no. 159 (March 1970).

3 Ingeborg Bachmann, *Malina* (Frankfurt am Main: Suhrkamp, 1997 [orig. 1971]), p. 258. In the novel's third section, the first-person narrator thematizes the association of fire and water (pp. 257–258). [All translations in this essay are my own.]

4 See the italicized fairytale-sections in Transdanubia in Chapter 1, "Happy with Ivan," pp. 64–69.

5 See Elfriede Jelinek/Ingeborg Bachmann, *Malina. Ein Filmbuch* (Frankfurt am Main: Suhrkamp, 1991).

6 See Werner Schroeter's chapter "*Malina*," in *Tage im Dämmer, Nächte im Rausch* (Berlin: Aufbau Verlag, 2011), pp. 260–266, esp. p. 261.

Callas and the media persona of Ingeborg Bachmann, Schroeter uses the mythologizing memes surrounding both divas—the images of these women that were propagated and copied to produce stars in the first place. The director projects these memes onto the female protagonist of his film. He thereby undermines the fundamental premise of biography, namely, that its basis is the absolutely singular, inimitable quality of an artist's life. In his film *Malina*, Schroeter incorporates such biographical memes in order to show how psychologizing readings of a star's existence inevitably fall short of explaining it. Instead, the director allows the mythologizing memes to dissolve into multiplicity. Rather than preserve particular moments in time, frozen in all eternity, he also carries them over into his later project, *Deux* (2002), which builds on *Malina*. Thus, as I will explain in greater detail below, the circulation of memes rather than any supposed depth psychology deserves our attention.

I. (CON FUOCO)
ABER MAN HAT FEINDE. / BUT ONE HAS ENEMIES.[7]

Werner Schroeter's film begins with a cryptic sequence that adumbrates the themes of the novel and introduces the film's *modus operandi* via *montage*. The color scheme (recurrent red and shades of black) and soundtrack provide the barest of connections among the disparate shots. A cut after the bright red credit announcing the production company reveals a close-up of a man's face (Fritz Schediwy) in three-quarter profile, framed against a dark background with little depth of field. All is black or gray around him, with the exception of his clean white shirt collar. A hazy silhouette of a building in the background seems to reflect cold light onto the right side of his face. Red dots, like drops of blood, carry over the red from the credit image into this sequence, lining the bottom of the screen. The man is shown from a slightly lower angle in close-up, his brown eyes fixating on someone beyond our ken. A buzzing insect lands on his lips, as he looks off-screen to the left and harangues his unseen interlocutor: "You think you are something better, don't you? Who do you think you are?" A quick cut to the nameless woman (Isabelle Huppert) follows as his hand strikes her face. Dressed in flaming red, she begins to scream as the slap echoes. A quick succession of close-up shots alternates between her supposedly "white hands," the man's malevolent grip, and a long shot of the rooftop locale, where a tussle ensues between the two that is acoustically overlaid with the woman's shrieks.

This long take is quintessential "Schroeter," devoid of realism and redolent with symbolism—a gray parapet lined with the *petit-bourgeois* flower, the red geranium, the hulking silhouette of a *Flakturm* (an above-ground anti-aircraft tower), and next to it a small white church steeple, as if made of *fondant*. A little girl (played by Huppert's daughter, Lolita Chammah), with her back toward us, is also attired in red and stands next to the wrangling man and woman,

7 Bachmann, *Malina*, p. 329. My headings refer to the musical designations present in the third chapter, "Of Last Things."

Malina (1991)

MALINA

who are locked in their violent embrace. A scene of shattered pots, staring child, and cowering woman ensues.

We are in the realm of the nightmare, with the radical presentism and condensed characters on which the horror genre relies; we are also on the operatic stage, where the *tableau* delineates the fraught relationship between the characters in the (absent) distance between figures. A cut to the street, where a worm's-eye view shows us a falling doll, dressed in red. The doll drops from the place where the middle-aged man jettisoned the blonde child over the ledge. Suddenly, the woman, now in a medium close-up, is shown on the ground as well, witnessing the fall, but no longer screaming. The scene resolves not with a shattered child-doll, but with a blood-spattered dark-haired man lying on the ground, broken geranium pots next to his wounded head and another man's legs akimbo behind him. A man's voice berates the woman for allowing her father to attempt to kill him—then this gentleman (Mathieu Carrière) grabs her in a two-shot, repeating the claustrophobic struggle that took place on the roof. The well-attired gentleman tries to force her to accompany him and leave the scene of mayhem. The enemy is everywhere, congealed in these bespoke patriarchs and concretized in Nazi architecture. Sound begins before the source becomes visible; voices of violence come from unknown places, to remind us that danger lurks beyond the frame.[8]

While this second male figure moves to send off the arriving police (explaining the incident as one of a rollicking "family party"), the red-dressed woman resists going along. Instead, she places her head on the wounded man's on the ground. As she does so, her red dress and the garish, viscous blood on his temple bind them together visually. The same cold white light we had witnessed with the first man bathes her face from above. Her dazed state already beckons toward the realm of the dead. Her gaze is that of the corpse she becomes in the last twenty minutes of the film, when she submits to the aggressions of the gray-haired Malina. She numbly intones the following lines: "How did I get here? In whose power? It cannot be a strange man. It cannot have been in vain, not have been deception. It cannot have been true."[9] Giacomo Manzoni's soundtrack further emphasizes the irreality of this horrific scene about the loss of spatial orientation, the gendered hierarchy of power, the nature of truth, and the outrageousness of the events.

This first montage is Schroeter's contribution, pulling the 82nd scene of Jelinek's script to

8 In the case of *Malina*, one should actually speak of two films: the French version with Isabelle Huppert's voice and the dubbing of the German-speaking actors; and the German version, with Lisa Kreuzer speaking Huppert's part. Since both versions engage in partial synchronization, the film space created via sound is particularly difficult to analyze. On the voice and (dis)embodiment, see Michel Chion, *The Voice in Cinema*, ed. and trans. Claudia Gorbman (New York: Columbia University Press, 1999).

9 The German varies the idiomatic phrase "das darf doch nicht wahr sein" ("but this is unbelievable") at the end: "Wie bin ich hierher gekommen? In wessen Macht? Es darf nicht ein fremder Mann sein. Es darf nicht vergeblich sein, kein Betrug gewesen sein. Es darf nicht wahr sein." Here the screenplay departs slightly from Jelinek's *Filmbuch* (p. 107) and Bachmann's novel (p. 215).

the very beginning. He augments the scene's brutality through the introduction of the child, both the woman's daughter and younger self. Instead of opening with the woman's waking life as in Jelinek's film book, Schroeter's montage introduces her night states, further fragmenting the already disconnected source narrative while alluding to its many themes. The novel *Malina*, part of Bachmann's "Ways of Dying" project,[10] charts the sexist microaggressions of everyday life in patriarchal Western society, which are inseparable from National Socialism's legacy. In Schroeter's dense montage, we find references to the woman's traumatization through patriarchal relations; the hush-up to maintain the veneer of propriety; the "third man" (an allusion to Carol Reed's 1949 film of the same title set in post-war Vienna) and his shadowy presence in the woman's life; the intergenerational witnessing of violence and its perpetuation and propagation across bodies; the threatening aspect of all masculine figures in their interactions with women; the conflagration reds ("red and seven times redder than red") and the glaciation whites ("in the rising moon, [...] white and estranging") that run like a *leitmotif* through the novel.[11]

10 The *Todesarten* ("Ways of Dying") project comprises the novels and stories Bachmann worked on from 1962/63 until her death. It includes *Das Buch Franza*, *Requiem für Fanny Goldmann*, and the only completed work, *Malina*.

11 Bachmann, *Malina*: "rot und siebenmal röter als rot," p. 25; "in dem aufgehenden Mond, [...] weiß und befremdlich," p. 67. The red and white imagery is brought together in the "blood-spattered white butcher's apron" ("blutbefleckten weißen Schlächterschurz") in the final dream of Chapter 2 (p. 246).

12 Bachmann, *Malina*, p. 314.

II. (AGITATO)

ES IST ABER WAHR. / BUT IT IS TRUE.[12]

As the police drive away and Huppert sends her deadened gaze upwards, moving close to the injured stranger on the ground, a bizarre sequence of spatial images follows in quick succession. Its relationship to what has just occurred remains unexplained. The dominant strings and otherworldly flute overlay the whistling wind on the soundtrack and the screeching of the police car's tires, creating a sound-bridge to this series of brief images. We are confronted with a vast expanse of flat grassland bordering a dominating white sky with dramatic clouds that emerge from the vanishing point in the center of the screen. The blood-red lettering of the opening credits and title unfurl on this luminous sparseness. Then comes a screen-filling image of two streams with murky water, flowing in opposite directions and separated by a stone barrier. Next, an androgynous youth strokes a pillar of ice, both his head and the ice dramatically backlit. Afterward a dusty, deserted room with a single high window, an old stool, and shattered mirror shards is shown in a long shot; the remains of a bird's skeleton are surrounded by bits of filthy glass in close-up; wooden doors creak open to reveal a grayish wall with scratch marks; finally, there is an elevated shot of the old roofs of a European city on a drab day. In this second *montage*, daytime emerges out of night, albeit with no end to the surreal images of decay and putrefaction. The theme of mirrors, which do not reflect but either block or generate images, is introduced. The hidden archive also literally enters the picture: the final images allude to the traces of writing, and its suppression behind closed doors, where these residues nonetheless remain for posterity to discover.

The *montage* by Juliane Lorenz augments the visceral content of these individual shots, increasing their potential to shock. The temporal jumps that *montage* tends to generate inject the disjointed nature of dreamtime into the representation of waking life. The anxiety associated with night states carries over into a natural landscape devoid of humans. Both culture and nature become repositories of traumatic inscription. Land, air, water—Schroeter's film picks up on the elemental nature of Bachmann's metamorphic figures and gestures toward their ephemeral shapes and states (grass, cloud, ice) in the service of revealing a new kind of truth. It is a truth of the "but" or "*aber*," an alternative knowledge arising from a non-rational, sensuous approach. *Malina*'s protagonist repeats the phrase "I do not know" myriad times in the novel (I noted thirty-seven instances), suggesting the limitations of Western reason. Lorenz's *montage* and Elfi Mikesch's camera movement are of a piece with this alternative knowledge practice, one that eschews fixities and erodes prior certainties.

Thus the *montage* in *Malina* resists synthesizing endeavors and suits the inebriated camera, which careens around the apartment. To the sound of clacking typewriter keys, a cut carries us from the exterior to the interior. The woman works furiously at a typewriter. She is first shown from the back, with smoke billowing up in front of her, a full ashtray as well as what looks like a glass of whisky amidst mountains of paper on the table before her. The camera immediately begins to circle her. Smoke floats up, as a female voice-over speaks: "Look, around me the angels are losing their wings and carrying me in the way in which one carries the sick. They are carrying me to heaven. And then, when I return one day and wander in this area, time and space become confused ... and you and I and others." While the woman removes the typewritten page from her machine, the camera continues its orbit, revealing a labyrinth of large late-19th century rooms, with French doors opening onto other rooms and mirrors reflecting bookshelves as well as a few pieces of antique furniture. The camera pauses 180 degrees from its point of departure, showing the woman from the front. She sloppily folds blue papers into grayish envelopes. The woman avoids looking up. The camera proceeds in its circular movement, while the woman hastily continues to stuff and lick envelopes. The slight pause in the music ends, a steady kettledrum beat begins, accompanied by high-pitched flutes, and suddenly the strings from the beginning build an auditory bridge to the film's opening *montage*. Her desk is full of blue letters, redolent in their iconography of the Romantics' blue flower of longing, love, and the infinite (present in the blue symbols of the novel's second chapter). Only the woman's furtive glance toward the sound of approaching footsteps arrests the camera's 360-degree turn. We see the tall gray-haired man from the opening sequence walk down a hall with many doors. Does apprehension, resignation, or diffidence register on the woman's face as she seems to await him at her desk? The layout of hall to room and of man to woman is purposefully confusing, and no eyeline matches establish the two figures in a spatial relationship to one another.

Together with the supposed quotation—the "angel" text is neither in the novel nor the screenplay—this sequence lays bare the porousness of the woman's life. It is always open to the stern Malina, who is presented as ghost-like *alter ego*, shadowy counterpart, lover, confidante, bully, and, finally, violator; it is open to fevered dreams of destruction and fears of emptiness. The sense of dislocation in both the introductory *montage* and this segment underlines her vulnerability: being porous means being exposed. Which room opens onto what? From which direction is Malina coming? He enters and crosses the room in the back, but then suddenly he emerges from the front of the image. The whole room has been made mobile through the camera's rotation, the wafting smoke, the mirrored reflections of entryways and doorframes. The highly active camera, which also travels through these very rooms as everything goes up in flames at the end, makes her febrile mental energy and her creative energy palpable. Like the sick person in the poetic passage cited above, viewers are whisked away with her through time and space into a melded time-space of artistic creation.

The second half of the film reprises both the beginning *montage* and the quick camerawork of the sequence just described. At the midpoint, 67 minutes into the 115-minute film, the woman shreds geraniums, before running—unkempt, sweaty, clothes disheveled—into a Catholic church. Her eyes agape and her faded lipstick a ghoul's smudge, she screams as she presses her face against the rood screen separating her from the sculpture of figures burning in Hell. In an intricate *montage* she runs back and forth through deserted nocturnal streets, smashing into doors and grates, casting her gaze up to the right, then up the left to match the segment's rhythm: run-crash-gaze up to the right, run-crash-gaze up to the left, and so on.

Malina

First we see her full-length figure, but increasingly we focus on her upturned face leaning against Ivan's entryway and then against her own apartment building's door. The tight editing now paradoxically underlines her loss of control.

After the street *montage*, we again move into interior space, but now not to the stereotypical writer's desk—instead, the woman is seen through an opened window, kneeling in her torn dress on the floor, amidst masses of scattered papers and dark-paneled walls. The camera observes her from the window ledge. It is immobile, indicating a departure from the close proximity of the prior encirclement. While she has been on the floor grabbing packing paper and wrapping books, the voice-over about the angels recurs, carrying viewers back to the beginning. She hastily covers a book and runs to throw it out the window. As the melding of "I" and "you" is spoken about on the soundtrack, the images of the grasslands and sky reappear, intercut with her skyward gaze through the opened window. Nature now appears to be a vast, empty expanse, without writing, without a message. However, her spoken words have taken over the function of the words in the credits. Her transcendent voice guarantees the legibility of the images. Significantly, the film cuts back to her face as she looks out, acknowledging and authorizing this vision of freedom as a horizon of possibility. The dissolution of "I" and "you" has occurred; the landscape evokes her poetic traces.

Thus all attempts to arrest the woman's flow and dam up her lyrical words come to naught. Jammed into envelopes, they will still arrive in a tomorrow; her public pronouncements cannot truly be fled; books thrown out windows grow metaphorical wings. The vivid *montages* and camera movement repeatedly undercut any efforts to stop her. Her amorousness, which is linked to overflowing emotion, brimming tears, and trickling menstrual blood, is an affront to the world of hard-edged subjectivities and clearly demarcated persons. "Don't let yourself go," Malina scolds her as he lifts her, soaked, from the bathroom floor, where she has washed herself with the mobile showerhead, splayed on the ground in a flowing dress with blood on her leg. She is not supposed to spread by word, gesture, or bodily fluid. The flowing camerawork underlines her liquidity. She cannot be channeled into tight, dark rooms at the end, which would circumscribe the radius into which she and, by extension, we can move. Swimming in Vienna's public Gänsehäufel Bath reveals the potential of this streaming; significantly, this beautiful love scene with Ivan is filmed on the banks of the Danube, in the luminescent fullness of the setting sun.

The anecdotes about Schroeter's own currents should be seen in this context—whether it be the director himself, who relays in conversation with Michel Foucault how he urinates in the bathwater as his mother washes him (at

13 Michel Foucault, "Passion According to Werner Schroeter," in *Foucault Live: Interviews 1961–1984 with Michel Foucault* (New York: Semiotext[e], 1996), pp. 313–321. The French original, "Entretien avec Werner Schroeter" (1981), can be found on Gérard Courant's website, www.gerardcourant.com/index.php?t=ecrits&e=162.

Malina

Malina

age 27),[13] or Jelinek, who describes Schroeter demonstratively passing water. For Jelinek, this experience during the filming of *Malina* stands in a direct relationship to the creator/God ("*Schöpfer*"), as she describes Schroeter in a 2010 homage, "Werner Schroeter in Person" ("Werner Schroeter als Person"). In her essay written for the 24th Teddy Award, the queer film prize of the Berlinale, Jelinek recounts: "In a break from filming the *Malina*-adaptation we walk through a little woods, he pulls out his dick and pisses mightily ahead of himself, without holding on to it or pointing the gush anywhere in particular. It flows unchecked into the ground. Werner says he sometimes watched one of my colleagues take a leak, it only dripped, for a long time, but rather thin, a trickle; he told him: No man pisses like that. This is the way one has to do it: so that it streams out mightily, uninhibited, so that you have no doubt that you might be different, someone weaker than you actually are. All of this [happens] on a small hike through the woods."[14]

She goes on to offer an interpretation of Schroeter's act, implicitly relating it to the philosophical conception of excess that Georges Bataille formulated in the 1940s. For her, Schroeter's behavior on the movie set follows this pattern, expending a surplus of energy beyond any economic constraints or considerations of propriety. She links the creative flows that the artist unleashes to the hefty gush Schroeter demonstrated on their walk: "In this act of fiercely letting-it-flow-out-of-oneself, squandering has become the only possibility. [...] Here a man has worked, there was no doubt. A great creator [*Verursacher*] of all things and producer [*Her-Steller*], no fly-by-night, who just does whatever [...]."[15] This powerful act of expenditure does not suggest a diminution, in Jelinek's interpretation. Instead, unhindered streaming increases power. With her colloquial

14 The full text is available on Jelinek's homepage, www.elfriedejelinek.com/fwernera.htm, and was republished in Schroeter's autobiography *Tage im Dämmer, Nächte im Rausch* (Berlin, Aufbau Verlag, 2011), in an opening chapter, "Werner Schroeter als Person" ("Werner Schroeter in Person"), pp. 9–10.

15 Jelinek homepage.

speech patterns, she shifts metaphorical registers from outflows to inputs, from one kind of current to another. Like a battery pack, the outflow recharges Schroeter in the potent act of creation. He creates precisely by letting go. Jelinek explicitly links Schroeter's art to a post-Freudian (or, more accurately, non-Freudian) stance on his part. Arrogating the power of the creative Father in a self-defining gesture, Schroeter circumvents the psychoanalytic Oedipal narrative of the jealous son.[16]

In Schroeter's conversation with Michel Foucault and Gérard Courant from 1981, translated into English as "Passion According to Werner Schroeter," the German director makes clear his dislike of psychology and Freudian depth psychology in particular.[17] In his words, psychology and specifically psychoanalysis are a "very dangerous system above our heads, one that all western society can use."[18] He resents the fact that this system "functions on guilt" and makes of sickness something to be hidden rather than exhibited freely. Foucault concurs with him. He lauds Schroeter's films, such as *The Death of Maria Malibran* (1972) and especially *Willow Springs* (1973), precisely because they are not interested in interiority, in confessing an inner being: "One knows nothing about what goes on among the women [in *Willow Springs*], about the nature of these little worlds, and yet, at the same time, there is a kind of clarity about the facts."[19] This statement could be applied to *Malina*: the psychology behind the figures remains opaque, if not to say peripheral. The film's "immediate" or "impassioned evidence" is aesthetic rather than psychological—the gorgeous hues, the beautiful costumes, the tasteful interiors, the camera's ballet, the arias sung by Jenny Drivala.[20] Enshrining beauty in the agitated (*agitato*) movements of *montage* and camera becomes Schroeter's way of "exiting altogether from psychological film," as Foucault argues. *Malina* evades categories of the self and self-knowledge as the precondition for truth.[21]

The focus on aesthetic truth befits the final image of the woman in the film. As she calls out to Malina, telling him that he should hold her tight or her disappearance will be considered murder, flames lick the sides of the screen. Because of the angled mirror against which she leans, we see her tripled, quadrupled, even quintupled, as she slowly walks out of the frame. First she seems to be in the foreground, then in the background, then both in the far back as well as near the lens. The flames, too, are behind, up close, on the side; they lap upward right in front of the camera. Majestically, Huppert glides out of the image like an opera

16 Jelinek homepage.
17 Foucault, "Passion," p. 319.
18 Foucault, p. 319.
19 Foucault, p. 318.
20 Foucault, p. 317. Foucault returns repeatedly to the evidentiary aspect of Schroeter's films.
21 See Foucault, who argues ("Passion," p. 318) that "[w]e have been taught throughout the 20th century that one can do nothing if one knows nothing about oneself. The truth about oneself is a condition of existence, whereas you have societies where one could perfectly imagine that there is no attempt at all to regulate the question of what one is and where it makes no sense, while the important thing is: what is the art of putting into a work what one does, for being what one is. An art of the self which would be the complete contrary of oneself. To make of one's being an object of art, that's what is worth the effort."

Malina

diva, and soprano Diane Rama's rendition of Giacomo Manzoni's "Omaggio a Josquin" (1985) ends. The pyrotechnics after this show-stopping exit—the apartment goes up in a crackling firestorm in the final sequence—cannot hide the unarticulated premise of the close: this phoenix rises from the ashes.[22] The stern Malina is left in the image's vanishing point in the exact middle, with the infinite regress delineated by a frame-within-the-frame-within-the-frame. When it becomes too hot, he must close the door behind him. With a wan smile he then departs centrally, walking toward the camera and making the screen go black—and blank.

III. (QUASI GLISSANDO)

DANN IST ALLES LÄDIERT, BESCHÄDIGT, GEBRAUCHT, BENUTZT UND SCHLIESSLICH ZERSTÖRT WORDEN. / THEN EVERYTHING WAS BRUISED, DAMAGED, USED, AND FINALLY DESTROYED.[23]

The circulation in this film—of fluids and flames, of specific images from Bachmann's mediatized presence during and after her lifetime, of real and fictive quotations and quotations of quotations[24]—adds to my sense that Schroeter has no interest in psychology, that is, in presenting the novel filtered through the life of the artist. For this is the charge most often leveled at the film: that it reduces the multifaceted novel into the biopic of an unhinged writer, that fiction becomes psycho-biography.[25] Especially in the last third of the film, the director seems to encroach on biographical terrain. Instead of having the woman disappear into a crack in the wall as in the novel, Schroeter spectacularly stages her self-immolation, alluding to Bachmann's death in October 1973 after a fire in her Rome apartment from a lit cigarette. The writer's life and death had become the stuff of legend, promulgated by talk-show hosts (the most notorious case is Marcel

22 See Christina Mandt's chapter "Unscreening Disintegration," in her dissertation *Unscreenings, Unwritings: Gender in Contemporary Adaptation Practice* (New Brunswick, NJ: Rutgers University, 2016), pp. 132–165.

23 Bachmann, *Malina,* p. 325.

24 On Ingeborg Bachmann's citation practice, see Jens Brachmann, *Enteignetes Material: Zitathaftigkeit und narrative Umsetzung in Ingeborg Bachmanns "Malina,"* (Wiesbaden: DUV, 1999), and the compendium of correspondences between Ingeborg Bachmann and Paul Celan in Sigrid Weigel, *Ingeborg Bachmann: Hinterlassenschaften unter Wahrung des Briefgeheimnisses* (Vienna: Zsolnay, 1999), especially pp. 420–435.

25 See Mittermayer, p. 235, where he relates this to the production company's marketing strategy. See also Kurt Bartsch, "'Mord' oder Selbstvernichtung? Zu Werner Schroeters filmischer *Malina*-Interpretation," in Robert Pichl and Alexander Stillmark, eds., *Kritische Wege der Landnahme: Ingeborg Bachmann im Blickfeld der neunziger Jahre* (Vienna: Hora, 1994), pp. 147–162; and Kathleen Komar, "'Es war Mord': The Murder of Ingeborg Bachmann at the Hands of an Alter Ego," *Modern Austrian Literature* (Houston, TX), vol. 27 no. 2 (1994), pp. 91–112, especially p. 99.

Reich-Ranicki), highbrow magazines (starting with *Der Spiegel*'s 1954 cover story that included an iconic image of the writer), and posthumous television documentaries, such as Gerda Haller's *Die Wahrheit ist dem Menschen zumutbar* (Truth Is Appropriate for Man, ORF, 1974), Peter Hamm's *Der ich unter Menschen nicht leben kann: Auf den Spuren Ingeborg Bachmanns* (For I Cannot Live Among People: On the Trail of Ingeborg Bachmann, NDR / SWR / WDR, 1980), and Martina Zöllner's *Keine Delikatessen* (No Delicacies, SDR Stuttgart, 1993).[26] The stress on the fragility of the author, present in many of her contemporaries' reminiscences, colors the presentation of the delicate woman in Schroeter's film, who is simultaneously befuddled and fiercely intellectual, versed in Heidegger and Wittgenstein.[27] Literary texts and non-literary representations create a feedback loop, gliding between biography and literature: "The adaptation of texts by Ingeborg Bachmann are thus repeatedly linked visually and via specific elements of the plot with the person of the author; in this manner, they help generate and further transport public images of Bachmann."[28] This generative looping of images related to decline and damage is actually what seems to interest Schroeter. While films based on Bachmann's texts may draw attention to the coordinates of her life, *Malina* draws attention to the "flow" of the diva's image.[29]

In his film, he sets in motion another current, namely a "meme" stream: those small cultural units of transmission that spread via copying or imitation when they fall on fertile socio-cultural ground.[30] He uses stereotypical images of the public persona of Bachmann as mini-citations in his film—a reading in 1971 serves as model for the lecture in the film; the chess game and the final woman-at-the-mirror-image follow the photos Heinz Bachmann took of his sister in 1962; her often upturned gaze cites the famous *Spiegel* cover of 1954 that proclaimed Bachmann a new literary celebrity.[31]

The filmmaker focuses on this memetic circulation from the very outset of his work, and he blends it with his affinity for opera and his

26 The dominance of biographical readings is amply documented in Constanze Hotz, *'Die Bachmann': Das Image der Dichterin. Ingeborg Bachmann im journalistischen Diskurs* (Konstanz: Ekkehard Faude, 1990). See also Manfred Mittermayer's résumé in "Gefilmt und verfilmt. Bewegte Bachmann-Bilder im Dokumentar- und im Spielfilm," in Wilhelm Hemecker and Manfred Mittermayer, eds., *Mythos Bachmann. Zwischen Inszenierung und Selbstinszenierung* (*Profile* 18) (Vienna: Zsolnay, 2011), pp. 222–240.

27 Bachmann devoted her dissertation to criticizing Heidegger's philosophy and wrote a radio essay on Wittgenstein in 1953. See Bachmann's essay "Sagbares und Unsagbares – Die Philosophie Ludwig Wittgensteins," in Ingeborg Bachmann, *Werke*, Vol. 4, Christine Koschel, Inge von Weidenbaum, and Clemens Münster, eds. (Munich/Zurich: R. Piper Verlag, 1978), p. 124.

28 See Mittermayer, "Gefilmt und verfilmt," p. 234.

29 One might also think of Michael Haneke's early television film *Drei Wege zum See* (*Three Paths to the Lake*, 1976) or his 2001 film *Die Klavierspielerin* (*The Piano Teacher*), which filters Jelinek's novel through a Bachmann-Schroeter sieve.

30 Richard Dawkins introduced the term "meme" in his 1976 book *The Selfish Gene* (Oxford: Oxford University Press). The term has been updated for the digital age in Limor Shifman's *Memes in Digital Culture* (Cambridge, MA: MIT Press, 2014).

31 I would like to thank Aleksandra Kudryashova for pointing out these correspondences.

admiration for the Greek-American diva Maria Callas.[32] In the nearly 13-minute, 8mm *Maria Callas Porträt* from 1968 (one of numerous short films he made on Callas, and now in the archive of Filmmuseum München), Schroeter intercuts photographic reproductions from newspapers and magazines with two operas that Callas sang, Verdi's *Il ballo in maschera* and Bellini's *I puritani*. Through his effective *montage*, Schroeter unmasks the collusion of media and *montage* in creating a star persona. The short begins with a static shot of Maria Callas staring at the viewer, with dramatically made-up eyes, hair, and lips; there is no sound. The screen goes black. The camera pans slowly to the right, revealing the same image of Callas. It then continues, however, resisting the lure of her face and panning further to the right, past her. Two strings of blurred lights are exposed behind and above her. As the music sets in, other images of Callas come into view, fragmented into pieces—a sleeve, a hand, another brightly colored close-up. Then a series of black and white shots, skillfully edited to keep pace with the aria and to bring together images and sound. Finally, more color images from glossy magazines fill different parts of the frame in a concerted effort to pick up and carry the music over to the level of visual form. The film takes as its basis another short film of Schroeter's, *Callas Text mit Doppelbelichtung* (Callas Text with Double Exposure, 1968)[33]: the media cycle of incorporation and (re)production is all-inclusive. The diva must be dramatically lit to appear as such. Without face paint, the mask would not suffice. The camera pries, cuts, and closes in as it erases the distance between viewer and viewed.

At approximately the 8-minute point, the short film switches: writing displaces the photo *collage*. What seems to be a cover story fills the screen. Above a close-up of Callas singing, her hand gesticulating dramatically, we read in capital letters: "DIESE STIMME"—perhaps best rendered in English translation by the more colloquial "What a voice!". This image flashes on screen twice; then, a few seconds later, the music track changes to an aria from *I puritani*, one of Callas's career-making roles. Out of the darkness of the screen appears black writing on a white box, zooming toward the foreground: "*Die Callas schwebt*" ("Callas floats") drifts toward the viewer. The white box is revealed to be a small aperture cut out of black paper. It then moves from right to left, sliding along a newspaper review of *Lucia di Lammermoor* that recounts how Callas floats onto the stage in a white, pleated gown, "a person who has already left this earth behind" ("*ein Mensch, der dieser Welt schon entrückt ist*"). The description of her movements is particularly striking in light of the grand gestures we have just witnessed in the photographs: she is described as "a marionette," with "circumscribed motions" ("*abgezirkelte […] Bewegungen*"), "cataleptic" ("*vom Starrkrampf befallen*"), yet sensitive ("*sen-*

32 See Marc Siegel's essay in this volume, "Longing Is Your Own Affair (I Always Remained Underground)," in which he discusses this short film in detail.

33 See Benjamin Halligan, *Desires for Reality: Radicalism and Revolution: Western European Film* (New York: Berghahn, 2016), p. 213, note 69.

sibel") and deeply mournful. The "cadences of insanity" ("*Kadenzen des Irreseins*") are musically interwoven with the sounds of the flutes. The singer avoids sentimentality ("sobbing sure of its effect"—"*wirkungssichere[s] Geschluchze*") in the scene of ultimate breakdown, where artistic bravura coincides with a "death cry" or "*Todesschrei*." The camera rests on the review's final word, *Todesschrei*, for emphasis. It flashes on screen three times, separated from the rest of the passage and coinciding with the last notes of the aria. The word fades out simultaneously with the music.

Rather than illustrating the text's content with pictures, the experimental short accentuates the price subtending artistic "masterpieces" (*Brillantstück*). Ekphrasis and gesture are used in lieu of frozen images, where the re-presentation of what is described might tilt into kitsch. In ending this way, *Maria Callas Porträt* forces the viewer to reckon with what should or should not be shown. The words supplement the singing, offering an explanation that itself dissolves into a kinetic gesture. With his fragmentation via cut-and-paste, Schroeter thrice pummels us with the final message, a visual fist pounding against the screen. The pre-digital circulation of memes requires a congealed image moving from recipient to recipient on the yonder side of artistic creation: the process freezes the creative subject into an object of veneration, a semi-divine presence circulating in increasingly stenographic images and signifying in a kind of stereotyped shorthand. A metaphorical death by other means.

But the quality of being citable or re-presentable also inserts the possibility of change, as is the case with Schroeter's "quotation" of frozen images of Callas, be it in reproduced image or printed word. He remains true to this aspect in his "diva-adaptation" of Bachmann. After all, he is working from a book that thematizes citability as the new *status quo* in mediated, memetic modernity. For stardom based on this kind of repeatability has pitfalls. As the first-person narrator of *Malina* states in an interview embedded within the novel, quoting both Honoré de Balzac (in translation) and Gottfried Benn (who used the German translation): "Fame does not have white wings."[34] In the novel, the frozen Balzac-Benn statement—for what else is such a quotation but a congealed phrase on the cusp of platitude?—is remediated within the fictive interview and placed in proximity with another quotation, actually a misquotation of Flaubert: "with my burnt hand, I write about the nature of fire"—this time in the original French, "Avec ma main brulée, j'écris sur la nature du feu." The citation of a translated quotation-of-a-quotation, next to another somewhat incorrect quotation, suggests the malleable and mobile meanings that can be achieved through *montage*, especially of the experimental kind. Citation then actually does take flight (with "white wings") or moves like wildfire ("*la nature du feu*").

Indeed, it is worth returning briefly to Schroeter's own slightly "off" quotations of *Malina* in his later work *Deux* (2002). Like the

34 Bachmann, *Malina*, p. 96.

Deux (2002)

letters flung into the sea breeze following the opening credits, this late film purposely scatters Bachmann and Jelinek's messages. In doing so, it insists on alternative ways of carrying forward their multiple legacies and adapting the themes from 1991 for 2002. Isabelle Huppert plays twin sisters, Maria and Magdalena, separated at birth, who are reunited. This is the skeletal plot line linking together surreal scenes of sexual pleasure, operatic excess, and poetic transmission (especially from Lautréamont's *Les Chants de Maldoror*, 1834; 2012 trans. *The Songs of Maldoror*). Aggression and fatality subtend all encounters in Schroeter's "ways of dying" work, to apply Bachmann's project title to *Deux*. Even in moments of amorous abandonment, cruelty and mortality enter in word or deed; battlefields and cemeteries return from scene to scene. The doubles pervading the film—as in the human sculpture of two men in the street or in an art gallery—comment on desire and the search for a complementary and/or narcissistic mirror-image. But the film breaks open dyadic structures, introducing various third figures. Like Ivan-Malina-Woman in the earlier film, we now have mother-twins or mother-lovers or mother-daughter-lover or daughter-multiple lovers. When the film narrows down to two, murder ensues: one half knifes the other, literally rending bonds. The image is also split down the middle, showing a child-like Maria-Magdalena in two separate rooms. Immediately thereafter, a singing adult Huppert (*Ave Maria*) is displaced by a dreamy close-up of her looking upwards, copying the newspaper photos of Marlon Brando and a young Queen Elizabeth II pinned to the walls in earlier scenes. The film, dedicated to "Isabelle Huppert" (as the writing before the closing credits informs us, when Huppert bows and the red curtain comes down), is interested in playing with her stardom, alternately dissolving it in watery images or freezing it in such head shots.

In the following sequence, Huppert is seen on a train, holding a blank piece of paper against the window and hastily scrawling a letter to the children she "never had." With this testamentary letter, she describes the mirroring function of family members and also echoes her mother's letter at the outset of the film. Family is archive, legacy, transgression, malevolence, subordination, dependency, transmission, and love in all forms. She stresses the oneiric aspect of the entire film: "I kiss you, not just as mother, but as the only beings who love me. Not a single day has gone when I didn't dream of you."[35] The letter then addresses the adored absent mother and the unknown, stern father. Significantly, Huppert's face at the end of the letter is only the reflection in the train window. Gender warfare, so strongly present in Bachmann and even more so in Jelinek, is emphasized: while violence is everywhere, the nuclear family is its most important locus and the point from which it radiates outward, de-materializing the virgin, the sinner, the diva. It turns her into a mere shadow of herself. However, as in *Malina*, one woman's evacuation is no univocal end; Maria / Magdalena / Isabelle remains on stage.

CODA.

I GET UP AND GO THROUGH THE ROOM SLOWLY, IN THE DOORWAY I TURN AROUND AND I DON'T HEAR MYSELF SAYING ANYTHING TERRIBLE, BUT SOMETHING ELSE, *CANTABILE* AND *DOLCISSIMO*: AS YOU WISH. / ICH STEHE AUF UND GEHE LANGSAM AUS DEM ZIMMER, IN DER TÜR DREHE ICH MICH UM UND ICH HÖRE MICH NICHT ETWAS ENTSETZLICHES, SONDERN ETWAS ANDERES SAGEN, *CANTABILE* UND *DOLCISSIMO*: WIE DU WILLST.[36]

These are the last words spoken by the first-person narrator in Bachmann's novel, shortly before she wills her disappearance into a crack in the wall. The film *Deux* closes with Huppert lying on a beach, whispering the words: "Je t'aime." Then there is a cut. The woman is standing again. Defiantly and mockingly, she stares at the camera. She begins to dance, waiting for the next curtain call as the credits stream across the screen.

35 The letter addresses the mother thereafter, the "dear unreachable mother," and the camera shifts to reveal Huppert mirrored in the window. Finally, as the letter moves on to the "unknown" father, whose "reproaches" she missed, the focus shifts once more: to the woman reflected in the train's window.

36 Bachmann, *Malina*, p. 352.

Poussières d'amour – Abfallprodukte der Liebe (1996): Gail Gilmore and Werner Schroeter

Roy Grundmann

"A Quivering Tremor, a Vibration in Space"

Voicing Utopia in Poussières d'amour – Abfallprodukte der Liebe *(1996)*

Werner Schroeter's *Poussières d'amour – Abfallprodukte der Liebe* (1996) approaches its main subjects, opera and the human voice, by relating them to larger questions about life, death, our erotic longings, our search for love, and the role that music plays in all of this. *Poussières d'amour* begins with the following epigraph, spoken by the filmmaker in voice-over: "The song I hear inside my body, what does it sing of? All that resonates within me, that frightens me or arouses my desire?"[1] The singers Schroeter invited to spend a few days with him at a Gothic abbey located north of Paris were tasked with exploring these topics in word and song—through conversations filled with personal anecdotes, in interviews prompting them to share their professional perspectives, and, most significantly, in intimate recitals of famous arias Schroeter had selected for each of his guests to sing in furtherance of the film's musical-philosophical quest. As he put it: "This film is based on the deeply held conviction that everything we express through the voice is the 'product' of our quest for closer contact with another person, with love and every possible expression of love. In order to verify this fundamental idea, I invited singers to the Abbey of Royaumont, to create situations and provoke debate between them and their companions, wives, husbands, lovers, girlfriends, and children. Every 'loving couple' stayed 1–2 days with me, and following the inspiration and alchemy of the moment, I directed planned situations which 'resolved' themselves through music."[2]

Schroeter's set-up shaped the hybrid character of the film, which has been characterized as part workshop, part therapy session, part great voices gala, and part diva worship.[3] As indicated in Schroeter's comment above, love, usually of the tragic kind, is opera's big theme, so it figures prominently in the film. Schroeter does not question love's centrality to human existence, but wonders on camera how true love can be recognized. Hence, his interest in the operatic voice. Only the voice is able to capture something deemed so essential—indeed, like

1 "Was singt mir, der ich in meinem Körper höre das Lied? Alles, was in mir widerhallt, mir Angst macht, oder was mein Begehren erweckt?" Translated by the author, based on his transcription of the soundtrack. The epigraph is reprinted in its original German, but with a syntax that differs slightly from its spoken version, in the liner notes of the film's DVD released by Filmgalerie 451.

2 Commentary attributed to Werner Schroeter, included in online information about *Poussières d'amour*, website of Filmgalerie 451. www.filmgalerie451.de/en/filme/abfallprodukte-der-liebe/.

3 Kuhlbrodt, Dietrich, "*Poussières d'amour*," *Filmzentrale* www.filmzentrale.com/rezis/poussieresdamourdk.htm. Initially published in *epd film* 12/96, n.p.

beauty, so transcendental—yet so elusive and tragic. Singing of tragedy and loss, the voice itself is not impervious to the vagaries of life and the vicissitudes of fate. In his stage work and films Schroeter repeatedly showcases the voice as a register of both triumph and failure. Since his early 8mm experiments Schroeter sampled arias by the greats of the genre, most of all Maria Callas, Schroeter's *prima donna assoluta*. In Callas's case, however, triumph and failure were not strict opposites, but, and this accounts at least in part for her appeal, existed in tension as the spectacle of supreme control and the looming spectre of its loss. Her very fragility constituted the exhilarating precarity of Callas's singing and defined her virtuosity.

The embracing of fragility also echoes through Schroeter's own approach to life, and helped him position art's place in it. For Schroeter, failure—both actual and potential—does not ruin life's beauty. It is something to be accepted and endured. The ability to do so reflects one's *contenance*, something Schroeter characterizes as a near-stoic inner strength, coupled with the recognition of one's own weaknesses, which one adopts in the face of insurmountable odds. This strength, so Schroeter explains, relativizes the concept of failure—it transmutes failure into a different kind of strength.[4]

In 2006, Schroeter directed a Düsseldorf stage production titled *Die Schönheit der Schatten* (The Beauty of Shadows), a fictional dialogue between writer Heinrich Heine and composer Robert Schumann, who wrote music to accompany several of Heine's poems.[5] Schumann, as Schroeter explains in *Mondo Lux*, one day decided to jump into the Rhine during Mardi Gras—an extravagant act that marked the beginning of Schumann's protracted psychiatric treatment. For Schroeter, this behavior reflects Schumann's passion and genius.[6] It indicates the composer's anxiety that his compositions may be failing music's spiritual essence of being the true language of lovers. To give expression to Schumann's torment, Schroeter instructed Alexis Bug, the actor playing the composer, to speak in an impassioned manner, but with a barely audible voice. Whether or not Bug's hoarsely intoned anguish, shown in a brief excerpt in *Mondo Lux*, truly invokes misunderstood genius is open to debate. Schroeter in-

4 The association of *contenance* with a certain aristocratic *noblesse oblige* is reinforced by the fact that Schroeter, in his on-camera interview with *Mondo Lux*'s director Elfi Mikesch, explains that his grandmother, from whom he acquired both the term and the attitude it denotes, was a Polish baroness. It should be noted, however, that with the rise of the bourgeoisie and its mimicking of aristocratic attitudes, *contenace* has also come to signify something less noble and more strategic, like a poker face. Schroeter, by contrast, uses the term to describe to Mikesch how he coped with his terminal cancer.

5 See Regine Müller, "Wuchernde Assoziationen," *taz NRW* (March 15, 2006), p. 4, online at https://www.schumann-portal.de/schoenheit-der-schatten-150306.html.

6 While Schumann's carnivalesque leap into the Rhine precipitated his institutionalization, Schroeter's decidedly feminine and non-*bourgeois* (read: non-respectable) obsession with opera earned him a reputation among the public that Schroeter himself characterizes by the likewise carnivalesque image of a "singing, frolicking little art cunt." ["Das singende, springende Kunstfötzchen." English trans. by the author, from *Mondo Lux*.] In both images, passionate artistry generates spirited animation that, in turn, registers as lunacy and/or (feminized) infantilism.

tended its exalted theatricality to express the artist's—all artists'—consummate dedication to their art. Far from being gimmicky, Schroeter's direction shrewdly uses the medium of voice to expand the notion of artistic performance and its subtending concepts of command and virtuosity.

The personal and professional converged for Schroeter in poignant ways during the production of *Die Schönheit der Schatten*, when he learned of his terminal cancer. Whether it was the specific diagnosis—cancer of the larynx—that motivated Schroeter to place so much emphasis on Schumann's voice remains unclear. The fact, however, that Schroeter directs his actor to make the composer's voice register both strength and weakness does seem suggestive in light of a comment Schroeter makes in another interview segment in *Mondo Lux*, about how he deals with his own illness. He states that, for him, embracing failure and mortality can only lead to something positive. It may produce uncertainty, he explains, but whether it hastens or delays death must not really be of concern to him. For Schroeter, the personal and artistic completely overlapped. No matter what the aspect of artistic performance, including musical and vocal performance, there are no weaknesses, no failures, no negatives. Cracking, collapsing, or (largely) absent voices carry no stigma for Schroeter. He does not juxtapose them to vocal virtuosity, nor is virtuosity tasked with redeeming what falls short of it.

Featuring the voice in all its manifestations, *Poussières d'amour* rejects traditional humanism for a more radically utopian proposition. Exploring this proposition is the purpose of this essay. Doing so demands attending to several interconnected aspects: the erotics of the voice and the intimacy of vocal performance, the rejection of perfectionism and the embracing of play, the reframing of virtuosity and the development of new forms (and formations) of vocal art, and, finally, the concept of utopia itself, as it emerges in the film's innovative featuring of voices and the architectural spaces through which they resonate.

THE EROTICS OF THE VOICE

Near the beginning of *Poussières d'amour*, Schroeter explains to arriving guests that the film explores why singers find expression via their voice. French theorist Roland Barthes is not explicitly mentioned, but given the film's focus on voice and music, his reflections on the voice permeate the whole project.[7] For Barthes, too, voice was closely linked to music. In a 1973 interview with *Le Nouvel Observateur*, he explains that the voice is an object that has hitherto been denied its own existence. Like language, it has the status of a tool, an anonymous, characterless transmitter. As a cultural object in its own right, it has had no presence.[8] When

7 The DVD liner notes claim that Schroeter here knowingly references Roland Barthes, but the claim remains unsupported.

8 Roland Barthes, "The Phantoms of the Opera," excerpt from an interview conducted with Hector Biancotti, in *Le Nouvel Observateur* (Paris), December 17, 1973. Reprinted in Barthes, Roland, *The Grain of the Voice: Interviews, 1962–1980*, trans. Linda Coverdale (Berkeley/Los Angeles: University of California Press, 1991). First English publication (New York: Hill and Wang, 1985), pp. 183–187; here p. 183.

Schroeter directs actors to speak with a hoarse voice and queries singers how they find expression in their voice, it echoes Barthes's quest to make the voice speak for itself, to make it signify independently of what it says. According to Barthes, one must "listen to the voice's text, its meaning, everything in the voice which overflows meaning."[9] At issue is what Barthes understands as "the grain of the voice," a quality that, since it lacks its own ontology, is best described with metaphors. This quality, as Barthes admits, is decidedly unscientific, as it implies an erotic relationship between the voice and the listener.[10] The role of the listener, of course, makes things vexingly subjective. One person may love a given singer's voice while another may find it objectionable. Barthes, never afraid of controversy, freely admits he dislikes the grain of Callas's voice, finding it "tubular" and "hollow, with a resonance that is just a bit off-pitch (a voice can be in tune while its grain is out of tune)."[11]

Schroeter, we may want to object, would have disagreed. But would he really? His avant-garde approach to music and film, broadly eclectic while frequently pursuing specific antitheses, reflects nothing so much as his intuitive embrace of internal difference. His objection to Barthes may well have limited itself to insisting that what Barthes calls "off-pitch" has its very own beauty, thus merely raising the bar on what Barthes deems subjective. But Schroeter does share Barthes's interest in the grain of the voice. As he explains with regard to *Poussières d'amour*, by asking his singers to open up to the arias selected for them, to bring their individual humanity and full expressivity to the task, he aims to remove masks, so as to discover the essence, the heart of music that must be uncovered with every new performance.[12]

Vocal intimacy demands every singer's unique approach to the material, but it is not confined to the level of the individual. It has a broader cultural-historical dimension. For Barthes, a voice's *grain* is to singing or speaking what *jouissance* is to language.[13] Both are connected in that the erotics of vocal performance lay bare the phonic structure of language. This connection, Barthes argues, has been sundered by the ascendancy of *bourgeois* culture with its normative tastes and social practices. The loss of erotic rapport between a voice and its listeners is mirrored on a socio-historical level by (French) society falling out of touch with its earlier musical traditions dominated by popular poetry and/or folk songs.[14] In opera, the vanishing of eroticism has been delayed. Opera is undeniably a *bourgeois* affair marred by high ticket prices and middle-class protocols of "background, ambiance, sophistication," which, as he points out, "are still class reflexes."[15] At the same time, opera has retained its spectacle character that gives it an "almost imperial sensuality."[16]

9 Barthes, "The Phantoms of the Opera," p. 184.
10 Barthes, "The Phantoms of the Opera," p. 184.
11 Barthes, "The Phantoms of the Opera," p. 184.
12 Claire Alby, "*Abfallprodukte der Liebe*," part of the pressbook accompanying the film's theatrical release in Germany, November 11, 1996, included in the liner notes for the film's DVD release by Filmgalerie 451.
13 Barthes, "The Phantoms of the Opera," p. 185.
14 Barthes, "The Phantoms of the Opera," p. 185.
15 Barthes, "The Phantoms of the Opera," p. 187.
16 Barthes, "The Phantoms of the Opera," p. 186.

Barthes's comments in this 1973 interview build on his earlier essay "Musica Practica," published in 1970. Here Barthes classifies sensual, intimate vocal performance and its reception as an altogether separate category of music that gives the essay its title: "It is the music which you or I can play, alone or among friends, with no other audience than its participants."[17] Barthes calls it "manual" and "muscular," as opposed to the other kind, the music one listens to in official or technologically controlled settings. "Kneadingly physical,"[18] *musica practica* is not played by the heart but the body, which functions as "inscriber and not just transmitter, simple receiver."[19] Mapping a historical shift analogous to the one he references in the later interview, Barthes then observes that *musica practica* has disappeared from modern life: "initially the province of the idle (aristocratic) class, it lapsed into an insipid social rite with the coming of the democracy of the *bourgeoisie* (the piano, the young lady, the drawing room, the nocturne) and then faded out altogether (who plays the piano today?)."[20]

Who plays the piano today? In *Poussières d'amour*, Elisabeth Cooper does. While gentle and measured, her playing is no mere "background" music. It asserts the role of the piano as the instrument that frames and guides the recital, but does so without undermining its intimacy. Mikesch's camera captures the joy with which Cooper plays. Her body language indeed signals the very physicality Barthes describes in "Musica Practica." Barthes's scenario of domestic music implies that the musicians do their own singing. The recital approach compels Schroeter to assign distinct roles to musician and singer, but clearly Cooper has no intention of competing with them. She is not interested in showcasing her own virtuosity. As she observes the singers and also listens to her own playing, she seemingly ratifies her own performance for the sake of creating the optimal conditions for the recital.[21]

The modest parameters and artisanal character of the recitals in *Poussières d'amour* are indicative of the way the film understands the music it features: it celebrates grand opera, but does so by scaling it down. There is no orchestra, only piano accompaniment; no big audience, only the performer, the pianist, and the small film crew; no grand stage, which does not mean Schroeter did not use the spaces available to him (including costumes, props, and surroundings) highly effectively. This downscaling makes for greater vocal intimacy, but also allows for an unfolding—of voices, of musical expression, of ways of looking at opera—into new possibilities and registers that, as will become clear, are closely linked to the film's critique of perfectionism.

17 Barthes, Roland, "Musica Practica," in *Image, Music, Text*, trans. Stephen Heath (New York: The Noonday Press, 1977), p. 149.
18 Barthes, "Musica Practica," p. 150.
19 Barthes, "Musica Practica," p. 149.
20 Barthes, "Musica Practica," p. 149.
21 Barthes uses the word "ratification" specifically with regard to the auditory faculty that characterizes *musica practica*. There, he states, "the part taken by the sense of hearing is one only of ratification" (Barthes, "Musica Practica," p.149). Barthes contrasts this mode of hearing to the *connoisseur's* activity of listening, which is an act of discerning musical virtuosity.

Poussières d'amour: Elisabeth Cooper (top), Anita Cerquetti (middle), Anita Cerquetti, and Trudeliese Schmidt (bottom)

One of the ways for the film to explore the erotics of the voice is by anchoring it to the body and everyday life. The connection becomes clearest through former opera singer Anita Cerquetti, one of several divas featured in the film. Her delicate yet strong and bright voice made her a distinguished soprano in postwar Europe and a Callas competitor in her home country, Italy. Cerquetti retired in 1964 at the peak of her career, while still at a young age. Appearing in Schroeter's film more than thirty years later, her singing voice has become breathy, at times raspy. Even her speaking voice is hoarse. As we learn from Schroeter, finding Cerquetti after a nearly three-decade search is a boon to him. Including her in his film serves him in several ways. Schroeter has no intention of denying us samples of Cerquetti's vocal brilliance during her heyday—these, as will be discussed further below, serve the film's meditation on virtuosity in an intriguing way. But rather than exploiting the contrast between Cerquetti's past and present-day voice for the *cliché* of the faded star, he assigns her present-day voice a crucial role: he embeds it in the film's dense tapestry of interviews, rehearsals, and performances featuring singers in solo performances and in varying duets.

Cerquetti's solo segment, in which we hear old recordings, is followed by a scene in which Trudeliese Schmidt sings an aria from Alban Berg's *Lulu* for the film. The scene is intercut with shots of Cerquetti being costumed while listening to Schmidt. Next, we see Schmidt and Cerquetti rehearsing together, after which they sing a duet from Vincenzo Bellini's *Norma.*

Several scenes later, Cerquetti is shown singing again, this time with her present-day voice, which is followed by an interview with her and her family. The film again returns to Cerquetti as she receives instructions from Schroeter to breathe along with Schmidt. They proceed with Schmidt doing the singing and Cerquetti mostly lip-synching. Schroeter accomplishes more than one feat in this loose string of scenes: he brings two renowned singers together for a duet, and uses their vocal performance to issue a resounding rejection of such divisive categories as "good" and "bad" voice, or "prime" and "defunct." The integrative fabric he weaves combines not only past and present, but also different vocal ranges and, by implication, the musical styles associated with them, i.e., the 19th century *bel canto*, in which Cerquetti excelled, and 20th century opera, exemplified by such composers as Alban Berg, which suits Schmidt's "modern" voice with its penchant for moving between dissonances and harmonies and between singing and speaking.

Schroeter here shifts emphasis away from vocal virtuosity towards less ostentatious aspects of vocal performance, such as breathing and what Barthes refers to as "the grain of the voice." This shift enables both singers to mobilize the erotic dimension of vocal expression in a display of sensuous homosocial art-making that carries artistic and political implications. Female singers, who ordinarily may compete with one another, are here shown to be mutually supportive. They shine together, but by other means—and for other meanings. One such meaning is already suggested by the musical material. The excerpt from "Oh! rimembranza!" from *Norma*, which Schmidt and Cerquetti sing together—"Reassure or rebuke me, but save me from myself, save me from my heart"—is about two women realizing they are in love with the same man, who, as they find out, has betrayed one with the other. This comes after the film has introduced us to two of Cerquetti's historic recordings of classic arias suffused with female suffering and pleading, "Vissi d'arte" from *Tosca* and "Casta diva" from *Norma*, and after Schmidt has sung of her character, Lulu, having been used by various men and forced to become a prostitute. While not essential to the enjoyment of the film, knowledge of the libretti of these operas reinforces the sense that Schroeter, by pairing two singers linked to different operatic styles and eras, aims at creating a vision of female identification across historical and class lines in the face of patriarchal oppression—something that resonates throughout his larger body of work.

Just as Cerquetti's duet with Schmidt serves as a reminder that operatic singing is an art of the whole body, not just the voice, as well as an inherently erotic art, Cerquetti's on-camera conversations reveal that her singing and her discovery were rooted in everyday life rather than being determined early on by professional considerations. As she tells her interlocutor, the actress Carole Bouquet, when she was growing up she only sang for herself and for friends. Her motive was self-gratification, not success. Her discovery happened not in a music school or during an audition, but when she was spotted singing at a friend's wedding. While such circumstances may be beyond an individual's control, they may well shape the attitude a singer adopts to manage a future career. Her discovery prompted Cerquetti to work with a professional voice coach, but she retained final say over her official career launch—just as the decision to end that career at its peak remained exclusively hers, responding, as she did, to her body, which had begun to strain under the pressures of professionalism. Defining success first and foremost in terms of profit and fame, professionalism gives rise to what Schroeter regards as virtuosity's evil twins: perfectionism and commodification.

PERFECTIONISM REJECTED, VIRTUOSITY REFRAMED

The duet that Cerquetti and Schmidt sing and breathe together flies in the face of conceptions of opera that are shaped by the logic of perfectionism. Their personal gratification of singing opera fuels their performance. They sing in a manner that redefines what constitutes a successful rendition of an aria. Schroeter here repeats an approach that informs all of his work, but particularly his early films: the replacement of normative standards of artistic brilliance with innovative approaches guided primarily by pleasure, communitarianism, and making art as part of everyday life. The logic driving perfectionism—which Schroeter defies—has been theorized by Herbert Marcuse as that of the "performance principle," a mode of organizing society and the individual through socio-economic competition and according to principles of acquisition and growth.[22] As Marcuse explains in *Eros and Civilization*—a text that became influential on the late 1960s counterculture in which Schroeter came of age—with the performance principle, the individual's "erotic performance is brought in line with his societal performance."[23] Libidinal energy is channeled for the maximization of speed, efficiency, and flawlessness. The rewards are wealth, fame, and power.

But the "off-beat" character of Schmidt and Cerquetti's duet aside, to what extent, we may ask, does the film's showcasing of opera really constitute a critique of the performance principle? Or, to put it another way: notwithstanding his diva worship, how does an opera aficionado like Schroeter celebrate the virtuosity of his favorite divas and, at the same time, avoid reenshrining opera as an institution of capitalist principles and *bourgeois* values? The question pertains to Cerquetti in particular, whose career, in contrast to Schmidt's more liminal experimental trajectory, is closely associated with the *prima donna* grandeur that remains a box-office factor at all the world's big opera houses. Cerquetti's entry into the film is underscored by one of her recordings of "Vissi d'arte" and prompted by Schroeter's beckoning call "Anita!" As he greets her with an embrace, the crackling record that echoes through the room is replaced by a remastered track that takes over the full soundtrack. After a brief external shot of a detail of the abbey, we see Schroeter and Cerquetti sitting side by side, listening to her

22 Herbert Marcuse, *Eros and Civilization: A Philosophical Inquiry into Freud* (Boston: Beacon Press, 1974; 1st ed. 1955), pp. 45–46.

23 Marcuse, *Eros and Civilization*, p. 46.

Poussières d'amour: Werner Schroeter and Anita Cerquetti

singing. Following further shots of the abbey's architecture and of religious motifs, the film cuts back to the diva and her fan, who now kneels before her, accompanying her singing with his hands, eventually raising them in rapture as the aria reaches one of its famous *crescendi*.

To understand this scene further, we need to compare the way Schroeter listens to Cerquetti with the way Barthes theorizes listening. Rapturous though it is, we should not mistake the manner in which Schroeter follows Cerquetti's recorded rendition of "Vissi d'arte" for what Barthes defines as the "liquid" and "effusive" listening that is indicative of *bourgeois* culture's appreciation of virtuosity.[24] In this process, virtuosity is discerned by an informed rehearsal of its structure before it is sanctioned, and thus contained, via *bourgeois* categories of quality and taste. Schroeter does not contain virtuosity. He matches it with purely physical excess. His play of gestures, "kneadingly physical" in their own right, lacks the purpose Barthes associates with *musica practica*, but it has a practicality of its own. If for Barthes practicality is what makes the musician a physical inscriber of the music she hears, in Schroeter's case it makes the gay fan an ecstatic transcriber of his diva's divinity. That the recipient of this rapture should also be its source is only fitting, for all that does (thereby completing the analogy to *musica practica*) is to keep the music in the house—and, thus, out of the circuits of commodification.

The relation between gayness and opera is a long-standing one. As we learn from Wayne Koestenbaum's influential study on opera and homosexuality,[25] for gay men opera has always been more than a pastime or a lifestyle—it has been a whole way of life, a philosophy, an ethic. This does not mean, however, that their love of opera has led homosexuals to forsake forms of *bourgeois* social expression. Twenty-five years after its publication, Koestenbaum's study still resonates with regard to the analogy between the precarity of the opera diva's performance and the way gay opera fans have known to insert themselves into the circuits of urban *bourgeois* consumption, in the process bending the rules of *bourgeois* society in provocative ways without, however, leaving that society. This, as can be gleaned quickly from his biography, was never Schroeter's world. His obituary of Maria Callas reflects his personal view that what links the homosexual to the diva is their shared alienation from what opera is today—the site of a disparity between the ecstatic artistic expressivity of its singers and the socio-economic privilege of its patrons.[26]

It is not, however, as though there is no overlap between Schroeter's relation to opera and the gay love of opera that Koestenbaum theorizes. Both share a passion and commitment that pivots on one and the same base, narcissism—in other words, on what heteronormative thinking has traditionally dismissed as arrested development leading to neurosis or

24 Barthes, "Musica Practica," p. 150.

25 Wayne Koestenbaum, *The Queen's Throat: Opera, Homosexuality and the Mystery of Desire* (New York: Poseidon Press, 1993).

26 Werner Schroeter, "Der Herztod der Primadonna," in *Der Spiegel* (Hamburg), September 26, 1977, p. 261.

psychosis or some other mental illness. In Schroeter's case, this narcissism is marked by the collapse of active and passive: as with Barthes' *musica practica*, loving art means living art, being an artist. Narcissism is here quite literally traceable to Narcissus, as well as to Orpheus, who in Marcuse's *Eros and Civilization* is posited as Narcissus's conceptual twin. In Orpheus's case, "his language is *song*. His work is *play*. Narcissus's life is that of *beauty*, and his existence is *contemplation*."[27] For Marcuse, both are figures of a non-repressive erotic attitude towards reality and, as such, practitioners of the "Great Refusal"—the refusal not to give in to the performance principle, symbolized by Prometheus, "the culture-hero of toil, productivity, and progress through repression."[28]

Emphasizing that Narcissus and Orpheus stand against the repressive order of procreative sexuality, Marcuse directly links them to homosexuality.[29] This is one reason why queer theory has recently embraced Marcuse.[30] Another reason is that Marcuse's systemic critique of Freud leads him to trace narcissism directly to Greek mythology rather than understanding it through Freudian logic, which merely pathologizes it—though, as Marcuse points out, Freud did not fail to note that primary narcissism, even after it gets repressed/sublimated as part of psychological maturation, continues to hold the faint promise of its "limitless extension and oneness with the universe."[31] In this sense, Marcuse insists, narcissism holds the key to a different reality principle—and, thus, a different vision of the world.[32] For Marcuse, repression is what enables the performance principle, through its use of fear and rewards. If we were able to rechannel our narcissism and negotiate our relation to the world in a non-repressive way, it might help us redefine our relation to that world, "transforming this world into a new mode of being."[33]

Here, we come to an epistemological *impasse*. Marcuse's argument, as is well known, dates itself through a lack of engaging with Jacques Lacan.[34] From a Lacanian perspective, which conceives of ego development as an irreversible emergence—or, rather, fall—into linguistic existence, non-repressive sublimation is a contradiction in terms. What the maturing subject irreversibly trades in for the acquisition of language is the unbridled freedom over meaning that primary narcissism still promised. Where Marcuse argues for non-repressive sublimation "which results from an extension rather than from a constraining deflection of

27 Marcuse, *Eros and Civilization*, p. 170.
28 Marcuse, *Eros and Civilization*, p. 160.
29 Marcuse, *Eros and Civilization*, p. 171.
30 See José Esteban Muñoz, *Cruising Utopia* (New York University Press, 2008). My approach to Schroeter is indebted to Muñoz's thinking about 1960s queer experimental art, some of which can be compared with certain aspects of Schroeter's work.
31 Marcuse, *Eros and Civilization*, pp. 168–169. Marcuse's reading of Freud focuses on *Civilization and Its Discontents* (London: Hogarth Press, 1949).
32 Marcuse, *Eros and Civilization*, p. 169.
33 Marcuse, *Eros and Civilization*, p. 169. Marcuse notes that it was Freud himself who acknowledged the central role of narcissism in helping the ego negotiate its relation to the world, even though this can only happen through sublimation, which is a form of repression.
34 The first publication date for *Eros and Civilization* is listed as 1955, a period in which Lacan's theories evolved and became popularized only gradually.

the libido,"[35] Lacanians would say he finds himself in the realm of utopia. And yet, the very existence of someone like Werner Schroeter and of the various countercultures, whose spirit he shared, seems to present incontrovertible evidence of concrete utopias—concrete because the various forms of non-repressive living associated with them have existed for no other reason than human resolve, even if those lived utopias had flaws and have not lasted.

The realm in which this epistemological *impasse* can be resolved—to the extent it can be resolved at all—is that of art. As Marcuse famously reminds his readers, "under the rule of the performance principle, art opposes to institutionalized oppression the image of man as a free subject."[36] Art-making affords Orphic-Narcissistic figures like Schroeter the opportunity to enact their version of the "Great Refusal," summarized by Marcuse as the refusal "to accept separation from the libidinous object (or subject)."[37] When Schroeter kneels before his diva in rapture, what looks like a homosexual's quasi-pathological attachment to his love object (his surrogate mother) may be read in Marcusian terms as an act of resistance, a refusal that "aims at liberation—at the reunion of what has become separated."[38] Whether this liberation reverses the separation or whether it rearticulates the pathos that confirms the irreversibility of the loss incurred (as a Lacanian reading of Schroeter is compelled to argue[39]) may be secondary. Schroeter's art leaves us with an economy of narcissism that, while organized in relation to rupture and separation, is decidedly non-etiological.

When Cerquetti's singing goes from well-worn record to remastered track, the past is not sublimated into an eternal present (a finality that would carry something akin to a morbid death wish). As she listens to her own voice, Cerquetti comfortably enjoys her own open-ended story: she is full of appreciation for her erstwhile virtuosity, but has no regrets about cutting her career short. While it stopped her from continuing to mine this aspect of her brilliance, it allowed her to free herself from the performance principle without having to give up her love of singing altogether. As we hear Cerquetti's voice in a spectrum of forms—on a crackling record, on a remastered track, in its present-day state as a hoarse speaking voice or when singing a breathy duet—it becomes clear that this diva's assimilation of her imperfect past has put her on a new temporal plane, an existence that moves forward without fear of looking back: a past imperfect. Also, as suggested earlier, the film's scaled-down

35 Marcuse, *Eros and Civilization*, pp. 169–170.

36 Marcuse, *Eros and Civilization*, p. 144. See also p. 174, where Marcuse theorizes the connection between art and social freedom via Kant's understanding of beauty. For Kant, beauty symbolizes freedom because it demonstrates intuitively the reality of freedom.

37 Marcuse, *Eros and Civilization*, p. 170.

38 Marcuse, *Eros and Civilization*, p. 170.

39 See Alice A. Kuzniar, *The Queer German Cinema* (Stanford, CA: Stanford University Press, 2000), chapt. 4, "The 'Passionate Evidence' of Werner Schroeter's *Maria Malibran* and *Der Rosenkönig*," pp. 113–138. Kuzniar argues, via the Lacanian concept of the *objet petit a* (pp. 126–129), that the emotional affect and beauty of Schroeter's images signify the subject's relation to the object as prohibited, lost, and impossible, while, at the same time, putting themselves in place of such loss.

version of opera and the intimate nature of its recitals produce a potentially salutary split between private and public. Schroeter places the music on a closed circuit between performer and listener that protects it from being subjected to conventional judgments about "quality" and economic categories of marketability.

Schroeter's celebration of Cerquetti's singing raises eyebrows—though, as mentioned, less for its enthusiasm than for the complete lack of restraint with which it gets conveyed. Not only does this rapture defy any expectation of transforming into an expert assessment of voice, *timbre*, or even "grain" (Barthes, too, was more comfortable with theorizing *jouissance* than with openly showing it), it also does the opposite: because Schroeter already does all the emoting for her, there is no need for Cerquetti to do it herself. There is little risk of Schroeter's flattery proving "unhealthy" to its recipient in that it might enthrall Cerquetti to her own voice the way silent-film diva Norma Desmond was enamored of her screen image in Billy Wilder's noir study of pathological narcissism, *Sunset Boulevard*. Schroeter's relation to his diva is free of false flattery and strategic exploitation. In other words, if William Holden's Joe Gillis in *Sunset Boulevard* had behaved to Gloria Swanson's Norma Desmond the way Schroeter acts towards Cerquetti, he would still be alive (and we would have no juicy noir exploitation of pathological narcissism). *Poussières d'amour* is the anti-*Sunset Boulevard*.

Cerquetti is not the only singer featured with a virtuoso performance in the film—but, importantly, the category itself is burst open by the range of voices Schroeter has included. The film's sole unifying category is that of the primacy of song. It shapes the recital format that critically blurs such binaries as work vs. play, product vs. process, and professional vs. amateur. Cerquetti's "Vissi d'arte" sequence is followed by her recording of "Casta diva." When we first hear the aria, we see Isabelle Huppert listening to it. She asks who sings. Schroeter tells her. They both listen to it until it ends with the recorded applause of Cerquetti's historical audience. The scene puts Huppert and us viewers in the same position, that of an intrigued but not fully knowledgeable group of laypersons whose admiration for the great voice is reinforced by the sound of an approving and seemingly expert audience. The scene is part of a loosely organized narrative vignette (there are several in the film devoted to various performers) that charts Huppert's arc from listener to singer. Huppert does not consider herself a singer, and although her effort is respectable, the film in no way suggests the star actress is in for a career change. What Huppert's story elegantly introduces, however, is the theme of the *amateur*.

AMATEURISM AND UTOPIA

In *Poussières d'amour*, Huppert fits the classic definition of the amateur, but the film also uses her participation as a segue into expanding that definition. Not surprisingly, the amateur is important to Barthes's characterization of "Musica Practica." According to Barthes, what characterizes the amateur is not the devout

Poussières d'amour: Martha Mödl

enthusiasm obtained by listening to a professional, but the irrepressible urge to make music. Amateurism is defined by a certain style more than by imperfection.[40] This shift is reflected in Huppert's decision to take up singing. While impressed by Cerquetti's skills, the diva's virtuosity would only have intimidated Huppert. What brings Huppert "around" is another guest of Schroeter's, Martha Mödl.

It is Mödl who illuminates Barthes' expanded concept of amateurism, though this is not for lack of a professional background. On the contrary, Mödl was one of the leading German Wagnerian sopranos from the late 1940s to the early 1960s. Her peak period closely overlaps with Cerquetti's, but while the latter decided to abruptly end her career, Mödl switched from leading soprano roles to supporting mezzo-soprano parts that suited her changing voice. A role in which she found great fame is the aging Countess in Tchaikosvky's *Pique Dame*. Schroeter asked two singers, Mödl and Rita Gorr, to sing the Countess's aria, "Je crains de lui parler la nuit," but he is more interested in Mödl, who gets to sing the aria twice in the course of the film. The first time, we see her in an extreme long shot walking across a hall towards the grand piano with Cooper behind it. She seats herself on a sofa in a half-reclined position that underscores her fading life and gives the aria a sense of melancholy. The second time, the camera is already in close range to Mödl's face when she begins to sing.

It is easy to see why Mödl continued to sing this role in recitals until shortly before her death in 2001 at the age of 88. Her mellowed voice still possesses beauty and expressivity, but there is more to it. The aria suits her by allowing her to move her vocal performance a bit further away from song and a bit closer to speech. Mödl fills it out nicely, adding an ornamental level of expression. Capitalizing on the fact that her stage character sings the aria to herself, she draws out the *tempi* just long enough to give expression to the character's melancholic dignity. The effect is reminiscent of what Schroeter has characterized as *contenance*. It projects inner strength without trying to claim power over others. It can be summed up by a phrase Marcuse uses to describe what differentiates Orpheus and Narcissus from

40 Barthes, "Musica Practica," p. 150.

Prometheus: "it is the voice which does not command but sings."[41]

As mentioned, my discussion is indebted to recent queer theory, specifically José Esteban Muñoz's reading of Marcuse's *Eros and Civilization* with regard to American experimental art of the 1960s. As Schroeter's artistic approach shows notable parallels to some of the artists Muñoz discusses, it is worth exploring another philosopher Muñoz draws on, Ernst Bloch, specifically his concept of utopia. Schroeter's utopianism is alluded to in the early literature on his films. One look at Schroeter's closely intertwined ways of living and art-making suggests that he inhabited a concrete utopia of the kind that could be glimpsed in liminal and countercultural circles in the 1960s.[42] Similar to the one that Muñoz links to 1960s queer experimental art, Schroeter's utopia is guided by both practical-material and ideational factors. Keenly aware of the inevitability of failure and tragedy, Schroeter never allowed his awareness to quell his stubborn sense of hope in the face of more reasonable-sounding calls for pragmatism and efficiency—values that, as we already saw, Marcuse identifies as central to the performance principle. Stubborn hope is exactly what Bloch theorized as a hallmark of the utopian impulse and also, more specifically, of what makes utopias concrete. The possibility of being disappointed is the factor that makes hope what it is in the first place—utopian—and also what grounds it in reality.[43] The disappointment of hope is unconditional. It lets hope "open in a forward [...] future-oriented direction; it does not address itself to that which already exists."[44] Thus, Bloch goes on to argue, "hope's methodology (with its pendant, memory) dwells in the region of the not-yet, a place where entrance and, above all, final content are marked by an enduring indeterminacy."[45]

In its attempts to imagine stubborn hope and utopia, art frequently resorts to illusion. It should be noted that neither Marcuse nor Bloch regard illusion as wholly negative. According to Marcuse, who relates it to Freud's notion of phantasy, illusion gets dismissed by the reality principle as utopian because it holds the key to the truth, only to be gleaned in phantasy, that humans can overcome their repressive, self-alienating existence. It is in the moment of artistic creation when we see that "behind the illusion lies knowledge [...], when phantasy itself takes form, when it creates a universe of perception and comprehension—a subjective and

41 Marcuse, *Eros and Civilization*, p. 162.

42 Schroeter encountered American queer countercultural art at the 1967 Knokke-le-Zoute Experimental Film Festival, though exact influences are hard to trace. While Muñoz's concept of utopia has proven inspiring for my reading of Schroeter, it is not the only possible approach to historical countercultures. My own analysis of the same segment of the 1960s New York queer art scene that Muñoz's discusses is not based on Marcuse's utopia but on Michel Foucault's concept of heterotopia. See Roy Grundmann, "The Tenderness of Scissors in *Haircut (No. 1)*," in Gary Needham and Glyn Davis, eds., *Warhol in Ten Takes* (London: Palgrave MacMillan/BFI Publishing, 2013), pp. 67–83.

43 Ernst Bloch, "Can Hope Be Disappointed?," in *Literary Essays*, ed. Werner Hamacher and David Wellbery (Stanford, CA: Stanford University Press, 1998), pp. 339–345; here p. 341.

44 Bloch, p. 341.

45 Bloch, p. 341.

46 Marcuse, *Eros and Civilization*, pp. 143–144.

at the same time objective universe."[46] Bloch, too, regards this creative moment as concrete and immanent, whereby "artistic illusion is not only mere illusion, but a meaning that is cloaked in images and can only be described in images, of material that has been driven further [...]."[47] For Bloch, this "driving further" of artistic material constitutes a basic exaggeration that inheres in any act of aesthetic rendering. The radical openness of this process constitutes the aesthetic correlative to hope—or, as Bloch terms it, art's "anticipatory illumination [...] of what is real."[48] It enables a glimpse of the object's—and thus, reality's—utopian potential, its quality of "not-yet."[49]

This anticipatory illumination and indeterminacy are instantiated in what Bloch describes as the quality of the ornamental. Bloch's ornament is less a concrete object or specific form than a relation, a deviation from functionalistic norms marked by expressive surplus.[50] Schroeter's aesthetics may be called ornamental by virtue of the centrality they accord to the gestural. Gestures in Schroeter's work are notable for combining the urge to express something with the insistence not to specify what is expressed, so as not to delimit it. This is in evidence particularly in his experimental films of the late 1960s and 70s, which feature slow, stylized gestures performed by Magdalena Montezuma, Christine Kaufmann, and Candy Darling. Suspending any narrative logic, these gestures are so self-contained that they defy any conventional function of gestures. They acquire the paradoxical character of non-gestural gestures.[51] What Bloch terms "anticipatory illumination" is almost literalized by Montezuma and Darling's acts of self-stylization. They generate what Schroeter himself once described as a certain incandescence that lends his images a shimmering, free-floating quality. But we also encounter the ornamental in the later films—even in *Poussières d'amour*, a film focusing on what is, in fact, a *bourgeois* art form (largely) practiced by *bourgeois* artists.

Poussières d'amour links the ornamental to two further aspects of utopia—imperfection

47 Ernst Bloch, *The Principle of Hope*, Vol. 1, trans. Neville Plaice, Stephen Plaice, and Paul Knight (Cambridge, MA: MIT Press, 1986), pp. 214–215. My quote, however, is taken from a more recent, modified translation of this passage, in Jack Zipes's introduction to Ernst Bloch, *The Utopian Function of Art and Literature: Selected Essays*, trans. Jack Zipes and Frank Mecklenburg (Cambridge, MA: MIT Press, 1988), p. xxiii.

48 Jack Zipes, introduction to Ernst Bloch, *The Utopian Function of Art and Literature*, trans. Jack Zipes and Frank Mecklenburg (MIT Press, 1988), p. xxxiii. The term "anticipatory illumination" is Zipes's retranslation of Bloch's term "Vor-Schein."

49 Jack Zipes, introduction to Ernst Bloch, *The Utopian Function of Art and Literature* (MIT Press, 1988), p. xxxiii.

50 Ernst Bloch, "The Creation of the Ornament" [orig. "Erzeugung des Ornaments" (1918), in *Geist der Utopie*; rev. ed. (Frankfurt am Main: Suhrkamp, 1973)], in *The Utopian Function of Art and Literature*, pp. 78–102. In this essay, Bloch traces the emergence of ornamental qualities through architecture and painting. Yet, as noted by Zipes and Mecklenburg in an explanatory section preceding the main text, "Notes on the Translation and Acknowledgments," "Bloch did not develop a systematic theory of aesthetics. Rather, he sought to comprehend how the apparent generic differences in art and literature were related to basic ontological and political questions underlying humankind's quest for utopia" (p. ix).

51 For a theorization of the gestural in Schroeter's films through Ludwig Wittgenstein, see Gertrud Koch's essay in this volume.

and failure, whether exemplified through small snafus, such as a painting falling on Kristine and Katherine Ciesinski mid-performance, or by tenor Laurence Dale's struggle to hit a high note. Indeed, in its meditation on the human voice the film's depiction of imperfection acquires its most Blochian dimension. While Cerquetti embodies imperfection through her broken voice, whose utopian potential unfolds in her breathy duet with Schmidt, it is Mödl who exemplifies the quality of the ornamental, as already indicated in the discussion of the aria of the aging Countess in *Pique Dame*. Her vocal performance, which expresses the impossibility of desire in a coldly realistic world through its wistful lilts and drawn-out *tempi*, identifies the ornament as a figure of fantasy, as that which points away from the present and towards an elsewhere, a world filled with imagination.[52] In addition, the latency of speech in Mödl's singing and the evidence of advanced age in her voice lend her vocal performance a mundane artisanal quality. It hints at a concrete utopia that is within reach for everyone.

Mödl's example indicates that the ornament bears within it a rejection of the performance principle and a love of impurity. As we learn from her interview segment in *Poussières d'amour*, Mödl is adamant in her skepticism towards perfectionism. Her attitude comes from working with two conductors, Wilhelm Furtwängler and Herbert von Karajan, the former held up by Mödl as an example of how to achieve musical greatness without falling prey to perfectionism, the latter exemplifying the opposite. The film here grants Mödl her own virtuoso moment. The camera pans down from a shot of the abbey's dome to focus on Mödl's face, as she listens to one of her old recordings of "Die Liebe wird es richten" from Beethoven's *Fidelio*. Mödl is visibly happy with her performance, though, as with Cerquetti, the prevailing attitude is critical appreciation, even puzzlement, rather than being enthralled and self-absorbed. It is a reflection of her modesty that, after the aria is over, Mödl draws attention away from rather than towards her singing: "At least now you know what Furtwängler was like." The reason for the conductor's uniqueness, as Mödl tells Huppert, is his highly individual modulation of *tempi* (something that has evidently influenced her own singing): "He was not overly strict." In a later scene, Mödl discusses Karajan. His reputation as a perfectionist and micromanager is notorious, but the Karajan anecdote merits repeating for what it says about perfectionism's dislike of the ornament. For a Wagner opera he conducted, Karajan placed Mödl on stage inside a space cut out from a rock, and became upset when Mödl did not recede far enough into her niche, blocking the lighting with her bosom. For Karajan, Mödl thus came to embody an actual ornament, whose curvature disturbed the perfectionist's master plan.

Mödl's anecdote is an amusing literalization of the ornament's excess, of how it sticks out. But Mödl literalizes yet another facet of the or-

52 Muñoz makes a similar point with regard to the imperfect dance routines of queer experimental dancer Freddy Herko. See Muñoz, *Cruising Utopia*, pp. 148–167, especially p. 151.

nament's being in the way—its refusal to go away—by delaying her retirement. When read against Marcuse's notion of Orphic-Narcissistic play, Bloch's utopia, and Barthes' notion of the amateur, this particular refusal is a consequence of the resolve to claim one's craft for oneself and, thus, to sing, first and foremost, for oneself. Mödl's decision not to retire should not be read as evidence of an oversized ego that can't let go, but simply as a refusal to revert from active to passive.

Admittedly, having enjoyed a career as a *prima donna* that leaves one with little to prove, these deliberations may lose some of their existential import. The question of wanting to prove oneself does, however, remain acute with regard to Huppert and her desire to sing opera. Sensing where things may be headed, Mödl cautions Huppert against trying to be a perfectionist, advising the actress to start with something simple. Huppert will never be a professional singer, but Mödl's observation that Huppert clearly sings from her heart establishes the actress as an *amateur* in the best sense of the word. Understanding amateurism this way, I do not mean to claim there is no such thing as bad singing, or that there are no professional standards worth upholding. The question is whether it is always a singer's lack of mastery of the musical material that denotes "bad singing," or whether the institutional environment—the apparatus of opera with a capital "O"—is as capable of producing the impression by quite literally dwarfing a singer. A case in point is Susan Alexander, Citizen Kane's second wife, who—forgive me for charting another connection to popular culture's story reservoir about divas—represents a conceptual opposite to Schroeter's singers. In contrast to Charles Foster Kane, still the most haunting embodiment of the (self-) destructive force of the performance principle, Schroeter rejects opera with a capital "O." While certainly giving virtuosity its due, *Poussières d'amour* uncouples it from its deleterious conceptual twin, perfectionism, which the film replaces with an expanded notion of amateurism. As conceived by Schroeter, amateurism does not stand for foolishly ignoring the limits of one's competence. The amateur embraces these limits so as to work with them. No matter at what level they perform and whether they are young or old, active or retired, the singers Schroeter has invited are invariably empowered by their craft and by the film's small-scale recital setting.

This setting deserves the final word. The Gothic abbey Schroeter chose as a setting may seem imposing. However, he skillfully uses its bigger spaces, such as the dome and the indoor equestrian ring, for the film's few spectacle-oriented scenes, while using the other rooms to create an intimate atmosphere that corresponds to the film's celebration of imperfection, amateurism, and play—in short, to its ornamental, utopian qualities. One reason for the perfect appositeness of the abbey's Gothic architecture is its inherent ornamentalism and impurity. As Bloch points out, Gothicism is filled with spiritual-psychical yearning—evident in the way the film repeatedly focuses on certain details, such as the round windows in the abbey's walls through which one can glimpse the sky, or the ornamental frame inside the steeple window that is turned by an unidentified hand. In his architectural history of the ornament, Bloch juxtaposes Gothicism to the Egyptian period. While Egypt, according to Bloch, "is the artistic congruence with the tomb," it is Gothicism that has "grasped life, is the spirit of resurrection [...]".[53] This characteriziation is nicely illustrated in *Poussières d'amour*. Elfi Mikesch's camera repeatedly comes to rest on an Egyptian stone head in one of the abbey's walls, which has water gushing from its gaping mouth. In addition to illustrating Gothicism's impurity by showcasing its zest for citing other periods, the image is suggestive of what Bloch describes as the "uncanny pathos derived from the vitalization of the inorganic."[54] Indeed, the film features numerous images of gushing fountains and related examples of vitalism.[55] It may thus not be surprising that the abbey, notwithstanding its imposing size, created a nurturing environment for Schroeter's artistic agenda. The ornamental nature of the Gothic line, characterized by Bloch as "the free spirit of the expressive movement as such,"[56] visually and conceptually supports the film's meditation, signaled in its title, on music and art as by-products of our search for love. What remains, as Schroeter tells Mikesch in *Mondo Lux*, is human expression: "A quivering tremor, a vibration in space."

53 Bloch, "The Creation of the Ornament," pp. 93–94.

54 Bloch, p. 92.

55 I would like to thank Gertrud Koch for first bringing the connection to vitalism to my attention.

56 Bloch, p. 94.

Edward Dimendberg

For and Against Interpretation: *Nuit de chien* (2008)

Vanquished revolutionary Barcala sits alone in his house, hiding from the opposition forces who comb the city looking for him in the midst of a brutal civil war. Before committing suicide, he tears apart a pillow, causing feathers to drift slowly through the air. Absent from the novel *Para esta noche* by Juan Carlos Onetti, this scene, introduced into the 2008 cinematic adaptation by Werner Schroeter, released in French as *Nuit de chien* and in German as *Diese Nacht,* exemplifies a film constructed by the accretion of moments that frustrate attempts to impose meaning on them.[1]

Schroeter was the post-war German director whose films most nimbly ascend on "the flight from interpretation" espoused by Susan Sontag in her 1964 plea to abandon hermeneutics for an erotics of art.[2] Every film Schroeter made contains myriad scenes in which color, music, dialogue, and dramatic gesture exceed plot and instill in viewers a heightened awareness of the visible and audible. These moments propose themselves as dominant structures, rather than isolated formal gestures, in the work of the director. Although Schroeter loved cinema, opera, music, and theater, he could scarcely be labelled a formalist, obsessed as he was with investigating love, sexuality, politics, and beauty in his work. His "erotics" of art was a philosophical project evident in his personal life and his creations. It realized a complex braiding of the aesthetic, the personal, and the political.

Schroeter resided in New York City during the 1970s, and may well have read Sontag's essay in English before the translation of her writings into German.[3] His extensive travel throughout the United States and familiarity with many levels of American culture—from popular music to film, literature, theater, theory and criticism—makes this supposition wholly plausible. Regardless of the circumstances in which he discovered Sontag's work, or indeed whether he knew it at all, the coincidence between her ideas and Schroeter's explorations in film, theater, and opera is striking.

1 Schroeter filmed *Nuit de chien* in French and later supervised the German overdub, *Diese Nacht*. The ambiguity which permeates his film is suggested by the existence of two versions.

2 Susan Sontag, "Against Interpretation", in *Against Interpretation and Other Essays* (New York: Farrar, Straus, and Giroux, 1966), pp. 3–14 (originally published in *Evergreen Review*, 1964).

3 Sontag's essay appeared as "Gegen Interpretation," in a collection of her essays entitled *Kunst und Anti-Kunst*, trans. Mark W. Rien (Munich: Carl Hanser Verlag, 1980). German cultural sociologist Eike Gebhardt notes that pirate editions of translations of theoretical texts appeared frequently during the 1960s and 1970s. He also thinks it likely that he could have introduced Schroeter to Sontag's work when they were friends in New York during the 1970s.

Nuit de chien (2008)

Contradictions pervade Schroeter's work. Indeed, one might understand them as driving his creations, albeit without ever culminating in dialectical resolutions, final syntheses, or direct answers. Working in a cultural context defined by the legacy of Bertolt Brecht, Schroeter might be grasped as the figure who introduced romanticism, affect, and gender into the Brechtian tradition of allegorical and pedagogical drama and its reliance on the *Verfremdungseffekt*.[4]

4 Michelle Langford ably pursues the Brechtian dimensions of Schroeter's work in *Allegorical Images: Tableau, Time and Gesture in the Cinema of Werner Schroeter* (Bristol, UK: Intellect, 2006), especially pp. 169–192.

Although set in an unspecified historical moment and country, Schroeter's final film is, among much else, a reflection by the filmmaker on the violent past and the years in which torture was practiced in his native Germany.

Directed when Schroeter was already critically ill from the cancer to which he succumbed on April 12, 2010, this German-Portuguese-French co-production includes music by Mozart, Beethoven, Schubert, and a Portuguese punk band; quotations from film noir; and allusions to literature and painting. Its plenitude of references, unusual even in the work of an artist known for unexpected juxtapositions and conspicuous borrowing across art forms, is formidable. Viewers accustomed to the fusion of media that Schroeter mastered by his careful study of opera may nonetheless find *Nuit de chien* among his most challenging films.

Whether spectators decide to follow the winding trails of Schroeter's intertexts to their philosophical summits or to forgo interpretation and allow the allusions in the film to wash over them, watching the film is to plunge into erudite melancholy, a grim meditation on mortality whose dense web of citations provides a counterpoint to the violence and terror expounded in its narrative. Intertextuality functions not as a form of bragging intended to burnish the intellectual credentials of Schroeter, but rather proposes the myriad cultural references in the film as viable escape routes—instructions for living—that enable aesthetic transcendence of an intolerable reality.

Late works invariably accrue meanings resulting from their position at the end of an artist's *oeuvre* or as the terminus of movements or periods associated with his or her work. Whether one understands them to be continuous with earlier efforts or as definitive formulations of implicit tendencies, chronology exerts a gravitational force capable of pulling even texts organized around resisting interpretation into the orbit of hermeneutics.[5] Schroeter's final film allowed him to reckon with his own mortality, and the many interviews he gave about it suggest that its exploration of politics, sexuality, and religion are rooted in his biography.[6]

Simultaneously eliciting and resisting interpretation, the film relegates its director to one strand of its meanings. The death of Schroeter and the death of the author as guarantor and originator of meanings realize an insoluble tension. Is *Nuit de chien* a culmination of Schroeter's career and life work, or does it comprise a larger constellation of histories and traditions, a Great Barrier Reef of culture, within which the filmmaker is but a single polyp?

Theodor W. Adorno suggests: "In the history of art late works are the catastrophes."[7] This is the catastrophic film of Schroeter's career, within which the feverish passage of time and the delirious accumulation of references become palpable. *Nachträglichkeit*, the sense of the present imprinting the past, continuously jostles against confinement in an unbearable here and now.[8] Set in an unspecified historical

5 See Theodor W. Adorno, "Late Style in Beethoven," in *Essays on Music*, ed. Richard Leppert, trans. Susan H. Gillespie (Berkeley/Los Angeles: University of California Press, 2002), pp. 564–569; and Edward W. Said, *On Late Style: Music and Literature against the Grain* (New York: Random House, 2007).

6 See "Gegen das Rohe und Brutale steht die Verfeinerung," www.artechock.de/film/text/interview/s/schroeter_2010.html; "Fragen Sie das Universum" www.zeit.de/2008/43/Schroeter-Interview; and "Ich such mich im Fremden," in *Welt am Sonntag*, April 12, 2009.

7 Adorno, "Late Style in Beethoven," p. 567.

8 A succinct definition of *Nachträglichkeit* (translated into English as "deferred action") is found in the definition and overview of its usage by Freud in J. Laplanche and J.B. Pontalis, *The Language of Psychoanalysis*, trans. Donald Nicholson-Smith (New York: W.W. Norton, 1973), pp. 111–114.

moment and country, the film draws on the past while suggesting the horrors that one might encounter on the front page of a contemporary newspaper.

Everything about this film is multilayered, and it abounds with refractions, displacements, and ambiguities. Some of these complexities are present in its literary source material. Others emerged in the process of its adaptation for the screen and its location filming and post-production. Porto provided an ideal location, standing in for the imaginary city of Santa Maria, situated somewhere between the Argentine provinces of Entre Rios and Corrientes, in which novelist Juan Carlos Onetti set works such as *El Pozo* (1939), *Tierra de nadie* (1941), and *La vida breve* (1950).

Consider how Onetti scholar Gordon Brotherson describes Santa Maria in Onetti's novel: "The city registered here, as a precondition of any imaginable life, in a way that from the start precludes enthusiasm for the New World and naive faith in its 'magic.' The river flowing by is irreversibly remote from any natural source, from the 'blooming wilds' and 'worlds of solitude' upstream. Natural America is not just overlooked but positively transmuted into the social, sordid, deprived and anonymous: a secondary unvirgin state."[9]

No hint of *costumbrismo*, the realism and edifying depiction of social types at the service of nation-building that long dominated the literature of Argentina, can be discerned in the Santa Maria of Onetti's early novels, where redemption is not an option.[10] Corruption is endemic in the city, whose most emblematic character is the prostitute. Like the fictional town of Bouville (probably modeled on Le Havre) in which Jean-Paul Sartre set *La Nausée* (1938), Santa Maria is a port, in principle open to the world, yet sealed off by political hostilities. Onetti admired and wrote about Faulkner, and Santa Maria is akin to the American writer's Yoknapatawpha County, the place where his characters play out their destiny, albeit in an urban guise and a Latin American context in which fallen humanity discovers its greatest challenge not in mastering nature but in overcoming its own history.[11]

Nuit de chien is also nestled within the (always complicated) legacies of German history and culture, but references are indirect. Schroeter endows the film with a polysemous quality that is traditionally the domain of literature more so than cinema, an expensive medium that generates pressure to recoup costs by making films that obtain maximum exposure. If in his earlier films, such as *Der Bomberpilot* (1970), Schroeter treated ordinary people and their relation to National Socialism, here he tackles the barbarism of its perpetrators.

9 Gordon Brotherston, *The Emergence of the Latin American Novel* (New York: Cambridge University Press, 1977), p. 65. Mario Vargas Llosa argues for the influence of John Dos Passos on Onetti. See his invaluable *Die Welt des Juan Carlos Onetti*, trans. Angelica Ammar (Frankfurt am Main: Suhrkamp, 2009), p. 39.

10 On *costumbrismo*, see H. Ernest Lewald, "Aim and Function of Costumbrismo Porteño," in *Hispania* (American Association of Teachers of Spanish and Portuguese), vol. 46 no. 3 (September 1963), pp. 525–529.

11 Onetti's writings on Faulkner are collected in *Requiem para Faulkner y otros Articulos* (Montevideo: Arca Calicanto, n.d.).

Onetti's gloomy and frequently violent fictions are widely compared to the works of Louis-Ferdinand Céline.[12] The atmosphere of decay and relentless movement permeating Céline's *Voyage au bout de la nuit* (*Journey to the End of the Night*, 1932) is also evident in *Para esta noche*. At one point in the film, Ossorio picks up a book and reads the lines, "This city sickens me. They all live as if everything lasts forever. They're proud of this endless mediocrity," possibly an allusion to the French writer.

Filmed in French and later dubbed into German, a mode of European production increasingly common today, *Nuit de chien* challenges earlier definitions of national cinema produced in a single language or cultural context.[13] *Nuit de chien* was adapted from Onetti's novel by Schroeter and French co-screenplay writer Gilles Taurand. The latter had previously worked with directors such as André Téchiné, Raúl Ruiz, and Benoît Jacquot, and wrote scripts that ranged from art films to martial arts movies to television productions. Paulo Branco, the film's producer, has worked with art-film directors, including Pedro Costa, Raúl Ruiz, Alain Tanner, and David Cronenberg, and realized 256 films. Co-producer Frieder Schlaich distributed the film though his company Filmgalerie 451, in whose offices Schroeter lived for four months while completing the editing. German cinematographer Thomas Plenert filmed the scenes in Porto with a Portuguese crew.

Speaking Spanish and having traveled in Latin America, especially Mexico and Argentina, Schroeter knew and admired Onetti's work. Branco's budget would not suffice to adapt and film in Paris Schroeter's first choice, James Baldwin's *Giovanni's Room*, so the producer suggested *Para esta noche*.[14] Schroeter's experience teaching in Buenos Aires in 1983 sensitized him to living in a society where violence and brutality were commonplace.[15]

Onetti has long been eclipsed by better-known Spanish-language writers such as Jorge Luis Borges, Julio Cortázar, and Mario Vargas Llosa. Yet, as a member of the generation that preceded—and for some commentators even commenced—the Latin American literary

12 On the significance of Céline as a literary model for Onetti, see Carlos María Domínguez, *Construcción de la noche. La vida de Juan Carlos Onetti* (Montevideo: Cal y Canto, 2009; 1st ed., Buenos Aires: Planeta, 1993), pp. 48–49, 62, 83. See also Fernando Ainsa and Cedric Busette, "Onetti's Devices," *Latin American Literary Review* (Ithaca, NY: Cornell University Press), vol. 3 no. 5 (Fall – Winter 1974), pp. 81–97. Schroeter discusses Céline as an inspiration for his film in the interview with Max Dax included in the DVD release of *Diese Nacht*.

13 On this contemporary mode of European film production, see Thomas Elsaesser, *European Cinema: Face to Face with Hollywood* (University of Amsterdam Press, 2005), esp. pp. 485–512.

14 This anecdote is related in Werner Schroeter, with Claudia Lenssen, *Tage im Dämmer, Nächte im Rausch* (Berlin: Aufbau Verlag, 2011), p. 313.

15 In Argentina Juan Perón returned from exile and to office on June 20, 1973, which precipitated the deleterious infighting of right-wing and left-wing followers and exacerbated the already existing economic and political instability in the country, ultimately resulting in the enactment of emergency decrees. After his death and the brief rule of his wife, Isabel Perón, violence intensified and culminated in the "Dirty War" of the period 1976–1983, associated with the National Reorganization Process. The imprisonment and "disappearance" of individuals deemed enemies of the state became commonplace during these years.

boom of the 1960s, he contributed much to the vitality of 20th-century Spanish-language literature.[16]

His novel was originally called *El perro tendría su dia* (The Dog Will Have Its Day), a title that was changed after his publisher feared that Argentine dictator Juan Domingo Perón would consider it an attack on his person.[17] The published title, *Para esta noche*, came from the newspaper *Critica: Para esta noche*, to which Onetti contributed. Its story takes place in a geographically ambiguous port city soon to be invaded by a general.

The plot centers on opposition members of an unspecified political party, likely Communist, who are engaged in an internal struggle. Former comrade Luis Ossorio Vignale, a medical doctor who has become increasingly disillusioned with politics, arrives in the city to seek his beloved, journalist Clara Baldi, and to obtain two tickets on a boat departing the city. He finds Baldi has disappeared, and commences his search for her, an archetypical film noir protagonist pursuing a quest in the city.

The man who promises Ossorio boat tickets commits suicide in a local bar with the picturesque name The First and Last. The head of the secret police, Morasan, raids the bar and tortures two of the prostitutes working there to learn the hiding-place of Barcala, the opposition leader. After visiting the head of the Army, Martins, Ossorio agrees to visit Barcala's hideout, with the intention of killing him. Barcala gives the boat tickets to Ossorio, who leaves without killing him, only to learn subsequently that the revolutionary has killed himself. Barcala's daughter Vittoria ends up in Ossorio's care. Martins is killed by enemy fire. Morasan takes his own life. Ossorio and Vittoria make their way toward the harbor, where they are killed.

This synopsis of Onetti's novel and Schroeter's film glosses over many of the intriguing differences between the first publication of the book in 1943 and the appearance of an edited version in 1966. Something of the ambivalence that Onetti maintained toward the novel is conveyed by the fact that it appeared in five different editions, which contain 400 textual variants; this complicates any discussions of a definitive text, which plausibly might be denied to exist.[18] Ossorio's fate in distinct versions and the complicated textual history of the novel suggests *Para esta noche* as a political allegory of some of the most desperate years of the 20th

16 For a discussion of Onetti in relation to the Latin American literary boom, see Donald L. Shaw, "Onetti and the 1940s," in Gustavo San Román, ed., *Onetti and Others: Comparative Essays on a Major Figure in Latin American Literature* (Albany: SUNY Press, 1999), 13–20. On the boom more generally, see Roberto González Echevarría, *Modern Latin American Literature: A Very Short Introduction* (New York: Oxford University Press, 2012).

17 I am grateful to Michelle Clayton for confirming that the title of the book alludes to a Spanish expression that can be loosely translated as "what goes around comes around," and that the phrase "every dog has its day," which suggests the malleability of fortune, comes from Shakespeare, *Hamlet*, Act V, Scene 1.

18 The variants of the five editions of the novel are discussed by Gabriel Saad in "Invariants et systèmes de production du récit dans l'œuvre de Juan Carlos Onetti. Etude comparée de cinq éditions de *Para esta noche*," in *Cahiers du monde hispanique et luso-brésilien* (Université de Toulouse – Le Mirail), no. 35 (1980), pp. 297–298.

century.[19] Its resonances include the rise to power of National Socialism in Germany, the defeat of the Republican government in the Spanish Civil War, the rise of Stalinism in the Soviet Union, the signing of the Hitler-Stalin Pact, and the collapse of the Popular Front. Schroeter filmed an alternate ending, in which Vittoria escapes the carnage at the harbor, but decided that it rang false. In the released film the petty functionary Captain Villar shoots both her and Ossorio. Onetti's novel was also adapted by another filmmaker, Italian director Carlo Di Carlo, whose version was released in 1977 as *Per questa notte*.

The first of Schroeter's many additions to Onetti's story appears in the credit sequence, in which the camera (wielded by a second-unit cinematographer Schroeter sent to the state museum in Kromeriz, in the Czech Republic) moves over the surface of *The Flaying of Marsyas*, the last painting Titian completed in the period 1570–1576. Nearly every cultural reference in the film addresses death, and this late work, produced at the end of the painter's life, after the plague in Venice, to which he succumbed, is no exception. Titian frequently adapted scenes from the work of Ovid, in this case the description in Book Six of the *Metamorphoses* of how the enraged God Apollo punished the satyr Marsyas, fearing he might have upstaged him in a musical duel between the double flute and the lyre.[20] In A.D. Melville's translation, this reads, "Apollo stripped his skin; the whole of him was one large wound, blood streaming everywhere, sinews laid bare, veins naked, quivering and pulsing. You could count his twitching guts, and the tissues as the light shone through his ribs."[21] Titian's painting troubled Erwin Panofsky, who called the little dog lapping up blood "gratuitous brutality."[22] He found this *"horror vacui"* aberrant in the painter's art, noting most damningly about the painting that "no square inch is vacant," a comment that positions the violence and visual density of Schroeter's film in the lineage of half a millennium of Western art. Edith Wyss interprets the severe punishment Apollo inflicted on the Satyr as retribution for disrupting the sacred and harmonious order of the universe, identified by the followers of Pythagoras with the seven strings of the lyre and a well-governed city.[23] In his posthumously published autobiography, *Tage im Dämmer, Nächte im Rausch*, Schroeter described the inclusion of Titian's painting in place of a prologue to his film as an allegory for the dilemma that people are not able to live in a community. "Music and cruelty, beauty and violence are close to each other in this mythological scene. [...] The wild music

19 On allegory in Schroeter's films, see Langford, *Allegorical Images: Tableau, Time and Gesture in the Cinema of Werner Schroeter*.

20 A lucid overview of the mythological themes and history of Titian's painting is found in David Rosand, "Most musical of mourners, weep again!": Titian's *Triumph of Marsyas*," *Arion*, 3rd Series, vol. 17 no. 3 (Winter 2010), pp.17–43.

21 Ovid, *Metamorphoses*, trans. A.D. Melville (New York: Oxford University Press, 1986), p. 133.

22 Erwin Panofsky, *Problems in Titian: Mostly Iconographic* (New York University Press, 1969), p. 171.

23 See Edith Wyss, *The Myth of Apollo and Marsyas in the Art of the Italian Renaissance* (Newark, DE: University of Delaware Press, 1996).

of Marsyas's flute comes from nature like the wind in the trees and does not accompany measured song and human language."[24] The death of Marsyas allegorically figures the tension between aesthetic expression and political order. Indeed, Titian's painting might be understood as a visual allegory of the erotics of art advocated by Sontag, a challenge to philosophy and the power of the state alike.

Rather than banishing poets from the city, as Plato advocated in *The Republic*, Apollo skins Marsyas alive, a torture whose sadistic and homosexual overtones are evoked in *The Black Cat* (1934, dir. Edgar G. Ulmer), a film produced in the Universal cycle of horror films, in which Bela Lugosi skins Boris Karloff alive.[25] It also evokes the sado-masochistic eroticism in 1970s photography by Robert Mapplethorpe.[26] Having several years earlier ceased making films in Germany, a country about which by the end of his life he felt ambivalent, Schroeter perhaps imagines himself as Marsyas, a martyr for his art. Significantly, Schroeter called Porto home at the time he made his film, and claimed he felt more comfortable in Portugal than in Germany.

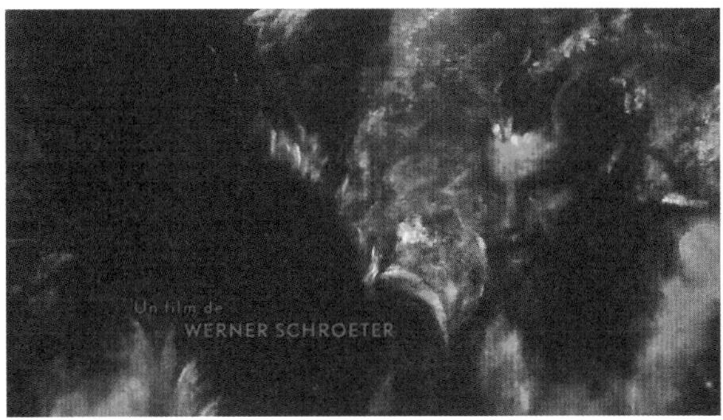

Nuit de chien

This identification is rendered plausible by the voice-over of Schroeter, who as the camera lingers on the Titian figure with donkey ears, recites a line from Act II, Scene 2, of Shakespeare's *Julius Caesar*: "Of all the wonders that I yet have heard, it seems to me the most strange that men should fear; Seeing that death, a necessary end, will come when it will come." Schroeter believed that fear leads people to commit acts of brutality. Hope resides in acknowledging the inevitability of death and validating the force of beauty. His romanticism oscillates between valorizing experiences of transcendence made possible by art, music, and sexuality, recognizing their insufficiency, yet nonetheless seeking heightened experiences of life.

Spatio-temporal indeterminacy—a trait common to many films noir and frequently encountered in the director's work—appears in the first scene in the film, depicting the skyline of Porto, with the spectacular 16th-century Serra do Pilar monastery, and the 1886 Dom Luis Bridge (see also p. 48). At the time of its construction, the 172-foot span of the bridge

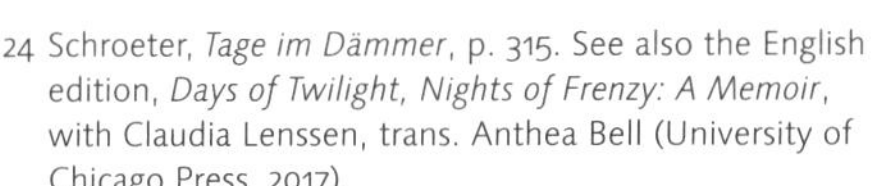
24 Schroeter, *Tage im Dämmer*, p. 315. See also the English edition, *Days of Twilight, Nights of Frenzy: A Memoir*, with Claudia Lenssen, trans. Anthea Bell (University of Chicago Press, 2017).

25 *The Republic of Plato*, trans. Allan Bloom (New York: Basic Books, 1968). See also Ramona A. Naddaff, *Exiling the Poets: The Production of Censorship in Plato's Republic* (University of Chicago Press, 2002).

26 On the relation between the painting by Titian and the photography of Robert Mapplethorpe, see Arthur Danto, *Playing with the Edge: The Photographic Achievement of Robert Mapplethorpe* (Berkeley/Los Angeles: University of California Press, 1995), pp. 68–73.

Nuit de chien

was the longest in the world. Its metal construction evokes the 19th century, and except for the airplanes flying over it, this scene could well be set in that period. With the arrival of a contemporary train on the station platform, *Nuit de chien* confirms its setting in the present. Yet passengers exiting the train are dressed in both contemporary and older styles of clothing. The young girl who sells Ossorio flowers wears her hair in dreadlocks, and at the row of taxis from different countries, he enters a black British Austin FX3 cab, a model introduced in 1948.

Production designers typically work to minimize, if not eliminate, such stylistic inconsistency, yet Schroeter and Alberte Barsacq, who designed the costumes for many of his previous films, intensified it. Unlike films such as *Chinatown* or *Il conformista* (*The Conformist*), identified by Fredric Jameson as "nostalgia films" exemplary of postmodernism,[27] the lack of a consistent visual style and period identity in *Nuit de chien* prevents the viewer from assimilating it as a retro art film. Contemporary reality seeps in to destroy the comfort of watching a past sealed off from the present.

As the taxi cab ascends a winding street, the atmosphere of film noir intensifies. The image of Ossorio's hat falling out of the car window onto the street conjures up the famous expressionist gesture of a hat landing in the gutter in Robert Siodmak's 1944 film noir *Phantom Lady*. Schroeter himself cites Robert Aldrich's 1955 *Kiss Me Deadly* and Orson Welles' 1958 *Touch of Evil* as inspirations for his film.[28] The hilly topography of the Los Angeles Bunker Hill neighborhood, movements by characters in and out of the city, and apocalyptic tone of *Kiss Me Deadly* are but more analogues. Moral corruption and the ubiquity of prostitution suggest *Touch of Evil*. These classic films noir feature dramatic conclusions in which their central protagonists, crazed by fantasies of omnipotence, are destroyed. Set in clearly recognizable locations, Los Angeles in the former, the two sides

27 Fredric Jameson, *Postmodernism, or the Cultural Logic of Late Capitalism* (Durham, NC: Duke University Press, 1992), pp. 27–28.

28 Schroeter, interview with Max Dax, *Diese Nacht*, DVD liner notes, Filmgalerie 451 (2010), p. 5.

of the border between California and Mexico in the latter, they compose two of the most iconic 1950s noir cityscapes.

Every scene in *Nuit de chien* but the final one was filmed at night. Schroeter and his cast and crew shot in Porto from six in the evening to six at dawn every day, and their working methods are evident in the finished film, whose claustrophobic airless quality and hallucinatory intensity—common to many films noir—permeate the film, which seems to unfold in a temporally distended eternal night.

The urban *patois* of Dashiell Hammett and Raymond Chandler clearly inflected Onetti's language. One could understand *Para esta noche* as a modernist novel that doubles as hard-boiled fiction, a familiar amalgam of urban perceptual investigation and the popular genre evident in the work of numerous 20th-century writers and the directors of the French New Wave. Ossorio is a detective, obsessed like so many noir protagonists, in this instance with finding Clara and maintaining his integrity in an existentially challenged environment. Onetti's novel suggests that organized politics, at least in the version represented by the revolutionary vanguard party, is corrupt and morally compromised. Comrades kill former comrades. The struggle for power, unsevered from any conception of morality, has become an end in itself.

Para esta noche contains no blueprint for rational collective action, no possibility for remaining in the city and continuing to fight. Famously, Onetti commences the first edition of his novel with a prologue that presents it as his own act of existential engagement, however imperfect: "All over the world in 1942 people were defending with their bodies various of the author's convictions when this novel was being written. The idea that only those people were living a life true to destiny was humiliating and difficult to accept. This book was written from the need—satisfied in a petty, non-compromising way—to participate in the pain, anguish and heroism of others. It is, then, a cynical attempt at liberation."[29]

Although Onetti was not a combatant in World War II, during the early 1940s in Montevideo he encountered two anarchists, a Spaniard and an Italian, exiles from Republican Spain, who recounted stories of torture and political treachery in Valencia as the Communists and anarchists murdered each other in advance of the arrival of Franco's troops at the end of the Spanish Civil War.[30] Their memories and accounts by opponents of the Nazis who survived torture made their way into his novel. If writing could be a form of action, perhaps even a demonstration of solidarity with suffering comrades, Onetti's understanding of it in literature shares little with the emphasis on heroism and morally uplifting characters present in socialist realism.[31]

Lacking heroic protagonists, Onetti's book negates the paradigm of socialist realism or engaged popular front literature. A striking fea-

29 Juan Carlos Onetti, *The Pit and Tonight*, trans. Peter Bush (London: Quartet Books, 1991), p. 33.
30 Schroeter, *Tage im Dämmer*, p. 314.
31 Jean-Paul Sartre, *What is Literature? and Other Essays* (Cambridge, MA: Harvard University Press, 1998).

ture of the novel is the absence of clearly articulated political principles. The reader never learns the ideals of any of the characters. What or why they fight is as shadowy as their national identity. Santa Maria, the putative setting of the novel, based on its continuity with other books by Onetti, is scarcely, if ever, mentioned by name. Its history, economics, geopolitics, or forms of governance are not specified. Lacking specific landmarks or recognizable urban neighborhoods, the city and the political crisis within it obtain a suggestive universality that clearly appealed to Schroeter.

Onetti's desire to participate in the pain, anguish, and heroism of others resonates with Schroeter's adaptation in which cynicism is tempered by romanticism. Suffering and a penchant towards masochism also figure prominently in *Der Rosenkönig* (*The Rose King*, 1986) and its unforgettable amalgam of male homosexual desire, bodily mutilation, and the exploration of operatic treatments of death. That Magdalena Montezuma, one of Schroeter's key actors, was dying of cancer during the production of that film lends its treatment of mortality the character of a practical exercise, the work of a small troupe of close friends seeking to reconcile themselves to death through the power of art. Yet Schroeter remains faithful to the bleakness of Onetti's novel, and perhaps regarded *Nuit de chien* as his own cynical—and thus level-headed—attempt at liberation.

Onetti's novel is a sustained exercise in modernist stylistics, an expunging of psychology, plot, and moralizing at the service of an ostensibly pure investigation of language. Consider the following sentence by Onetti, describing Morasan's interrogation of an unnamed prostitute who had briefly sheltered the fugitive Barcala: "He looked at her again—he had taken his eyes off her as soon as he started asking her whether she had lived with Barcala—thinking about his hatred for that filthy world of pimps and prostitutes, a hatred going back to his adolescence, for the dark mystery he sensed but which escaped him, hidden within those existences, that whole world of people in rented rooms, hotels, night clubs, his hatred for the appearances of that were all he could know, revealing and concealing the mystery that enraged him, dates, in the early hours in late-night restaurants, women with love in their eyes, the obscene, concrete words with which they expressed their love for men and the silence they defended them with when questioned in the police station, their servile determination to die rather than disturb even the sleep of men."[32]

Conjuring scenes glimpsed through urban windows or imagined behind grimy walls, Onetti moves from concrete perception to introspection, from present to the past, swinging from affectless description to enraged invective. A typical Onettian sentence plunges the reader into a maze of complex syntax. Schroeter's film style and its predilection for elaborate pans and camera movements that survey a scene in long takes might be understood as a cinematic correlative to Onetti's prose, a manner of discerning points in space and time yet holding them in the same thought, not unlike the conjunctions

32 Onetti, *The Pit and Tonight*, p. 121.

and punctuation skillfully deployed by the writer.

Although Onetti worked as an editor for the Reuters News Agency in Montevideo and Buenos Aires from 1941 to 1946, the period in which he composed the novel, he developed a literary style that rejected the journalistic logic of neutral reporting. Rare is the scene in which who, what, when, where, and why can be reconstructed with clarity. Even more so than Franz Kafka, whose office writings suggest tantalizing parallels with his fictions, Onetti practiced two unique styles of writing at the same time.[33] That Schroeter directed both fiction films and documentaries suggests that he also possessed the ability to work in multiple styles and modes.

Simultaneously fascinated and repelled by the prostitute and the civilization of the metropolis whose inscrutable surfaces she exemplifies, Morasan is a torturer. Denied a name, his female victim becomes a cipher for all that is unknowable, yet which Morasan cannot stop looking at. Onetti's gerunds—asking, thinking, revealing, concealing—and his elegantly worded clauses chart an inexorable movement toward investigating and punishing the woman as pathological and inflicting violence on her body. It evokes the psychosexual dynamics of classic film noir that culminates with the destruction of the woman.

33 Franz Kafka, *The Office Writings*, Stanley Corngold, ed. (Princeton, NJ: Princeton University Press, 2008).

34 Schroeter, *Tage im Dämmer*, p. 319. The line appears in Goethe's poem "Harzreise im Winter," www.kisc.meiji.ac.jp/~mmandel/recherche/goethe_harzreise.html.

35 Schroeter, p. 320.

Most difficult to watch is the scene in which the prostitute Irene dies slowly of wounds inflicted by Morasan and his torturers. Revealingly, Schroeter increases the prominence of prostitutes in his film. Irene shelters Barcala's child after his murder. Juan, a hustler, presents himself as a willing collaborator of the secret police, against whom he later turns in vain. These characters suggest even the most subjugated individuals possess agency and dignity. Schroeter maintained a continual interest in victims—prostitutes, ostracized foreigners, and the mentally ill—across his career.

Responding to critics after the premiere of the film at the 2008 Venice Film Festival, Schroeter invoked Goethe's incitement in *Faust: Part II* to "open your clouded-over eyes," and argued that his mannerist art should be understood as an engagement with the reality of violence.[34] Locating the torturers in a church and cutting frequently between scenes of Christ on the cross to victims, he cited "the history of mistakes and crimes of the church, a catastrophe, against whose treachery the film rebels."[35]

Taking as his credo Tchaikovsky's dictum that art works on "the unsublated contrast between pain and beauty," Schroeter is unabashed in his romantic faith in beauty, yet intransigent in his anarchist indictment of institutions. After the deaths of Barcala, Martins, and Morasan, a remaining rebel leader attempts to convince Ossorio to become head of the revolution, an offer he rejects.

Another rebel leader complains "the whiff of humanity stinks," and with its constant

Nuit de chien

moment. Screwing leads not to fusion with the other but culminates in unscrewing.

At the end of Onetti's novel, Ossorio and Vittoria are killed by a bomb on the way to the harbor. In a late version of the text, Ossorio turns back to help the child, a quasi-religious suggestion that he dies embracing something beyond himself. Realizing a circular structure, the film concludes with a black frame and Schroeter reading the quotation from Shakespeare's *Julius Caesar* with which it began, as if speaking directly to the viewer. The boat, without Ossorio and Vittoria as passengers, sails off into the dawn. Acknowledging the inevitability of death, his own included, does the director convince the audience to conquer fear, or does he register this as an impossibility?

It would be overly simple to read the film as devoid of hope and to label Schroeter as obsessed with death and mortality. His film places its faith in art. A deeply religious Catholic, Schroeter rarely bothered himself with consistency, noting famously, "I am a fatalist, I am a Stoic, I am a Christian, I am an Existentialist. I accept the path and not the end as the goal. I observe life and people as a complex image. That is not a contradiction."[37] Tenderness and

invocation of death, the film evinces little sympathy for humanism. For Schroeter, the original human sin is fear of death, with which he associates a morally catastrophic willingness to compromise and a removal from the here and now. Reinforced with music by Liszt, Beethoven, Rossini, Haydn, and Schubert, he concretizes Cicero's edict that to study philosophy is to prepare oneself to die.[36] *Nuit de chien* is simultaneously an affirmation of faith and a recognition of its insufficiency.

This may well explain the fascination with children throughout Schroeter's film, a theme wholly absent in Onetti's novel. In their vulnerability, spontaneity, and rootedness in the present, children suggest a direct relation to time—and a relative freedom from the weight of history—denied their adult counterparts. A case in point is the scene in which Ossorio and the prostitute Maria furiously copulate in a bathtub, only to be interrupted by Vittoria, who requests help opening a jar of juice. Here erotic passion, including the love that motivates Ossorio on his quest to find Clara, appear diversions from Vittoria's immersion in the

36 Cicero, *Tusculan Disputations*, 1:30:74. See www.gutenberg.org/files/14988/14988-h/14988-h.htm. Some of the musical allusions to death included on the film soundtrack include Beethoven's *Missa Solemnis*, Rossini's *Violin Concerto in D*, Schubert's *Stabat Mater* and *Death and the Maiden*, Heinrich Proch's *Deh torna mio bene*, sung by Maria Callas, and Haydn's *The Seven Last Words of Christ on the Cross*.

37 Schroeter, interview with Max Dax, *Diese Nacht*, DVD liner notes, p. 2.

utopian romanticism co-exist with a lacerating cynicism about human institutions in his films. Living without a fixed address and out of two suitcases, Schroeter may well have been the least materialistic of post-war German filmmakers. By the end of his life, he traveled from one theater or opera engagement to another, finding in his colleagues and co-workers the family and stability he lacked in his personal life.

The bourgeois value Schroeter most respected, and around which his life revolved, was work, perhaps the reason he commanded fanatical loyalty from actors such as Isabelle Huppert, Bulle Ogier, and Pascale Schiller, who cherished his precise direction and the security he provided. Fusing creation, love, and politics in his life, Schroeter embodied his art to a degree unusual among contemporary German filmmakers. Indeed, it is difficult not to regard him as one of the last German filmmakers who lived the avant-garde project of overcoming the separations between art and life.

Finding myself seated across from Schroeter at a dinner in 2010, I asked him what he remembered most fondly about the explosive political and cultural atmosphere of Berlin in the 1960s and 1970s. Without any trace of affectation, he replied that it was the sex he enjoyed in those years. His path towards an erotics of art inevitably engaged the body and fused the sensual and the intellectual.

Nuit de chien cost 4 million Euros to produce, 20 percent of which came from German film subsidies.[38] Unusually, the production received no initial support from German television, traditionally a major funder of ambitious art films. Only much later did co-producer Schlaich complete a sale to the 3sat/ZDF channels. Despite positive reviews, including a half-page in the *Frankfurter Allgemeine Zeitung*, the film did poorly at the box office and lost Schlaich's firm a six-figure sum.[39] Long regarded as "box office poison" (*Kassengift*) by the German film industry, Schroeter's films appear unlikely in the near future to attain mass popularity, despite what his *New York Times* obituary acknowledged as their prescient investigation of the performance of gender.[40]

As the film celebrates its tenth anniversary, and the planet confronts the most severe refugee crisis since World War II, the prescience of Schroeter's final film shows no signs of diminishing, even as the loss of his activism, commitment, and sensibility are more keenly felt than ever. Reading the daily newspaper, one encounters accounts of many people who overcome the fear of death and demonstrate great courage and bravery in their search for a

38 Author's interview with Frieder Schlaich, May 17, 2012.

39 Yet the film generally received positive reviews in both Germany and France. See, for example, Bert Rebhandl, "An das Nichts genagelt," *Berliner Zeitung* (April 2, 2009); Fritz Göttler, "Zitternde Bebung in der Luft, *Frankfurter Zeitung* (April 9, 2016); Andreas Kilb, "Absagebrief eines politischen Ästheten," *Frankfurter Allgemeine Zeitung* (April 2, 2009); Jean-François Rauger, "L'horreur séduisante du moment où tout bascule," *Le Monde* (January 7, 2008); Philippe Azoury, "Schroeter, le retour d'outre-nuit," *Libération* (January 7, 2009).

40 Dave Kehr, "Werner Schroeter, German Film and Stage Director, Dies at 65," *New York Times* (April 10, 2010). One might also note how Schroeter's work anticipates many of the concerns of contemporary affect theory.

better life. Participating in the pain, anguish, and heroism of others can involve collective political behavior that does not always devolve into corruption and violence. Schroeter's romanticism, aestheticism, and anarchism leave open the question of how to live in a community and how art—including the art of film—might facilitate solidarity.[41] In this openness tinged with urgency, the continued relevance of his work seems assured.[42]

41 Filmmaker Elfi Mikesch offers an incisive assessment of the film when she notes "Despite their differences, this film has a certain affinity with *Malina*. Everyone in it tries to save themselves, get aboard the ship, but no one knows where the journey goes. There is fear. The film is visionary. It represents our era. Werner's films are prescient. They let us know that certain events will have consequences." (Interview with Elfi Mikesch for this volume, by Christine N. Brinckmann and Roy Grundmann. See Chapter 11.)

42 I am grateful to Roy Grundmann, Eike Gebhardt, and Michelle Clayton for sharing their expertise and commenting on earlier drafts of this essay. Producer Frieder Schlaich of Filmgalerie 451 kindly allowed me to interview him about the production of the film. Noa Steimatsky provided access to the films of Carlo Di Carlo.

Interview with Elfi Mikesch

by Christine N. Brinckmann and Roy Grundmann

(Conducted in Berlin in the summer of 2016)

ROY GRUNDMANN: When and how did you meet Werner Schroeter?

ELFI MIKESCH: I remember my second encounter with him, on the street, accompanied by Magdalena Montezuma. It was in 1966. He showed his early Super-8 films in my friend Anke-Rixa Hansen's storefront apartment in Kreuzberg. From then on, we saw each other continually, including Magdalena. I also remember first meeting Ulrike Ottinger around the same time, with Tabea Blumenschein, standing at an intersection at Kurfürstendamm and Uhlandstrasse. I wanted to meet them personally—and, serendipitously, it happened. They looked so unconventional and beautiful.

RG: Were you part of an art scene?

EM: Only later it got labeled a scene—Munich, Berlin, Ulm....

CHRISTINE NOLL BRINCKMANN: When you met Werner Schroeter and saw his films, did you already make plans to work together?

EM: I don't recall. At the time I was mainly involved with photography. I didn't shoot my first Super-8 film until 1972. There are photos with me and Werner from that time. I also remember the premiere of *The Rose King* at the cinema Delphi in Berlin, but that was much later, 1986. Around 1968 I sometimes visited Werner and Magdalena in Munich. In 1971 Werner went to Lebanon to shoot *Salome* for which I did costumes, make-up, and still photography.

RG: In his autobiography, Werner mentions you not only as a camera person, but also as one of three important photographers, along with Roswitha Hecke and Digne Meller Marcovicz.

EM: In 1987/88, I had the good fortune to photograph one of his stage productions. I learned a lot. Werner's style favored physical acting, and I was able to get very close to the actors to take my pictures. I had immediate access to their faces and gestures, and my photographs benefited from their dynamics. Just as intensive was the designing of the costumes and the collaboration with the set designer Alberte Barsacq. Whether we had to develop a *motif* from scratch or were working in a studio or on stage, we needed few or no words. Magdalena Montezuma's presence reinforced this bond. If we hadn't complemented and suffused one another in our work, films like *The Rose King* could never have been made. Everyone was fully on the job with complete passion. This was essential, since Magdalena was already very ill, though full of energy to the very end.

CNB: Initially, Schroeter often operated the camera himself. When you took over, did he have any requests as to how to visualize his ideas?

EM: Werner had a strong visual sense, and a real sense for the "here and now," for the actual nature of a site and the situations that could unfurl there. He knew exactly what he wanted. At the same time, he gave actors a lot of freedom. What will the actors do, how will they play their parts? How does a scene develop, and where will it go? That's what I had to attune my camera to, and what shaped the use of equipment. Werner liked long takes, so as to generate time itself. There may have been suggestions or sketches as to how to break down a scene, but the long take had to be finished before we decided about the editing. The cinematographer would then propose additional takes, so the narrative could be structured in the cutting room.

CNB: Schroeter liked to work with the same actors again and again.

EM: Yes, he valued consistency. He generated his cinematic language organically. He developed extensive sequences, no fragments. On a theater stage there are no cuts. This is also how Werner shot his films.

RG: Does this mean that it made little difference to him whether he was directing a film or a play?

EM: He knew exactly what the differences are between the two media. He studied Dreyer's work, and many other films. He made very deliberate use of close-ups, and determined whether to move the camera or keep it still. The important thing was always to let the camera support the gestures, the physical presence, and the musicality. Werner used music by *living* with music; music was his life. It never served to merely underscore a scene; its content was always precise and integral to the film. Music existed in its own right, entering into a dialogue with the film. Werner created something that had been pretty much non-existent in Germany: he combined the great spectrum of music with the language of cinema to develop a new form of poetic expression. At the same time, there was something simple or even crude about his work. He created incredibly hair-raising ruptures by his stubbornness—humorous, challenging and provocative as well. It is these contrasts that constitute his aesthetics. This becomes clear in the conversation between Werner and Michel Foucault. They talk about love, passion, the art of living. From there one can draw a direct line to *Poussières d'amour*, a documentary that, among other things, deals with stage work, opera, art, friendship, and life itself. In this film, we get insights into Werner's complex attitude towards the language of cinema and the language of theater. We begin to understand both, and also how he develops a scene, how friendship becomes palpable, which was an essential component and prerequisite of his work. His friendships were deep and passionate and they shaped his work. Nothing was disconnected from life, everything was smoothly or sometimes painfully connected. Sometimes Werner could be harsh and uncompromising, making uncompromising demands. Only friendships that withstood this prevailed. Tolerance was required and this exacted a price. Such intensities have a price.

RG: You two were friends.

EM: I believe so.

RG: The kind of relationship you just described—did it apply to you as well?

Werner Schroeter during a film shoot (early 1980s)

EM: It applied to many people with whom Werner collaborated. He had very close friendships, as with Magdalena or Antonio Orlando, with Marcelo Uriona and Monika Keppler. The intensities generated by such relationships become very perceptible in the films. Isabelle Huppert—a close friend, as different as both were from each other. Or his friendship with Rosa von Praunheim: one cannot imagine greater opposites. Still, their friendship lasted, no matter how disparate and contradictory. In my film *Mondo Lux*, the two of them meet again after a long time. A strange, funny encounter, in which their contradictions come to the fore—as well as the wit, the humor, the impishness. What emerges are different concepts of life, of ideas, of art. There was tension, cross-fertilization, rivalry, real strife—all of this came together.

CNB: Were they aware of how different they were from each other?

EM: Yes, they were. And yet, there was something new about it every time. In *Mondo Lux* you see the familiar wit, the playfulness that linked both from the beginning—but also what separated them, namely art. I worked closely with both of them. I cannot think of anything more different than doing camera for Werner and doing camera for Rosa. I could enjoy both exactly because they are so contradictory. How can one reconcile these two approaches?—but, of course, one doesn't have to. This is a way of life for me—two worlds in which I have had the fortune to live. It shows that the impossible is possible, that it can grow on the same tree. How can opposites be combined without turning creativity into murderous rivalry? Through friendship.

RG: Rosa von Praunheim was initially very important for Schroeter.

EM: Rosa is an extremely generous person. He always wants to lend support, but sometimes does so in a rather aggressive manner. Some can stand it, others can't. It was fascinating for me to know two such different characters, each having made, in his very own way, very important films. They reflect history and retell the specifics of their own time in highly personal ways. Their lifestyles and their notions of politics and aesthetics differ drastically, and so do their ways of tackling problems. Werner animates, thematizes, and lives grand drama, probing what these dramas are about. And what does Rosa do? The film *It Is Not the Homosexual Who Is Perverse But the Society in Which He Lives* launched an incredible movement, a gaining of consciousness. It shows a reality that had been silenced and suppressed. The film's language is stiff, stuffy, clunky. Werner has a different way of narrating. We need both talents, both sensibilities. Rosa's television films were brittle, frayed, broken, making one wonder why a network consented to show them. Television back then had gutsy commissioning editors. Both Werner's and Rosa's films have a quality that steers clear of acquiescence and conformity; they are unique and radical. They were an important force that spawned the vividness of German cinema, together with Ulrike Ottinger's or Helke Sander's work, the *auteur* cinema of this unruly period.

RG: You have worked with many of these filmmakers. What was unique about operating the camera for Werner Schroeter?

EM: I have also worked with Monika Treut and others—all very idiosyncratic people. Their visual languages and concepts are highly specific.

CNB: You just mentioned that long takes were of particular importance for Schroeter. But the close-ups of faces also have a unique quality. Perhaps this is due to the way the scenes were filmed. Were the close-ups done together with the long takes, or, as in Hollywood, at some other time?

EM: For Werner, continuity was always very important, so that the actors are not interrupted and the creative space remains operative, allowing expressivity to unfold and take hold. Surely, we also had to do a few retakes here and there. But there was no fragmentation, experience retained an organic, coherent quality.

CNB: But the lighting of the close-ups is carefully thought through.

EM: Yes, we did take breaks to adjust the lighting, among other things. But it was important to Werner that we would keep going without much fussing around. At the same time, precision was always required for a take, for the composition of the images. Lighting is psychology, mood, or it follows the dramaturgy of movement. I always took care not merely to light a scene but to illuminate it according to its contents. There is also darkness and blackness. And natural light is full of beauty and nuance; I always made an effort to utilize it. How does light fall onto a face, a body? How does a room speak in which someone lives and something happens?

RG: So Werner would do a long take that would be briefly interrupted for you to do a close-up and to adjust the lighting, after which the filming of the scene would be resumed?

EM: Exactly. Sometimes the long take would last three, four, five, six minutes, so we had to think about how its individual parts would combine. How to break up a scene, how to condense it, recharge it with emotion and meaning. In Werner's close-ups, the action that preceded them is still present and palpable, carried over by the unrelenting intensity of the way he coached the actors.

RG: You have already established the comparison to music. Werner's films tend to be choreographed and musical. As a cinematographer, did you regard yourself as a kind of instrument in a concert, as one of the musicians? Does it make sense to describe your work in these terms?

EM: The comparison to a small orchestra or a quartet appeals to me very much, and I include the lighting crew and other technicians as well. As a team we had to find the right tone and proper phrasing, the sounds that fit together.

CNB: You also did costumes and make-up. Was double-tasking common?

EM: I did it once, for *Salome*. Do-it-yourself was common back then, especially in the theater. For many years actors did their own make-up.

CNB: Did Werner design the color schemes for his films, or did you or Alberte propose certain color effects?

EM: All of the above. Camera work opens many options. We started by scouting the locations without settling on anything right away. We surveyed the possibilities. Werner was often extreme in his ambitions and visions. So was Alberte Barsacque, who, for *Malina*, actually had a whole apartment built to the very last detail, first as a miniature, then as a studio set. She chose the colors and created the painted walls, so the atmosphere of the novel could emerge. Keeping in mind what Bachmann and Jelinek wrote, Alberte asked herself what kinds of space does the protagonist traverse? There are not merely four walls, there is patina—in other words, time itself—with a story behind the present, all of which had to be visualized. And there is the crack in the wall that is so uncanny and threatening. Then there were the costumes—a second skin, so to speak. And then there are the rooms.... Malina's room, swallowed up by darkness.

RG: *Malina* has some spectacular features. A very fluid camera, but also those unbelievable close-ups Noll mentioned, and the amazing reflections, which must be your work. Sometimes one has no idea what kind of space one is looking at.

EM: We tried to express interior space, something unknown. The important question was, what is happening with the woman in *Malina*? What happens in the first take? The apartment is a maze, and the woman walks around in circles while the camera circles around her. Consider the dynamics of the highly physical Isabelle Huppert. There was also the question of approach: how do I move within the labyrinthian apartment where nothing is concrete? Glass and mirrors, refractions of light, shadows, doors, walls: Alberte created wonderful options for the camera. The painted walls lacking any discernible corner. There are no two identical shots; every angle is new. We sustained this approach almost 100 percent. There was to be no repetition, only disorientation.

CNB: I would not be able to draw a floor plan of the apartment.

EM: In this story there are no floor plans. What kind of space does the woman from the novel inhabit? At first glance, it seems to be a typical Vienna apartment. But what exactly is that? What transpires, disintegrates here? So we were creating ways to make this inscrutability work in a studio. There is the novel *Malina* by Ingeborg Bachmann, and there is the film *Malina*. Combining them allows something completely new to emerge, freeing up new perspectives the way a film can develop them. Both works correspond with each other. It is great how Werner and Isabelle tackled the story so that it unfolds its own cinematic life.

CNB: What was Jelinek's role, how autonomous was she in writing the screenplay? Was Schroeter involved here? Was the screenplay complete by the time shooting commenced?

EM: I don't know what Werner and Jelinek discussed. I read both the novel and the screenplay, and of course I stuck to the screenplay, but always with Ingeborg Bachmann's work in mind. The enigma that manifests itself in the film through the visuals and the acting can be traced back to the source, the novel.

RG: Does the screenplay already convey a sense of the location, a location that actually does not exist as such, but is totally fragmented?

EM: The novel is all about language. But how could this language re-emerge in the film—which defines itself through space, through real and fictional spaces for people and for the protagonist? That is a mystery.
RG: An open form.
EM: Yes, and it stands on its own. A film is autonomous. What is fidelity? In the cinema, there is a large gap if a fiction film is an interpretation of pre-existing material. In this case, Werner Schroeter interprets Ingeborg Bachmann, via a screenplay by Elfriede Jelinek, who, in turn, had interpreted the novel. And so on. A creative spiral.
CNB: And continued through the editing.
EM: Yes. At the beginning, the outcome was very much in the dark, because the beginning of a project is always abstract, a mere idea. Fortunately, not everything is calculable in advance. Sometimes we will be baffled and shocked: what has happened, what has gone wrong? And sometimes the work comes out deeply satisfying and convincing.
CNB: Was it you who arranged the array of mirrors in *Malina*? They are fantastic and inscrutable. At times, one totally loses orientation.
EM: It's about getting immersed in the potential of *Malina*, about a track waiting to be found. In the end, the protagonist walks mysteriously through the wall. Werner had a scene in mind from Jean Cocteau's *Le Sang d'un poète* (*Blood of a Poet*), a leap into a mirror. We had a long discussion how to solve this problem technically. Werner mentioned that Cocteau back then had poured mercury into a tub. As long as you don't swallow the mercury, there seems to be no mortal danger. Such bizarre ideas represented the kinds of challenge we had to face: to find unusual solutions for the film. Today, everything is done through special effects. Not with Werner, however.
CNB: And how did you solve the problem?
EM: I always had [Lewis Carroll's] *Through the Looking-Glass* in mind—a wall as image and metaphor—for Jelinek, a vision of the woman. This wall begins to crack. Something opens up, rather violently.
RG: At first, the woman uses Scotch tape to mend the crack.
EM: Yes, she tries.
CNB: Then the plaster comes off.
EM: Yes. There's a rupture in the continuum. As if a fish, while leaping into the air, is able to catch a glimpse of the world—for just a moment, since being out of the water is deadly for fish. This anecdote, which has made a big impression on me, is told by the physicist Michio Kaku. He began to study physics after having observed a fish that briefly leaped up into the air and had incredible news to report upon returning to the aquatic realm. Today I would say that the woman in *Malina* is driven by this longing to experience and understand something that is beyond the limits of her continuum.

We are always faced with such challenges. At 3,000 meters we develop trouble breathing; at 8,000 meters we can hardly survive. We are always dealing with this border area between life and death. *Malina*, I think, is about crossing the border. How does the protagonist fare in her continuum? What moves her, what is she looking for? She pursues our existential questions. And she is in search of a trail, a language of love. But her high ambition makes her fall short. That's when we get to Werner. He, too, says: My ambition must proceed. The utmost must be possible in the art that I pursue.

RG: This ambition is the opposite of adapting to the *status quo*. Which also holds for the fish at its moment in the air.

EM: During the three seconds the fish spends in the air, it is possible for it to catch a glimpse of the unusual. Retreat is inevitable, but the fish can now tell its fellow creatures about the experience. This is what the film shows us. Leaving the cinema one can say: "I have seen something incredible."

RG: And how did you solve the problem with the wall?

EM: With a mirror. The fire is essential too. Threatening. If I walk into fire, I burn.

CNB: Looking at the images, one wonders how you could bear the heat.

RG: And your shoe was on fire, too.

EM: True.

CNB: At certain moments, the flames seem unreal, perhaps superimposed. If it had been scorching hot on the set, the door would have caught fire. But in at least one shot the wall is blackened with soot, which makes the fire credible.

EM: There really was a fire, and it was hot. In *The Rose King* the fire was real, too. And the ocean. For Werner, the elemental was essential. Fire, water, air, breathing. Love and passion. Breathing was important in *Poussières d'amour*. We were shooting in a Cistercian abbey near Paris. The courtyard wall had big windows that weren't real windows, but round openings that looked like wells in the sky. I associated these openings with a human throat, and hence with singing, the singing of singers, their voices as instruments. Vocal chords. Breathing. How long can breath be held? Werner and I had spoken about these *motifs* and found images for the film. Why do we see a water-wheel at this point in the film? Because it looked pretty and happened to be there? No. It is its relation to a particular place and to the story that is about to be told. A place where we live and work for a while, that inspires us to experience something about "love's debris." About friendship. The singers were all friends of Werner's. They came with their partners to talk with him about their art. It was all about our commitment to what we did at this unique and beautiful place.

RG: The personal relationships are very perceptible in the films.

CNB: And the passion.

EM: What is friendship? What separates us, and what links us? This is why I think the conversation with Foucault is the key to Werner's work and life. *The Rose King*, Magdalena's last film, is a key as well. She died soon after the shooting was complete. Her friendship with Werner was for life, and she contributed a lot to the film—the script, the idea. There is also a consuming fire in *The Rose King*. And other things, often very basic ones: flowers and animals. Gestures. The unknown. Eroticism. Every key opens something. That's Werner for me. He gives us the keys. Also in his last film, *Nuit de chien*. Despite all differences, this film has a certain affinity with *Malina*. Everyone in it tries to save

Werner Schroeter on the set of *Nuit de chien* (2008)

themselves, get aboard the ship, but no one knows whereto the journey goes. There is fear. The film is visionary. It represents our era. Werner's films are prescient; they let us know that certain events will have consequences.

RG: The film is not overtly political, but more broadly philosophizes about life. In contrast, Rosa von Praunheim's work is explicitly political and tackles specific issues. You've worked with many filmmakers, and have been able to adapt to each one—something not everyone can do. Some cinematographers work with one director exclusively.

EM: My collaboration with Rosa and Werner was certainly shaped by my background and that I became friends with them almost at the same time. Both supported me in my own work. Werner paid for the first prints of my

Super-8 films. Rosa made contacts with the commissioning editor of *Das Kleine Fernsehspiel* at the ZDF, Maya Faber Jansen, who oversaw my first documentaries. And one day Werner said, "I saw your film *Execution*, would you like to do the camera for me? Can you shoot *The Rose King* in 35mm? At that time, I had next to no experience with a 35mm camera.

RG: He had a lot of confidence in you.

EM: Yes! And he saw something in my visual language that he thought would befit his films. This is where we came together.

RG: Was working with him adventurous?

EM: Of course. I approached our collaboration pragmatically, along the lines of "let's see how it goes." I also had good assistants, which is important. My eye has been trained for a long time, mainly through photography. That's where my potential lies. As for cinematography, I had to learn everything step by step.

RG: Of course you had done other things before you worked with Werner Schroeter.

EM: Yes. Photography and documentary films were my training. Photography remains the center of my work.

RG: For *The Rose King* and other films, did you choose any of the locations—Sintra for *The Rose King*, and the abbey in *Poussières d'amour*? There's the abbey with the garden, but also the bleak settings in the film.

EM: That depended. In the case of *Poussières*, the location had been selected before my arrival: an old Cistercian abbey that these days houses a music school. Werner walked me through the rooms and I kept taking Polaroids, from the hip, so to speak, without having time to engage with the multiple layers and nuances of the place. Only afterwards, when I examined the Polaroids, I detected interesting colors and shades generated by the light. I tried to reproduce these effects when I did the lighting.

In the course of this I actually photographed a ghost. I had put the Polaroid into my bag without really looking at it until later. In the library there was a big Baroque book stand with latticed book cases, all very colorful. And in the background there was someone sitting on a bench. I hadn't noticed the white-robed figure when I took the picture. It is a very mysterious image. Gradually I realized I had photographed a resident ghost, a Cistercian monk—they are dressed in white. Years later, in his final months, I gave the Polaroid to Werner. He carried it with him, and included it in his photo exhibition. He told the visitors that the Cistercian monk was his ghost, who constantly followed him. There is something intense but also mysterious about scouting locations for a film about passion, love, and friendship.

RG: Was it Werner Schroeter who found the abbey?

EM: I don't know. The producers tend to make suggestions, they know the locale. For this film it was very important to give musicians a space to play—the pianist Elisabeth Cooper needed a grand piano. We were only allowed to film in certain rooms, but in order to create long shots, I opened doors to other rooms we were not allowed to photograph, we had not paid for them. But I felt we should be allowed to look through the doors.

RG: Where did you shoot the scene with the

nude young man on horseback? Was it on the premises of the abbey?

EM: Nearby there is a riding hall. Werner wanted the young man to ride in a circle in the arena. But the owner didn't allow it because he felt that one should not sit on a horse in the nude. There was supposedly something shameful and debasing about it, I'm not exactly sure what, but in any case, it was not to be. I already saw the problem coming, so I instructed my assistant to stand by with another cartridge.

RG: You had already finished filming the scene?

EM: We had filmed the rehearsal. The owner came stomping in, angry that his holy hall was defiled by the naked man, and screamed, "Material!" We gave him a cartridge, but not the one we had used.

RG: There is also the mysterious scene with the naked man in the large wheel.

EM: We shot that in Düsseldorf. We lit the scene with car headlights. We had run out of money, and we only had ten or eleven days for the whole shoot.

For *The Rose King* we looked at houses together. The Portuguese were wonderful, they opened their doors and showed us their impressive, mysterious homes. I really enjoy location scouting. But it becomes a challenge when you are pressured for time, and time was running out because of Magdalena's condition. When a Portuguese house looked usable from the outside, its inside also tended to be good for us; the atmosphere seemed to permeate the walls. Working with Werner meant having four eyes, his and mine. Sometimes I tried to backlight the actors to create plasticity. But he said, "the scene takes place in the forest; there is no light. And as you know, Elfi, my actors shine from within."

RG: And it was your job to put this onto film. But it is true: Magdalena's close-ups in *The Rose King* really shine from within. And her face is an homage to silent cinema, her large eyes and prominent brows.

EM: Call it Expressionism. The face is a projection screen. The body language, the gestures.

RG: As a cinematographer, do you take your time to get acquainted with a face?

EM: When I work in non-fiction film, a face is front and center; there's nothing in between. Shyness in a person is part of his or her expression. As soon as the camera is focused, a face closes up, but after ten minutes the face usually opens up again. Whether and how this happens also depends on the atmosphere of the interview. In a fiction film, actors are usually more comfortable with the camera, they have certain means of control at their disposal. There is potential for a rich dialogue between the camera and the look of the person *vis-à-vis*. These dialogues don't need words. For me, the eyes of an actor are central. My favorite example is Roman Polanski's eyes in *The Tenant*. He plays the main part, and he is capable of creating charisma and empathy. Polanski's gaze creates something that sparks a connection, a direct alertness or attention. To establish a rapport with the actors is one of the most important concerns for a cinematographer.

CNB: Some people seem to think with their eyes; they turn their eyes sideways or upwards while thinking. But it is hard for actors to get this right. Do you always know immediately how you want to light an actor's face?

EM: It depends on the story.

CNB: Yes, but beyond the story. Magdalena's face has a certain shape which has to be taken into account.

EM: The standard setting for the camera is at eye level. Fine. But every face is uniquely proportioned, which always fascinates me. What do I read into a face? How does it maintain its authenticity? The camera follows and interprets a story. Its function in a non-fiction film differs from that in a fiction film. A person in front of a camera reacts to the camera. With this reaction I conduct an imaginary "dialogue," I see how the intensity of the person across from me emerges through and for the camera. I see beauty, pain, joy, all kinds of expression, changing every second. Plus the body and its gestures. It is through colors, light, and shadow that I experience the face as a cinematic image. Magdalena's face is an unusual image, an image that speaks to us.

RG: Did you shoot anything Werner didn't like, so it had to be reshot?

EM: Not with Werner. Nor with Rosa. I may sometimes be uncertain myself, thinking there might be another way of filming a scene. But reshooting is always a problem. I *do* want things to go right the first time.

RG: We should talk about *Deux*, the last film you made with Schroeter.

EM: Another re-encounter with friends. The story is incredible. I have no idea how the script evolved, but all of a sudden it was there, this story of twins, and then with Isabelle Huppert. Mysteriously, she plays both twins. It is nowadays hard to get hold of the film, someone should try to bring it back into distribution. The shoot took place in Lisbon and Paris, and parts in Sintra, which has a special microclimate, an atmosphere uniquely suited to the surrealness of the story. It is all rather labyrinthian. And then there is the double figure of the sisters, two identities that couldn't be more different from each other, full of mysteries, as mysterious as *Malina*.

RG: Was it difficult to photograph Isabelle Huppert playing both characters?

EM: No, she acted completely schizophrenic. But you can also regard the two personalities she plays as one. Depending on what key you insert, a new side of the story gets unlocked. Like in *Persona* by Ingmar Bergman. This kind of double character is very contemporary, the essence of human discord. The film works like an ambiguous image. Its reversibility allows the sisters' lives to mirror each other, which is more than uncanny. *Deux* is a very personal film about the tragedy of love.

CNB: I've noticed that in his early films Schroeter often kept the actors' first names for the parts they played. What was the meaning of this, and why did he stop doing it?

EM: I think one of the reasons was the pleasure he took in friendship and the language of friendship. On the one hand, there is the fictional story that needs to be taken care of. On the other hand, there are the friends, personal relationships, love, work, the intimacy one enjoys.

CNB: Fictionalization and de-fictionalization in one and the same figure.

EM: Plus a little bit of trash, meaning *joie de vivre* and a little drama. To disregard conventions, to express one's assertion of a certain way of life, to withstand discrimination. And there is theatricality, the world of homosexuality, the fantastic, a certain aesthetics of role-play, of transformation. Werner and Rosa had different views as to how to tackle homosexuality. Rosa was aggressively political and demanded a free gay life in society. But Werner also made a socially conscious film with *Palermo or Wolfsburg*. In 1979, it was way ahead of its time. Or *Nel regno di Napoli*—a lot of death and a lot of life. And always an eye on diverse *milieux*. Thomas Mauch did the camera.

RG: *Palermo or Wolfsburg* is Werner's most overtly political film. Parts are almost semi-documentary.

EM: At the same time, Werner always saw himself committed to beauty, no matter how he interpreted it or visualized it. *Diese Nacht* is a meditation on politics. Juan Carlos Onetti's novel has a political agenda. Werner rearticulates Onetti's ideas. There is a plague, a shop, a tyrant, and the concrete apparatus of the enemy.

Werner knew a lot about dramatic potential, whether in the theater, in opera and music, or in everyday life. He had an incredibly rich life, but also one filled with drama. How many friends did he see die? But he drew from that for his work. It was his way of mourning. And using art as a means of survival means resisting conformity.

Passion According to Werner Schroeter[1]

MICHEL FOUCAULT: Watching *The Death of Maria Malibran* and *Willow Springs*, it struck me that these films are not about Love, but about Passion.

WERNER SCHROETER: *Willow Springs* is based on the idea of an obsession of dependence linking four characters, with none of them knowing the exact reasons for the dependence. For example, Ila von Hasperg, who plays the role of the servant and the maid, doesn't know why she's the victim of a relationship of dependence with Magdalena. I see it as an obsession.

FOUCAULT: Except for a single word, I think we're talking about the same thing. First, one can't say that these two women love each other. Nor is it love in *Maria Malibran*. What is passion? It's a state, something that falls on you out of the blue, that takes hold of you, that grips you for no reason, that has no origin. One doesn't know where it comes from. Passion arrives like that, a state that is always mobile but never moves toward a given point. There are strong and weak moments, moments when it becomes incandescent. It floats, it evens out. It's a kind of unstable time that is pursued for obscure reasons, perhaps through inertia. In the extreme, it tries to maintain itself and to disappear. Passion gives itself all the conditions necessary to continue, and, at the same time, it destroys itself. In a state of passion one is not blind, one is simply not oneself. To be oneself no longer makes sense. One sees things differently.

In a state of passion there is also a quality of pleasure-pain that is very different from what one can find in desire or in what is called sadism and masochism. I see no sadistic or masochistic relationship between the women, whereas there exists a completely indissociable state of pleasure-pain. These are not two qualities that are mixed together, but a single and same quality. In each one of the characters, there is a great suffering. One cannot say that one of them makes the other suffer. It's three types of permanent suffering, which, at the same time, are entirely willed, for there is no necessity there that they be present.

These women have been entwined in a state of suffering that links them, and from which they don't succeed in detaching themselves even though they do everything to liberate themselves from it. All that is different from

1 Originally published in Gérard Courant, ed., *Werner Schroeter* (Paris: Goethe-Institut/Cinémathèque Française, 1982). First English-language edition: Michel Foucault, ed. Sylvère Lotringer, *Foucault Live: Interviews, 1961–1984*, trans. Lysa Hochroth and John Johnston (New York: Semiotext(e), 1989, 1996), pp. 313–321. [Discussion originally recorded by Gérard Courant in Paris on December 3, 1981.]

Werner Schroeter on the set of *Palermo oder Wolfsburg* (1980)

love. In love, there is, in some way or another, a beloved, whereas passion circulates between partners.

SCHROETER: Love is less active than passion.

FOUCAULT: The state of passion is a missed state among different partners.

SCHROETER: Love is a state of grace, of distance. In a discussion several hours ago with Ingrid Caven, she was saying that love is an egotistical feeling because it doesn't consider the partner.

FOUCAULT: One can perfectly well love without being loved in return. It's an affair of solitude. For that reason, love is always full of solicitations toward the other. That's its weakness, for it always demands something of the other, whereas in a state of passion among two or three people it's something that allows intense communication.

SCHROETER: Which means that passion contains in itself a great communicative force, whereas love is an isolated state. I find it very depressing to know that love is a creation and interior invention.

FOUCAULT: Love can become passion, that is to say, the kind of state we have talked about.

SCHROETER: And therefore this suffering.

FOUCAULT: This state of mutual reciprocal suffering—it truly is communication. It seems to me what happens between these women. Their faces and bodies are not traversed by desire, but by passion.

SCHROETER: In a discussion several years ago someone said to me that *Willow Springs* was like Albert Camus's *Malentendu*.

FOUCAULT: I was thinking that your film came from Camus's book. It's the old story that one finds in many narratives of European literature, about the red auberge run by women who kill travelers wandering into their domain. Camus used it in his novel.

SCHROETER: I didn't know the story when I was shooting *Willow Springs*. Later, when I read Camus's book, I realized that what mattered in the narrative was the mother / son relationship. The *auberge* was run by a mother and sister who were waiting for the son. When the son returns, the mother and sister kill him because they don't recognize him.

Willow Springs was instigated by Christine Kaufmann, who had just been working with me on the *mise-en-scène* for Gotthold Ephraim Lessing's *Emilia Galotti*. One day, Tony Curtis, her ex-husband, came to take their two children, whom she had cared for for five years. We didn't have the money to fight this irresponsible husband. At that moment I had proposed a small-budget film for German television entitled *The Death of Marilyn Monroe*. I left for America with Christine Kaufmann, Magdalena Montezuma, and Ila von Hasperg, for I had the idea, with Christine, of getting the kids back. It was my first time in Los Angeles and California. The idea for *Willow Springs* came during my sessions with the lawyers, and while discovering the area. In Germany, certain people saw in it a critique of the fear of homosexuals. In the end we found ourselves in the same situation as the protagonists of the film. We were in a little hotel six miles from Willow Springs and completely cut off.

FOUCAULT: Why are the three women living together?

SCHROETER: What I want to say first is that we were together. *Willow Springs* is the reflection of the situation we were living and that I had felt while working for several years with the three women, Magdalena, Ila, and Christine. In a poetic way, Ila put her ugliness up front, Christine was coldly beautiful and very friendly, and the third, Magdalena, very depressive and dominant. The situation had been created in a very unfavorable political space, with fascists living all around. The town was run by an American Nazi. A really scary place....

Do you have a tendency for passion or love?

FOUCAULT: Passion.

SCHROETER: The conflict between love and passion is the subject of all my plays. Love is a lost force, a force that must lose itself immediately because it is never reciprocal. It is always suffering, total nihilism, like life and death. The authors I love are all suicides: Kleist, Hölderlin—who is someone I think I understand, but outside the literary context....

Ever since childhood I've known I had to work, not because I was told it was necessary—I was too anarchistic and turbulent to believe that—but because I knew that there were so few possibilities to communicate in life that it was necessary to profit from work to express oneself. In fact, to work is to create. I knew a very creative prostitute whose behavior, with her clientele, was very artistic and socially creative. It's my dream. When I don't attain this state of passion, I work....

What about your life?

FOUCAULT: Very wise.

SCHROETER: Can you speak about your passion?

FOUCAULT: I lived for eighteen years in a state of passion in relation to someone, for someone. Perhaps at a certain moment this passion took a turn toward love. In truth, it's a matter of passion between the two of us, a permanent state with no other reason to end than itself, which passes through me, and in which I am fully invested. I believe there isn't a single thing in the world, nothing whatever, that would stop me when it's a question of finding him again, of speaking to him.

SCHROETER: What differences have you noticed between a passion lived by a man and a passion lived by a woman?

FOUCAULT: I would tend to say that it's not possible to know if it's stronger among homosexuals, in this state of communication without transparency that is passion, when one doesn't know what the other's pleasure is, what the other is, what is happening with the other.

SCHROETER: I have my passion in Italy. It's a passion not definable in exclusively sexual terms. It's a boy who has his friends, who has his lovers. It's someone who also, I believe, has a passion for me. That would be too beautiful if true! I have been saying it since my childhood: for me it's an advantage to be a homosexual because it's beautiful.

FOUCAULT: We have objective proof that homosexuality is more interesting than heterosexuality: there are a considerable number of heterosexuals who would like to become homosexuals but very few homosexuals who really feel like becoming heterosexuals. It's like passing from East Germany to West Germany. We could love a woman, have an intense relationship with a woman, perhaps more intense than with a boy, but never feel like becoming heterosexuals.

SCHROETER: My great friend Rosa von Praunheim, who has made many films on the subject of homosexuality, said to me one day, "You're an unbearable coward," because I refused to sign a petition against the repression of homosexuals. In response to a press campaign launched by the magazine *Der Stern*, homosexuals had to declare their coming out. To Rosa I replied: "I will gladly sign your petition, but I cannot write something against the repression of homosexuals, for if there is one thing for which I have never suffered in my life, it is my homosexuality." As I was already much loved by women, they were even more attentive to me personally since they knew that I was homosexual.

Perhaps I filmed *Willow Springs* out of guilt, for I have made a lot of films and plays with women. I see very clearly the difference between my passion for a woman like Magdalena Montezuma, with whom I will maintain a deep friendship until the end of my days, and my passion for my Italian friend. Perhaps psychologically—and I know nothing about psychology—it's anxiety with men and guilt with women. My motivation is quite strange. I can't define it. In Prague, for my film *Tag der Idioten*, I worked with thirty women from among all those with whom I have collaborated since I was thirteen years old.

FOUCAULT: Could you say why?

SCHROETER: No.

FOUCAULT: One of the most striking things about your film is that one knows nothing about what goes on among the women, about the nature of these little worlds, and yet, at the same time, there is a kind of clarity about the facts.

SCHROETER: I can't define the cause of my feelings. For example, when I saw this Italian friend again, it put me in a state of passion.

FOUCAULT: Consider this example. When I see a film by Bergman, who is equally a film-maker obsessed by women and the love between women, I'm bored. Bergman bores me because I think he wants to try to see what goes on between women. Whereas in your work there is a kind of immediate evidence which doesn't try to say what is happening and what allows one not to even raise the question. And your way of exiting altogether from psychological film seems fruitful to me. At that exact moment one sees bodies, faces, lips, eyes. You make them evidence of passion.

SCHROETER: Psychology doesn't interest me. I don't believe in it.

FOUCAULT: We have to go back to what you were saying a little while ago about creativity. One is lost in life, in what one writes, in the film one makes, precisely when one wants to investigate the nature of the identity of something. At that exact point one "fails," for one enters into classifications. The problem is to create precisely something that happens between ideas, and to which one can't give a name. At every instant, therefore, it's trying to give a coloration, a form and intensity to something that never says what it is. That's the art of living. The art of living is to eliminate psychology, to create, with oneself and others, individualities, beings, relations, unnameable qualities. If one fails to do that in one's life it isn't worth living. I don't distinguish between people who make of their existence a work and those who make a work during their existence. An existence can be a perfect and sublime work. That's something the Greeks understood, whereas we have completely forgotten it, above all since the Renaissance.

SCHROETER: It's the system of psychological terror. The cinema is made up solely of psychological drama, of films of psychological terror. I have no fear of death. It is perhaps arrogant to say it, but it's the truth. Ten years ago, I was afraid of death. To look death in the face is an anarchist feeling dangerous to established society, which depends on terror and fear.

FOUCAULT: One of the things that has preoccupied me for some time is the realization how difficult it is to kill oneself. Let's consider the small number of means of suicide we have available, each one more disgusting than the others: gas is dangerous for the neighbors, hanging is disagreeable for the maid who discovers the body the next morning, throwing oneself out the window dirties the sidewalk. Moreover, suicide is considered in the most negative way possible by society. Not only are we told that it's not good to kill ourselves but also that if someone commits suicide it's because things were going badly.

SCHROETER: It's strange, what you are saying, because I had a discussion with my friend Alberte Barsacq, the clothes-designer for my films and plays, about two friends who committed suicide not long ago. I don't understand how somebody very depressed would have the strength to commit suicide. I could kill myself only in a state of grace or extreme pleasure, but above all not in a state of depression.

GÉRARD COURANT: The thing that surprised some people about the suicide of Jean Eustache[2] is that in the days before his suicide he was feeling better.

FOUCAULT: I'm sure that Jean Eustache killed himself when he was in good shape. People don't understand it because he was feeling well. Actually, it's something one can't admit. I am a partisan of a true cultural combat for re-instructing people that there is no conduct more beautiful, that merits more reflection with as much attention, than suicide. One should work on one's suicide all one's life.

SCHROETER: Do you know Amery, the German writer who wrote a book several years ago about suicide, and who proposed something like the same ideas? Afterwards, he killed himself.

We live in a system that functions on guilt. Consider sickness. I lived in Africa and India, where people feel no compunction about exhibiting their sickness to society. Even the lepers exhibit themselves. In our Western society the moment one is sick, one must be afraid, hide oneself, and no longer live. It would be ridiculous if sickness were not a part of life. I have a completely schizoid relationship with psychology. If I pick up my lighter and a cigarette, it's a banal act. The important thing is the

2 Jean Eustache, a French filmmaker, who made *La Maman et la putain* (*The Mother and the Whore*, 1973), committed suicide on November 4, 1981. [Ed.]

gesture. It's what gives me my dignity. Knowing that my mother smoked too much when I was five years old has no bearing on knowledge about my own personality.

FOUCAULT: It's one of the fundamental choices that one has not in relation to Western societies. We have been taught throughout the 20th century that one can do nothing if one knows nothing about oneself. The truth about oneself is a condition of existence, whereas you have societies where one could perfectly imagine that there is no attempt at all to regulate the question of what one is, and where it makes no sense, while the important thing is: what is the art of putting into a work what one does, for being what one is. An art of the self which would be the complete contrary of oneself. To make of one's being an object of art, that's what is worth the effort.

SCHROETER: I recall the phrase from your book *The Order of Things* that I love very much: "If these arrangements [of the episteme] were to disappear..., then it would be a good bet that man would be effaced, like a face drawn in sand at the edge of the sea." I have never been angry with anyone. I do not understand how one can accept the *bourgeois* system of psychology which ceaselessly plays one individual against another. I can easily argue with someone and the next day return to normal relations. (I'm not talking about a relationship of love or passion.) Each day I am another. Psychology, for me, is a mystery. Freud constructed a very dangerous system above our heads, one that all Western society can use.

I'd like to cite a revealing example of a harmless act that would be negatively interpreted in a Freudian sense. When I returned from America after the shooting of *Willow Springs*, I was very tired and my mother wanted to wash me, because it gave her pleasure. At a certain moment I began to pee in the bathtub. Imagine the situation: a mother of sixty years and her son of twenty-seven. I laughed a lot. (In any case, I always pee in the bathtub.) Why not pee? It's the only thing to say. Ours is not an incestuous relationship; we're like buddies; I've never imagined an erotic relationship with my mother. I see no problem there unless I reduce the action to a *bourgeois* psychological context.

Novalis wrote a poem that I love: *Night Elegies*. He explains why he prefers the night to the day. That's German Romanticism....

When I shot *Lohengrin* three years ago in Kassel, they asked me about my idea of *mise-en-scène*. My only response was to say that the music of *Lohengrin* is extremely beautiful, that it's a romantic music that can be forced because Wagner already had the consciousness of the industrial century. I explained that I would not give them the pleasure of playing with them the little devil who denounces Wagner's work and music, for I found it so overcharged with interpretations, above all ideological, that I decided to give it a rather childish representation in a very primitive *mise-en-scène* like the Marionette theater. The sky was studded with a thousand bright stars above a golden pyramid and sparkling costumes. I worked almost alone with the orchestra director to make the music as beautiful as possible. My left-wing friends from Berlin asked me how I could do Wagner

Candy Darling and Werner Schroeter on the set of *Der Tod der Maria Malibran* (1972)

in this way. I responded that I refuse to do Wagner like Patrice Chéreau, who uses evening gowns and industrial machines in the *Ring of the Nibelungen* in order to denounce Wagner, to make of him a precursor of the Third Reich.

FOUCAULT: I don't think Chéreau would have wanted to do as you say.[3] What seemed to me strong in Chéreau's work is not that because he makes industrial visions appear that he is denouncing something. To say that there are elements of that reality present in Wagner is not a simple critique and denunciation of the type: "Look at Wagner's reality, it's *bourgeois* society."

SCHROETER: I always work with the ambience. The Kassel theater where I did the *mise-en-scène* has a good musical ambience. I made the *mise-en-scène* a function of the actors and singers. If there is an enormous singer in the cast, like the

3 See Michel Foucault, "19th Century Imaginations," in Sylvère Lotringer, ed., *The German Issue*, *Semiotext(e)* (New York), no. 11 (1982). [Ed.]

one Elsa played, I don't try to camouflage her with a black shadow and white clothing. I conceived the *mise-en-scène* in such a way that when Elsa, in the first act, is accused of having assassinated Godefroi and she recounts her visions, I show them as collective visions, as if Elsa with vision made up part of a loving, passionate collective. At the end, when Lohengrin is discovered as a masculine being, one realizes that he is someone real, and it's no longer a question of a collective vision. At that moment Elsa commits suicide, and Ortrude, who represents the old culture, triumphs. For me, Ortrude is the positive passionate woman of the piece.

It's a music that one has to "attack" naïvely. I very much like the way Boulez directs Wagner, but it's not at all the way I see Wagner's music. His interpreters have shamefully missed his genius ... and finally they miss everything. Wagner was like everyone else, with a lot of talent and a great idea, to be sure. One should not begin by respecting him, although one should respect the quality of the work, but the genius that is behind it. The music of *Lohengrin* is very musical, like Viennese music. That's what I tried to show in the *mise-en-scène*, for I didn't like either the luxuriousness or Bayreuth.

FOUCAULT: When you shot *Maria Malibran*, did you think first about the music?

SCHROETER: Before anything else, I was thinking about suicide, about the people I loved and with whom I experienced passion, like Maria Callas, whom I've always loved. *The Death of Maria Malibran* also came into existence as a result of reading a Spanish book on Maria Malibran, a text on Janis Joplin's death, and another on Jimi Hendrix's death—people I admired enormously.

Maria Callas was the erotic vision of my childhood. At fourteen, in my erotic dreams, I imagined her pissing while I watched her. This was always outside the image of Maria Callas, for whom I felt friendliness and respect. She was *the* erotic woman. Maria Callas was a total passion. Oddly, she never frightened me. I remember a discussion I had with her in Paris in 1976, when she told me that the only people she knew were afraid of her. I asked her: "How is it possible to be afraid of you?" She had an exceptional gentleness, like a little American Greek girl. At fifty she was the same thing. I asked her if she wanted an article published in *France-Soir*, "Maria Callas looking for a man"? You would see a hundred men turn up! She laughed. People were so afraid of her that they didn't come to see her. She lived a very solitary life. Which was too bad, since, her genius apart, she possessed a sympathy and fabulous gentleness.

One thing fascinates me, which I find unimaginable. For the twelve years I have worked with the same dozen people, within this group there has been practically no interest on the part of one member for another. There is no deep interest between Magdalena Montezuma and Christine Kaufmann, between Christine and Ingrid Caven, etc. Between Magdalena and Ingrid, who love and admire one another, there is a vital interest, but it's the exception. If there were no director among them there would be no vital communication.

Translated by John Johnston

Appendix

Filmography Werner Schroeter

Researched and compiled by Stefan Drössler

This filmography is divided into three sections. The first lists all existing films by Werner Schroeter; the second, studies, tests, fragments, lost films, and unfilmed projects; and the third, films by others in which Schroeter appears.

The credits were taken from the prints and video copies in the Werner Schroeter Collection at Filmmuseum München. Since most of the films shot before 1978 do not have titles with credits or do not specify the functions of the named persons, the sources for additional information were conversations with Werner Schroeter or other people involved in their production.

Werner Schroeter's 8mm films were first shown at private screenings; it is thus impossible to specify premiere dates. The running times of the 16mm and 35mm films are calculated based on a projection speed of 25 frames per second, as they were shown on television. The term "separate sound" is used for entries about films for which Schroeter did not record sound on the filmstrip but on a separate sound carrier. His choice was usually music cassettes or consumer tapes.

KEY

DIR = director
ASST DIR = assistant director
SC = writer
PH = photography
ED = editor
MUS = music (only original score)
SD REC = sound recordist/recording
DES = set design, art direction
COST = costumes
CAST = cast
PROD = producer
LINE PROD = line producer
CO-PROD = co-producer
P.C. = production company
LANG = original language
PREMIERE = première
SD = sound

I. Films by Werner Schroeter

1967

VERONA / also known as **ZWEI KATZEN**
DIR, PROD, SC, PH, ED: Werner Schroeter – 8mm, 12 min. (18 fps), silent, color, 1.37:1

1968

SALOME'S DANCE / also known as **CARLA SALOME**
DIR, PROD, PH: Werner Schroeter – **CAST:** Carla Aulaulu – 8mm, 5 min. (18 fps), silent, color, 1.37:1

MAGDALENA
DIR, PROD, PH: Werner Schroeter – **CAST:** Magdalena Montezuma – 8mm, 2 min. (18 fps), silent, black & white, 1.37:1

ICA VILANDER
DIR, PROD, PH: Werner Schroeter – **CAST:** Ica Vilander – 8mm, 5 min. (18 fps), silent, black & white, 1.37:1

VERNER
DIR, PROD, PH: Werner Schroeter – 8mm, 5 min. (18 fps), silent, black & white, 1.37:1 – **LANG:** no text

CARLA / also known as **CARLA SINGT CALLAS**
DIR, PROD, PH: Werner Schroeter – **CAST:** Carla Aulaulu, Rosa von Praunheim – 8mm, 5 min. (18 fps), sd, color, 1.37:1 – **LANG:** no text and no dialogue

HOME MOVIE
DIR, PROD, PH: Werner Schroeter – **CAST:** Werner Schroeter, Daniel Schmid, Carla Aulaulu, Elfi Mikesch, Vassiliev – 8mm, 4 min. (18 fps), silent, color, 1.37:1 – **LANG:** no text

CALLAS WALKING LUCIA
DIR, PROD, SC, PH, ED: Werner Schroeter – 8mm, 3 min. (18 fps), silent, black & white, 1.37:1 – **LANG:** no text

MARIA CALLAS PORTRÄT / also known as **CALLAS COMMERCIAL**
DIR, PROD, SC, PH, ED: Werner Schroeter – 8mm, 13 min. (20 fps), separate sound, black & white + color, 1.37:1 – **LANG:** German

MONA LISA
DIR, PROD, SC, PH, ED: Werner Schroeter – 8mm, 32 min. (20 fps), separate sound, black & white + color, 1.37:1 – **LANG:** songs in Italian and German

MARIA CALLAS SINGT 1957 REZITATIV UND ARIE DER ELVIRA AUS *ERNANI* 1844 VON GIUSEPPE VERDI (CALLAS I, II, III, IV)
DIR, PROD, SC, PH, ED: Werner Schroeter – **CAST:** Werner Schroeter – 8mm, 11 min. (20 fps), separate sound, black & white, 1.37:1 – **LANG:** German

LA MORTE D'ISOTTA
DIR, PROD, SC, PH, ED: Werner Schroeter, using Lautréamont's "Les Chants de Maldoror" – **CAST:** Rita Bauer, Knut Koch, Werner Schroeter, Joachim Bauer, Truùla Bartek – 8mm, 37 min. (22 fps), separate sound, color, 1.37:1 – **LANG:** German

HIMMEL HOCH
DIR, PROD, SC, PH, ED: Werner Schroeter – **CAST:** Steven Adamczewski, Rita Bauer, Joachim Bauer – 8mm, 10 min. (18 fps), separate sound, black & white, 1.37:1 – **LANG:** no text and no dialogue

PAULA – "JE REVIENS"
DIR, PROD, SC, PH, ED: Werner Schroeter – **CAST:** Heidi Lorenzo, Rita Bauer, Suzanne Sheed, Truùla Bartek, Knut Koch, Werner Schroeter – 8mm, 31 min. (20 fps), separate sound, color, 1.37:1 – **LANG:** no text – **PREMIERE:** November 20, 1969 (Die Maininger, Frankfurt am Main)

AGGRESSION
DIR, PROD, SC, PH, ED: Werner Schroeter – **CAST:** Heidi Lorenzo, Knut Koch – 16mm, 22 min., separate sound, black & white, 1.37:1 – **LANG:** German

NEURASIA
DIR, PROD, SC, PH, ED: Werner Schroeter – **ASST DIR:** Rosa von Praunheim – **CAST:** Carla Aulaulu, Magdalena Montezuma, Rita Bauer, Steven Adamczewski – 16mm, 37 min., sd, black & white, 1.37:1 – **LANG:** no text – **PREMIERE:** December 27, 1968 (Das andere Kino, Munich)

1969

ARGILA

DIR, PROD, SC, PH, ED: Werner Schroeter – **ASST DIR:** Rosa von Praunheim – **CAST:** Gisela Trowe, Magdalena Montezuma, Carla Aulaulu, Sigurd Salto – 16mm double projection, 33 min., separate sd, color + black & white, 2.66:1 – **LANG:** German, songs in English, Italian, and German – **PREMIERE:** March 7, 1969 (Hamburger Filmschau)

EIKA KATAPPA

DIR, SC, ED: Werner Schroeter – **ASST DIR:** Magdalena Montezuma – **PH:** Werner Schroeter, Robert van Ackeren (Part 8, "für Violetta") – **CAST:** Gisela Trowe, Carla Aulaulu, Magdalena Montezuma, Knut Koch, Alix von Buchen, Rosy-Rosy, Rita Bauer, Joachim Bauer, René Schönberger – 16mm, 143 min., sd, color, 1.37:1 – **LANG:** no dialogue, only music (songs in German, Italian, English) – **PREMIERE:** October 10, 1969 (Internationale Filmwoche Mannheim)

1970

DER BOMBERPILOT

DIR, SC, PH, ED: Werner Schroeter – **ASST DIR:** Daniel Schmid – **CAST:** Carla Aulaulu, Mascha Rabben, Magdalena Montezuma, Suzanne Sheed, Werner Schroeter, Daniel Schmid – **PROD:** Werner Schroeter, for ZDF – 16mm, 65 min., sd, color, 1.37:1 – **LANG:** German – **PREMIERE:** November 3, 1970 (ZDF)
Working title: DREI MÄDCHEN

1971

SALOME

DIR, SC: Werner Schroeter, based on the play by Oscar Wilde – **ASST DIR:** Harry Baer – **PH:** Robert van Ackeren – **ED:** Ila von Hasperg – **COST:** Elfi Mikesch – **CAST:** Mascha Elm-Rabben (*Salome*), Magdalena Montezuma (*Herodes*), Ellen Umlauf (*Herodias*), Thomas von Keyserling (*Jochanaan*), René Schönberger (*Narraboth*), Joachim Paede (*Page*) – **LINE PROD:** Wolfgang von Fumetti – **P.C.:** Ifage Filmproduktion GmbH, for ZDF – 16mm, 81 min., sd, color, 1.37:1 – **LANG:** German – **PREMIERE:** June 11, 1971 (ZDF)

MACBETH

DIR, SC: Werner Schroeter, based on the play by William Shakespeare and opera by Giuseppe Verdi – **ASST DIR:** Mascha Elm-Rabben – **PH:** Horst Thürling, Dieter Gasper, Rolf Schilling, Frank Reich – **ED:** Brigitte Siara – **COST:** Magdalena Montezuma – **DES:** Rainer Schöne – **MUS:** Horst Franke – **SD REC:** Kurt Lange – **CAST:** Annette Tirier, Susi, Stefan von Haugk, Michael Bolze, Sigurd Salto, Ingrid Seidenfaden, Suzanne Sheed, Christine Rech, Magdalena Montezuma – **P.C.:** Hessischer Rundfunk – video, 61 min., color, sd, 1.37:1 – **LANG:** German – **PREMIERE:** December 18, 1971 (HR III)

1972

DER TOD DER MARIA MALIBRAN

DIR, SC, PH: Werner Schroeter – **ASST DIR:** Ila von Hasperg – **ED:** Werner Schroeter, Ila von Hasperg – **CAST:** Magdalena Montezuma, Christine Kaufmann, Candy Darling, Manuela Riva, Ingrid Caven, Annette Tirier, Einar Hanfstaeng, Joachim Bauer, Gabor Lessner – **PROD:** Werner Schroeter, for ZDF – 16mm, 104 min., sd, color + black & white, 1.37:1 – **LANG:** German – **PREMIERE:** March 7, 1972 (ZDF)
English title: THE DEATH OF MARIA MALIBRAN

1973

WILLOW SPRINGS

DIR, SC, PH, SD: Werner Schroeter – **ED:** Werner Schroeter, Ila von Hasperg – **COST:** Anna Spaghetti, Daisy, Goodwill – **CAST:** Magdalena Montezuma, Christine Kaufmann, Ila von Hasperg, Michael O'Daniels – **PROD:** Werner Schroeter, for ZDF – 16mm, 78 min., sd, color, 1.37:1 – **LANG:** English, German – **PREMIERE:** April 3, 1973 (ZDF)
Working title: DER TRAUM DER MARILYN MONROE

1974

DER SCHWARZE ENGEL

DIR, SC, PH, SD REC: Werner Schroeter – **ASST DIR:** Paul Helfer – **COST:** Luis Urquidi – **ED:** Werner Schroeter, Christine Leyrer – **CAST:** Magdalena Montezuma, Ellen Umlauf, Carlos da Muna – **PROD:** Werner Schroeter, for ZDF – 16mm, 71 min., sd, color, 1.37:1 – **LANG:** German, English, Spanish – **PREMIERE:** May 7, 1974 (ZDF)
English title: THE BLACK ANGEL

1975

JOHANNAS TRAUM

DIR, PROD, SC, PH, SD REC: Werner Schroeter – **CAST:** Magdalena Montezuma, Christine Kaufmann, Candy Darling – 16mm, 19 min., sd, color, 1.37:1 – **LANG:** German

1976

LES FLOCONS D'OR

DIR, PH, DES: Werner Schroeter – **SC:** Werner Schroeter, Carlos Clarens – **ASST DIR:** Rainer Will, Cheryl Carlesino – **MUS:** Werner Schroeter, Peter Van Hornbeck, Andréa Ferréol – **ED:** Werner Schroeter, Ila von Hasperg, Cécile Decugis – **CAST:** Magdalena Montezuma, Ellen Umlauf, Christine Kaufmann, Irena Staup, Bulle Ogier, Andréa Ferréol, Ila von Hasperg, Isolde Barth, Udo Kier, Carlos Clarens, Rainer Will, Klaus Prochyzycha – **LINE PROD:** Lena Schroeter – **PROD:** Werner Schroeter, for ZDF / Les Films du Losange / I.N.A. (Institut National de l'Audiovisuel) – 16mm, 160 min., sd, color + black & white, 1.37:1 – **LANG:** Spanish, French, German – **PREMIERE:** May 20, 1976 (ZDF)
English titles: GOLDEN FLAKES; GOLDFLAKES

1978

NEL REGNO DI NAPOLI

DIR: Werner Schroeter – **ASST DIR:** Gerardo D'Andrea – **SC:** Werner Schroeter, Wolf Wondratschek, Gerardo D'Andrea – **PH:** Thomas Mauch – **ED:** Werner Schroeter, Ursula West-Messinger – **MUS:** Roberto Pregadio – **SD REC:** Tommaso Quattrini – **DES:** Franco Calabrese – **COST:** Alberte Barsacq – **CAST:** Liana Trouche, Antonio Orlando, Renata Zamengo, Dino Melé, Margareth Clementi, Raúl Gimenez, Cristina Donadio, Ida Di Benedetto, Patricio Rispo, Maria Antonietta Riegel, Gerardo D'Andrea, Laura Sodano, Tiziana Ambretti, Romeo Ciro, Anna Segnini, Percy Hogan – **LINE PROD:** Michelangelo Ciafre, Peter Berling – **PROD:** Dieter Geissler Filmproduktion / Peter Berling Cinematografica / Werner Schroeter, for ZDF – Super-16mm blow-up to 35mm, 131 min., sd, color, 1.66:1 – **LANG:** Italian – **PREMIERE:** May 24,1978 (Quinzaine des Réalisateurs, Cannes)
English title: THE KINGDOM OF NAPLES

1980

PALERMO ODER WOLFSBURG

DIR: Werner Schroeter – **ASST DIR:** Horatio Torrini, Ursula West – **SC:** Werner Schroeter, Giuseppe Fava, Orazio Torrisi – **PH:** Thomas Mauch – **ED:** Ursula West, Werner Schroeter – **DES:** Roberto Laganá, Edwin Wengobowski – **COST:** Magdalena Montezuma, Alberte Barsacq – **SD REC:** Heiko von Swieykowski – **CAST:** Nicola Zarbo, Ida di Benedetto, Magdalena Montezuma, Brigitte Tilg, Gisela Hahn, Otto Sander, Johannes Wacker, Calogero Arancio, Antonio Orlando, Cavaliere Comparato, Padre Pace, Salvatore di Vincenzo, Roberto Laganá, Domenico Salerno, Giovanni Marongin, Rosa Maria Cani, Giuseppe Morganá, Pino Deiana, Harry Baer, Ula Stöckl, Tamara Kafka, Josef Hoff, Marie-Luise Marjan, Gisela Bartels, Rainer Will, Claude-Oliver Rudolph, Isolde Barth, Ines Zamurovič, Juliane Werding – **LINE PROD:** Renée Gundelach, Gertraud Göres – **P.C.:** Thomas Mauch Filmproduktion / Artco-Film Eric Franck / ZDF – 35mm, 173 min., sd, color, 1.66:1 – **LANG:** Italian, German – **PREMIERE:** February 28, 1980 (Internationale Filmfestspiele Berlin)
English title: PALERMO OR WOLFSBURG

LA RÉPÉTITION GÉNÉRALE

DIR: Werner Schroeter – **ASST DIR:** Mostéfa Djadjam – **SC:** Werner Schroeter, Colette Godard – **PH:** Franz Weich – **ED:** Catherine Brasier – **SD REC:** Christian Betz – **CAST:** Mostéfa Djadjam, Catherine Brasier, Colette Godard, Lew Bogdan, Pat Olesko, André Engel, Kazuo Ohno, Sankai Juku, Pina Bausch, Reinhild Hoffmann, Franz Weich, Christian Betz, Werner Schroeter – **LINE PROD:** Thomas Schühly – **P.C.:** Laura Film, for ZDF – 16mm, 89 min., sd, color, 1.37:1 – **LANG:** French, English, German – **PREMIERE:** September 7, 1980 (Mostra del Cinema di Venezia)
English title: DRESS REHEARSAL

WEISSE REISE

DIR, SC, PH, ED: Werner Schroeter – **DES:** Harald Vogl, This Brunner – **COST:** Ursula Rodel – **MUS:** Trudeliese Schmidt – **CAST:** Jim Auwae, Tilly Söffing, Margareth Clementi, Maria Schneider, Ursula Rodel, Marion Varella, Werner Schroeter – **PROD:** Eric Franck, Werner Schroeter – 16mm, 51 min., sd, color, 1.37:1 – **LANG:** French – **PREMIERE:** December 10, 1980 (Action-République, Paris)
English title: WHITE JOURNEY

1981

TAG DER IDIOTEN

DIR: Werner Schroeter – **ASST DIR:** Tamara Scheuffelen, Drahuse Králová – **SC:** Dana Horaková, Werner Schroeter – **PH:** Ivan Slapeta – **ED:** Catherine Brasier, Moune Barius – **MUS:** Peer Raben – **SD REC:** Wilhelm Schwadorf, Karl Mösbauer – **DES:** Zbynek Hloch – **COST:** Alberte Barsacq, Christine Kaufmann – **CAST:** Carole Bouquet, Ida di Benedetto, Ingrid Caven, Christine Kaufmann, Tamara Kafka, Hermann Killmeyer, Dana Medrická, Magdalena Montezuma, Marie-Luise Marjan, Mostefa Djadjam, Jana Plichtova, Carola Regnier, Fritz Schediwy, George Stamkost, Ula Stöckl, Ursula Strätz, Annette Tirier, Ellen Umlauf, Zoe Zag – **LINE PROD:** Harry Kügler, Jan Balzer, Peter Genée – **P.C.:** OKO-Film Karel Dirka / Bayerischer Rundfunk – 35mm, 106 min., sd, color, 1.66:1 – **LANG:** German – **PREMIERE:** October 31, 1981 (Internationale Filmtage Hof)
English title: DAY OF THE IDIOTS

1982

LIEBESKONZIL

DIR: Werner Schroeter – **ASST DIR:** Sophie Thoros, Antonio Orlando – **SC:** Dietrich Kuhlbrodt, Roberto Lerici, Horst Alexander, based on the play by Oskar Panizza – **PH:** Jörg Schmidt-Reitwein – **ED:** Catherine Brasier – **DES:** Klaus Meyenberg, Pietro Martin – **COST:** Bruno Garofalo, Magdalena Montezuma – **SD REC:** Christian Moldt, Sandro Zanon – **CAST:** Antonio Salines, Magdalena Montezuma, Kurt Raab, Margit Carstensen, Kristina van Eyck, Dagmar Aberle, Renzo Rinaldi, Agnès Nobécourt, Roberto Tesconi, Gabriela Gomez-Ortega, Ofella Meier, Hanja Kochansky, Solvie Stübing, Daniella Metternich, Margarete Rauhut, Johannes Grützke, Corinna Clauß, Walter Schoof, Heinrich Giskes – **LINE PROD:** Peter Berling – **P.C.:** Saskia Film GmbH – 35mm, 90 min., sd, color, 1.37:1 – **LANG:** German – **PREMIERE:** February 21, 1982 (Internationale Filmfestspiele Berlin)
English title: LOVER'S COUNCIL

1983

DER LACHENDE STERN

DIR, PH: Werner Schroeter – **ASST DIR:** Bibiena Houwer – **SC:** Werner Schroeter, Peter Kern – **ED:** Christel Orthmann, Werner Schroeter – **LINE PROD:** Peter Kern – **CO-PROD:** Franz Christoph Gierke, Paul Simon – **P.C.:** Luxor-Film Beteiligungs GmbH / ZDF – 16mm, 109 min., sd, color, 1.37:1 – **LANG:** Tagalog, German, English – **PREMIERE:** October 27, 1983 (Internationale Filmtage Hof)
English title: THE SMILING STAR

1985

DE L'ARGENTINE

DIR, SC: Werner Schroeter – **ASST DIR:** Martha Serrano, Mauricio Jose Skorulski, Marcelo Uriona – **PH:** Werner Schroeter, Carlos Bernardo Waisman, Juan Vera, Gérard Legrand, Olivier Petitjean – **ED:** Catherine Brasier, Claudio Martinez – **SD REC:** Abelardo Kuschnir, Victor Gonzales – **CAST:** Ernesto Sábato, [Pope John Paul II], Cipe Lincovsky, Alejandra Conti, Marcelo Conti, Norma Aleandro, Oriana Fallaci, Gregorio Glusmann, Jorge Alberto Solanas, Werner Schroeter, Hebe de Bonafini, Isabel Chorovic de Mariani, Enrique Broquen, Elvira del Valle Juarez de Coley, Daniel H. Cervino, Marta de Salinas, Elisa Elena de Tossa, Norman Briski, Paco Jamandreu, Alberto Morán, Libertad Leblanc, José Nait, Enrique Pinti, Graziela Fernandez Meijida, Enrique Fernandez Meijide, Monsignor Laguna, Adolfo Pérez Esquivel, Pater Trivinio, Augusto Conte, Luciano B. Menéndez, Osvaldo Bayer, Ruth Marie Kelly, Fernando Noy, Mario B. Menéndez, Mariano Grondona, Nahuel Moreno, Rabanaque Caballero, Elvira Orphée, Sául Ubaldini, José Luis García, Julio Cezar Urien, Monsignor Novak – **LINE PROD:** Richard Takvorian – **P.C.:** Out One / FR 3 – 16mm, 94 min., sd, color, 1.37:1 – **LANG:** Spanish – **PREMIERE:** December 2, 1985 (Cinémathèque Française)
English title: ABOUT ARGENTINA

1986

DER ROSENKÖNIG

DIR: Werner Schroeter – **ASST DIR:** Rainer Will – **SC:** Werner Schroeter, Magdalena Montezuma, Rainer Will – **PH:** Elfi Mikesch – **ED:** Juliane Lorenz – **SD REC:** Joacquim Pinto, Vasco Pimentel – **DES, COST:** Caritas de Witt – **CAST:** Magdalena Montezuma, Mostéfa Djadjam, Antonio Orlando, the children of Sintra and Montijo – **LINE PROD:** Udo Heiland, Paulo Branco – **P.C.:** Udo Heiland Filmproduktion / Metro-Films / Werner Schroeter Filmproduktion / Juliane Lorenz Filmproduktion / Futura Film – 35mm, 98 min., sd, color, 1.66:1 – **LANG:** German, Portuguese, Italian, English, French, Arabic – **PREMIERE:** February 1, 1986 (Rotterdam Film Festival)
English title: THE ROSE KING

1987

AUF DER SUCHE NACH DER SONNE

DIR: Werner Schroeter – **SC:** Werner Schroeter, Juliane Lorenz – **PH:** Wolfram Pilgrim – **ED:** Juliane Lorenz – **SD REC:** Louis Gimel – **CAST:** Ariane Mnouchkine, Hélène Cixous, Erhard Stiefel, Maitrey, Georges Bigot, Odile Cointepas, Maurice Durozier, Myriam Azencot, Guy Freixe, Bernard Martin, Serge Poncelet, Clémentine Yelnik, Andres Peres Araya, Pedro Guimaraes, Jean-François Dusigne, Baya Belal, Simon Abkarian, Christian Dupont, Paul Golub, Catherine Schaub, Mario Chiapuzzo, Bernard Poysat, Jean Louis Lorente, Sophie Piollet, Fabien Gargiulo, Mauricio Celedon, Marc Dumétier, Ly Nissay, Zinedine Soualem, Jean-Pierre Henin, Sophie Moscoso, Liliana Andreone, Naruna de Andrade, Beate Blasius, Jean-Claude Barriera, Nathalie Thomas, Jean-Jacques Lemêtre, Véronique Gargiulo, Pierre Launay, Maria Albaiceta, Baudoin Bauchau, Kim San, Claude Forget, Jean Noel Cordier, Carlos Obregon, Eugênio Sampaio, Thierry Meunier, Laurence Aucouturier, Joaquim Pedrosa, José Vasconcelos, Manuel Cunha, Robert Catenacci, Hector Ortiz, Orlando, Selahattin Öter – **LINE PROD:** Carlo Rola – **P.C.:** Regina Ziegler Filmproduktion, for ZDF – 16mm + video, 94 min., sd, color – **LANG:** French, German – **PREMIERE:** January 13, 1987 (ZDF)
English title: IN SEARCH OF THE SUN

1991

MALINA

DIR: Werner Schroeter – **ASST DIR:** Dana Cebulla – **SC:** Elfriede Jelinek, based on the novel by Ingeborg Bachmann – **PH:** Elfi Mikesch – **ED:** Juliane Lorenz – **MUS:** Giacomo Manzoni – **SD REC:** Georg Krautheim, Vasco Pimentel – **DES, COST:** Alberte Barsacq – **CAST:** Isabelle Huppert, Mathieu Carrière, Can Togay, Fritz Schediwy, Isolde Barth, Libgart Schwarz, Elisabeth Krejcir, Peter Kern, Jenny Drivala, Wiebke Frost, Lolita Chammah, David Philipp Kotai, David Salomonowitz, André Müller, Idl Graf Kinski, Gerhild Didusch, Sabine Schmeller, Nicolin Kunz, Hanno Pöschl, Fritz von Friedel, Daniela Leupold-Löwenthal, Stefan Holzer, Grete Öschlmüller, Bernd Stegemann, Brigitte Antonius, Sascha Ploner – **PROD:** Thomas and Steffen Kuchenreuther – **LINE PROD:** Gerhard Czepe – **CO-PROD:** Peter Pochlatko – **P.C.:** Kuchenreuther Filmproduktion GmbH / Neue Studio Film GmbH – 35mm, 121 min., sd, color, 1.66:1 – **LANG:** German, French – **PREMIERE:** January 16, 1991 (El Dorado, Munich)

1996

POUSSIÈRES D'AMOUR – ABFALLPRODUKTE DER LIEBE

DIR: Werner Schroeter – **ASST DIR:** Tonio Arango – **SC:** Werner Schroeter, Claire Alby – **PH:** Elfi Mikesch – **ED:** Juliane Lorenz – **MUS:** Elisabeth Cooper – **SD REC:** Vasco Pimentel – **DES, COST:** Alberte Barsacq – **CAST:** Anita Cerquetti, Martha Mödl, Rita Gorr, Katherine Ciesinski, Kristine Ciesinski, Laurence Dale, Jenny Drivala, Gail Gilmore, Serguej Larin, Trudeliese Schmidt, Isabelle Huppert, Carole Bouquet, Werner Schroeter – **LINE PROD:** Jean-Pierre Bailly, Anne Cauvin, Christoph Meyer-Wiel, Wieland Schulz-Keil – **CO-PROD:** Jean-Pierre Saire – **P.C.:** MC 4 Production / Imalyre-VT COM France Télécom / Schlemmer Film – 35mm, 125 min., Dolby Stereo, color, 1.66:1 – **LANG:** French, German, English, Italian – **PREMIERE:** August 15, 1996 (Festival del Film Locarno)
English title: LOVE'S DEBRIS

2000

DIE KÖNIGIN

DIR: Werner Schroeter – **ASST DIR:** Linda-Morena Schenk – **SC:** Werner Schroeter, Monika Keppler – **PH:** Thomas Plenert, Alexandra Kordes – **ED:** Florian Köhler – **MUS:** Peer Raben – **SD REC:** Bernhard Albrecht – **DES, COST:** Antje Wennigmann – **CAST:** Marianne Hoppe, Evelyn Künneke, Lola Müthel, Judith Engel, Ursina Lardi, Maren Eggert, Martina Gedeck, Einar Schleef, Elisabeth Minetti, Martin Wuttke, Robert Wilson, Barbara Nüsse, Gerti Blacher, Benedikt Hoppe – **LINE PROD:** Meike Kordes – **P.C.:** MIRA Filmproduktion GmbH – 16mm blow-up to 35mm, 97 min., Dolby Stereo SR, color, 1.66:1 – **LANG:** German – **PREMIERE:** February 18, 2000 (Internationale Filmfestspiele Berlin)
English title: THE QUEEN

2002

DEUX

DIR: Werner Schroeter – **ASST DIR:** Paolo Trotta – **SC:** Werner Schroeter, Cedric Anger – **PH:** Elfi Mikesch – **ED:** Juliane Lorenz – **MUS:** Thomas Dorschel – **SD REC:** Philippe Morel – **DES, COST:** Alberte Barsacq – **CAST:** Isabelle Huppert, Bulle Ogier, Manuel Blanc, Annika Kuhl, Arielle Dombasle, Robinson Stévenin, Philipp Reuter, Pascal Bongard, Jean-François Stévenin, Philippe Carta, Dominique Frot, Rita Loureiro, Zazie de Paris, Tim Fischer, Hovnatan Avédikian, Elisabeth Cooper, Delphine Marque, Alexia Voulgaridou –

LINE PROD: Alexandre Oliveira, Nicolas Picard – **CO-PROD:** Ulrich Felsberg, Frank Graf – **P.C.:** Gemini Films / France 2 Cinéma / Road Movies / Madragoa Filmes / Les Films du Camélia – 35mm, 117 min., Dolby Stereo SR, color, 1.85:1 – **LANG:** French – **PREMIERE:** May 19, 2001 (Festival de Cannes)
English title: TWO

2008

NUIT DE CHIEN

DIR: Werner Schroeter – **ASST DIR:** José Maria Vaz da Silva – **SC:** Gilles Taurand, Werner Schroeter, based on the novel **PARA ESTA NOCHE** by Juan Carlos Onetti – **PH:** Thomas Plenert – **ED:** Julia Grégory, Bilbo Calvez – **MUS:** Eberhard Kloke – **SD REC:** Pierre Tucat – **DES, COST:** Alberte Barsacq, Isabel Branco – **CAST:** Pascal Greggory, Bruno Todeschini, Amira Casar, Eric Caravaca, Nathalie Delon, Marc Barbé, Jean-François Stévenin, Bulle Ogier, Laura Martin, Mostefa Djadjam, Lena Schwarz, João Baptista, Pascale Schiller, Oleg Zhukov, Filipe Duarte, Sami Frey, Elsa Zylberstein – **LINE PROD:** Eileen Tasca, Ana Pinhão Moura – **CO-PROD:** Eric Franck – **P.C.:** Alfama Films Production / Filmgalerie 451 / Clap Filmes – 35mm, 117 min., Dolby Stereo Digital, color, 1.85:1 – **LANG:** French – **PREMIERE:** September 2, 2008 (Mostra del Cinema di Venezia)
English title: THIS NIGHT

II. Studies, tests, fragments, lost films, unfilmed projects

1968

CALLAS-TEXT MIT DOPPELBELICHTUNG

DIR, PROD, SC, PH: Werner Schroeter – 8mm, 5 min., silent, black & white, 1.37:1 – **LANG:** German. Unedited studies.
Preliminary study for MONA LISA. Was not included by Werner Schroeter for his program of Callas films as part of his 1970 Bochum retrospective.

ÜBUNGEN MIT DARSTELLERN

DIR, PROD, SC, PH: Werner Schroeter – **CAST:** Magdalena Montezuma, Steven Adamczewski – 8mm, 12 min. (24 fps), silent, black & white + color – **LANG:** no text. Unedited studies.
Magdalena and a young woman rehearse gestures of falling down; Steven Adamczewski lies on the floor with his arms spread out and is awakened with a kiss; Magdalena Montezuma stands at the window and turns to the camera; pictures of Alain Delon and Elvis Presley.
Uncut and unconnected studies. Original is at Filmmuseum München.

GROTESK – BURLESK – PITTORESK

DIR, SC, PH: Werner Schroeter, Rosa von Praunheim – **ED:** Werner Schroeter – **CAST:** Magdalena Montezuma, Rosa von Praunheim – 8mm, 60 min. (40 min.?), separate sound, color + black & white. Lost film.
In 1999, Schroeter brought this film along to the Internationale Kurzfilmtage in Oberhausen, where it was shown. When he left, the film was in his possession, but it has since disappeared.

DIE GRABSCHÄNDUNG

DIR, SC: Werner Schroeter – 8mm, 10 min., color. Lost film.
The film is listed by Wim Wenders in the journal *Filmkritik* in 1969. There is no further information on the film and no footage exists.

MARLENE KOCH

DIR, SC: Werner Schroeter – 8mm, 10 min., black & white. Lost film.
The film is listed by Wim Wenders in the journal *Filmkritik* in 1969. There is no further information on the film and no footage exists.

FACES

DIR, PROD, SC, ED: Werner Schroeter – **PH:** Rosa von Praunheim – **CAST:** Heidi Lorenzo – 8mm, 18 min. (18 fps), silent, black & white. Study.
According to Werner Schroeter, this is a fragment and a preliminary study for AGGRESSION. Original is at Filmmuseum München.

VIRGINIA'S DEATH

DIR, PROD, SC, PH, ED: Werner Schroeter – **CAST:** Magdalena Montezuma, Heidi Lorenzo – 8mm (16mm?), 9 min., black & white. Lost film.
"An unreleased fragment that evidently hasn't been seen by anyone" (Walter Schobert). The film itself is lost. There only exists an exact description of a fragment of the film from the year 1971.

1969

NICARAGUA

DIR, SC, ED: Werner Schroeter – **PH:** Robert van Ackeren – **CAST:** Carla Aulaulu, Magdalena Montezuma, Gavin Campbell – **PROD:** Peter Berling – 35mm, 18 min. (14 min.?), black & white, CinemaScope. Lost film.
According to Werner Schroeter, the film was shot, edited, and sound mixed at the studio of Schonger-Film in Inning am Ammersee, but it was never released. The production costs were 6,000 DM. Peter Berling said that he was unable to pay the costs for printing the film (according to Schroeter, the company in charge of printing was Arri). No material remains. Some sources list it wrongly as an 80-minute 16mm black & white film.

1970

ANGLIA

DIR, SC: Werner Schroeter – **ASST DIR:** Ulli Lommel – **PH:** Jörg Schmidt-Reitwein – **CAST:** Magdalena Montezuma, Carla Aulaulu, Mascha Elm-Rabben, Kathrin Schaake, Ulli Lommel, Stefan Hurdalek, Hannes Gromball – **P.C.:** Atlantis Film – 16mm, color. Unedited; lost film.
According to Werner Schroeter the film was never finished, because producer Ulli Lommel's "funds dried up halfway during production." The shoot lasted for 9 days. According to Ulli Lommel, Schroeter did not edit the film because he lost interest in it. According to Schroeter, Lommel has the footage. The footage is lost.

1971

FUNKAUSSTELLUNG 1971 – *HITPARADE*

DIR, SC: Werner Schroeter – **CAST:** Christian Anders, Mary Roos, Erik Silvester, Costa Cordalis, Lena Valaitis, Annette Tirier – **P.C.:** ZDF – video, black & white. Unedited; lost film.
The footage filmed by Schroeter was not used and no longer exists. According to Schroeter, the coverage was shot on black & white video, which was sent to Mainz to the ZDF, but when he was ready to edit it there, the tapes had been erased, allegedly by accident. Schroeter recalls having filmed visitors to *Hitparade* before, during, and after the show. The footage showed the harsh handling of the young audience by studio security. The singers apparently were interviewed by children. According to Schroeter, he asked Lena Valaitis to perform the lyrics of her song as a poem.

1977

IM DUNKLEN HERZEN DES NACHMITTAGS

DIR: Werner Schroeter – **SC:** Wolf Wondratschek. Unfilmed.
During the 1962 summer vacation, a 15-year-old student falls in love with an older woman. The budget for this German-French co-production was 1 million DM. Unrealized project.

1981

QUERELLE

DIR: Werner Schroeter – **ASST DIR:** Rainer Will – **SC:** Werner Schroeter, Burkhardt Driest, based on the novel by Jean Genet – **PROD:** Dieter Schidor. Filmed by Rainer Werner Fassbinder.
According to Werner Schroeter, Dieter Schidor approached him in Venice in 1980 about making the film. There was a preliminary contract. The budget was set at 800,000 – 1 Million DM. Shooting was scheduled to start in November 1981. Locations were La Spezia (Italian navy port) and Berlin (a studio soundstage and an old hotel near the Berlin Wall). The screenplay had been awarded subsidies from the Ministry of the Interior. According to Peter Berling, Schroeter started casting the film in Berlin in November 1981, but Werner Schroeter claims he was already ousted from the project in September 1981.

1982

NIJINSKY, HOCHZEIT MIT GOTT

DIR: Werner Schroeter – **SC:** Werner Schroeter, Meir Dohnal, based on the diaries of Vaslav Nijinsky – **CAST:** Lobomir Kafka, Juraj Kukura, Jane Birkin, Jeanne Moreau – **PROD:** OKO-Film Karel Dirka. Unfilmed.
This project was never realized due to a lack of funding. What remains is a promotional poster, NIJINSKY DIARIES. One page of the screenplay was published in *Cahiers du Cinéma* no. 400 (1987). "In my opinion Nijinsky's diaries belong to the most poetic pieces of modern literature. The film will show the world from the perspective of someone allegedly insane." (Schroeter)

1986

PRONOTEOCOLOSSAL

DIR: Werner Schroeter – **SC:** Pier Paolo Pasolini. Unfilmed. Pasolini's final screenplay, an 80-page treatment. An old man and his servant "pursue a comet in order to find Jesus. Through all of human history. This is really amazing. Fortunately, it is somewhat comical. It is much more bitter than SALÒ, but at the same time there is more comedy in it" (Schroeter). Allegedly, there was already a contract for the project, but nothing came of it.

III. Werner Schroeter in films by others

1969

ALABAMA: 2000 LIGHT YEARS

DIR: Wim Wenders – **P.C.:** Hochschule für Fernsehen und Film – 35mm, 21 min.

SCHWESTERN DER REVOLUTION

DIR: Rosa von Praunheim – **ASST DIR:** Werner Schroeter – 16mm, 20 min.

1971

WARNUNG VOR EINER HEILIGEN NUTTE

DIR: Rainer Werner Fassbinder – **P.C.:** Antiteater-X-Film GmbH – 35mm, 103 min.

1973

WELT AM DRAHT

DIR: Rainer Werner Fassbinder – **P.C.:** WDR – 16mm, 210 min.

1975

WERNER SCHROETER IM ÖSTERREICHISCHEN FILMMUSEUM I

DIR: unknown – **P.C.:** Österreichisches Filmmuseum – video, 33 min.

1978

VIVRE À NAPLES ET MOURIR

DIR: Gérard Courant – **P.C.:** Les Amis de Cinématon / La Fondation Gérard Courant – video, 85 min.

WERNER SCHROETER IM ÖSTERREICHISCHEN FILMMUSEUM II

DIR: unknown – **P.C.:** Österreichisches Filmmuseum – video, 32 min.

1980

IL FAUT LE SAUVER!

DIR: Gérard Courant – **P.C.:** Les Amis de Cinématon / La Fondation Gérard Courant – video, 59 min.

RAINER WERNER FASSBINDER: MEIN TRAUM VOM TRAUM DES FRANZ BIBERKOPF
DIR: Rainer Werner Fassbinder – **P.C.:** Bavaria Atelier GmbH / RAI, for WDR – 16mm, 112 min.

1981

ZWISCHEN MOND UND SONNE
DIR: Recha Jungmann – **P.C.:** Susanne Osterried Filmproduktion, for ZDF – 16mm, 101 min.

1982

DAS GESPENST
DIR: Herbert Achternbusch – **P.C.:** Herbert Achternbusch Filmproduktion – 35mm, 88 min.

CHAMBRE 666
DIR: Wim Wenders – **P.C.:** Gray City, Inc., for Antenne 2 – 16mm, 50 min.

1986

WERNER SCHROETER
DIR: unknown – **P.C.:** Inter Nationes – 16mm, 9 min.

1989

"DER CHARME, DER AUS DER FREIHEIT KOMMT - -". WERNER SCHROETER ÜBER VIOLETTA, MEDEA, NORMA, CARMEN - -
DIR: Alexander Kluge – **P.C.:** dctp – video, 31 min.

LES MINISTÈRES DE L'ART
DIR: Philippe Garrel – **P.C.:** Lasa Production, for La Sept – 16mm, 52 min.

1990

SOLANGE ICH FLIEHEN NOCH KANN, DA SCHÜTZE ICH MICH
DIR: Peter Kern – **PROD:** Axel Glittenberg and Peter Kern – 16mm, 50 min.

SEX, LEAR AND SCHROETER
DIR: Peter Kern – **P.C.:** Corazon Film – video, 25 min.

THEATER DER LEIDENSCHAFT – WERNER SCHROETER IM PORTRAIT
DIR: Mathias Haentjes – **P.C.:** WDR – video, 45 min.

1998

DIE WIEDERGEBURT DES TRISTAN AUS DEM GEISTE DER REVOLUTION. WERNER SCHROETER INSZENIERT *TRISTAN UND ISOLDE* IN DUISBURG
DIR: Alexander Kluge – **P.C.:** dctp – video, 24 min.

1999

... WELL, THERE WAS ALWAYS MÖDL! – WERNER SCHROETER IM KINO DER HFF
DIR, SC: Alexander Riedel – **P.C.:** Hochschule für Fernsehen und Film – video, 36 min.

WELCHE CHANCEN HAT DIE NAVIGATION IM MEER DER LIEBE? WERNER SCHROETER ÜBER DEN UNTERSCHIED ZWISCHEN LIEBE UND UNFALL
DIR, SC: Alexander Kluge – **P.C.:** dctp – video, 15 min.

2002

DIE VIERTE WAND
DIR: Alexandra Gulea – **P.C.:** Hochschule für Fernsehen und Film – 35mm, 16 min.

PFUI ROSA!
DIR: Rosa von Praunheim – **P.C.:** Rosa von Praunheim Filmproduktion, for NDR, ZDF, Arte – video, 68 min.

2003

LIEBESVERSUCHE – PORTRAIT WERNER SCHROETER
DIR: Claudia Schmid, Birgit Schulz – **P.C.:** Bildersturm Filmproduktion GmbH, for WDR, Arte – video, 64 min.

DIE TOCHTER DES MIRACULIX. VINCENZO BELLINIS GENIALE OPER *NORMA*
DIR: Alexander Kluge – **P.C.:** dctp – video, 45 min.

BEGEGNUNG MIT WERNER SCHROETER
DIR: Monika Treut – **P.C.:** Hyena Films – video, 14 min.

2004

LIEBE UND VERZWEIFLUNG
DIR: Robert Fischer – **P.C.:** Fiction FACTory Filmproduktion – video, 12 min.

LE FANTÔME D'HENRI LANGLOIS
DIR: Jacques Richard – **P.C.:** Les Films Elémentaires / La Cinémathèque française – 35mm, 210 min.

2006

WERNER SCHROETER INSZENIERT *KATZELMACHER* (TEASER)
DIR: Frieder Schlaich – **P.C.:** Filmgalerie 451 – video, 8 min.

2008

INTERVIEW MIT WERNER SCHROETER
DIR: Gudula Moritz – **P.C.:** ZDF / 3sat – video, 6 min.

DIETRICH KUHLBRODT IM GESPRÄCH MIT WERNER SCHROETER I + II
DIR: Stefan Drössler – **P.C.:** Filmmuseum München – video, 20 min. + 8 min.

WOLF WONDRATSCHEK: LAUDATIO AUF WERNER SCHROETER
DIR: Stefan Drössler – **P.C.:** Filmmuseum München – video, 20 min.

WERNER SCHROETER ÜBER *PALERMO ODER WOLFSBURG* 02.12.2008
DIR: Frieder Schlaich – **P.C.:** Filmgalerie 451 – video, 11 min.

2009

WERNER SCHROETER SYNCHRONISATION *NUIT DE CHIEN*
DIR: Elfi Mikesch – **P.C.:** Filmgalerie 451 – video, 39 min.

WERNER SCHROETER ÜBER *DIESE NACHT*
DIR: Elfi Mikesch – **P.C.:** Filmgalerie 451 – video, 7 min.

DAS LETZTE JAHR
DIR: Klaus Wyborny – **P.C.:** Typee-Film – video, 124 min.

LA TRAVERSÉE DU DÉSIR
DIR: Arielle Dombasle – **P.C.:** Fondation Cartier – video, 71 min.

2010

DANIEL SCHMID – LE CHAT QUI PENSE
DIR: Pascal Hofmann, Benny Jaberg – **P.C.:** T&C Film AG – digital, 83 min.

WERNER ET NENAD
DIR: Gérard Courant – **P.C.:** Les Amis de Cinématon / La Fondation Gérard Courant – video, 77 min.

AUF DER RASIERKLINGE DES LEBENS. WERNER SCHROETER INSZENIERT *DON GIOVANNI* AN DER OPER LEIPZIG
DIR: Alexander Kluge – **P.C.:** dctp – video, 24 min.

2011

MONDO LUX – DIE BILDERWELTEN DES WERNER SCHROETER
DIR: Elfi Mikesch – **P.C.:** Filmgalerie 451, for ZDF – digital, 97 min.

AUTREFOIS ET TOUJOURS – DIE FOTOARBEITEN DES WERNER SCHROETER
DIR: Elfi Mikesch – **P.C.:** Filmgalerie 451 – digital, 10 min.

DIALOGO SULLA CALLAS
DIR: Elfi Mikesch – **P.C.:** Filmgalerie 451 – digital, 14 min.

EINE HOMMAGE AN *LAUTRÉAMONT* VON WERNER SCHROETER
DIR: Elfi Mikesch – **LINE PROD:** Frieder Schlaich – **P.C.:** Filmgalerie 451 – digital, 14 min.

2012

WERNER SCHROETER
DIR: Rosa von Praunheim – digital, 11 min.

Selected Bibliography

Compiled by Frankie Vanaria

ANGER, CÉDRIC. "Werner Schroeter: Les belles manières," in *Cahiers du Cinéma* (Paris), numéro hors-série 23, "Cinéma 68" (1998), p. 98

BARTSCH, KURT. "'Mord' oder Selbstvernichtung? Zu Werner Schroeters filmischer *Malina*-Interpretation," in Robert Pichl and Alexander Stillmark, eds., *Kritische Wege der Landnahme: Ingeborg Bachmann im Blickfeld der neunziger Jahre* (Vienna: Hora, 1994), pp. 147–162

CORRIGAN, TIMOTHY. "Werner Schroeter's Operatic Cinema," in *Discourse* (Los Angeles), no. 3 (Spring 1981), pp. 46–59

CORRIGAN, TIMOTHY. *New German Film. The Displaced Image* (Bloomington/Indianapolis: Indiana University Press, 1994), pp. 169–183: "Schroeter's *Willow Springs* and the Excesses of History"

COURANT, GÉRARD. "Entretien avec Werner Schroeter," www.gerardcourant.com/index.php?t=ecrits&e=159. [Interview first published in *Cahiers du Cinéma* (Paris), no. 307 (1978).]

COURANT, GÉRARD. "Le décor, les visages, la mort," in Gérard Courant, ed., *Werner Schroeter* (Paris: Goethe-Institut / Cinémathèque Française, 1982)

EHRENSTEIN, DAVID. "Werner Schroeter," in David Ehrenstein, *Film: The Front Line 1984* (Denver, Colorado: Arden Press, Inc., 1984), pp. 65–74

ELSAESSER, THOMAS. *New German Cinema: A History* (Brunswick, NJ: Rutgers University Press, 1989)

FASSBINDER, RAINER WERNER. "Chin-up, Handstand, Salto Mortale — Firm Footing: On the Film Director Werner Schroeter, Who Achieved What Few Achieve, with *Kingdom of Naples*," in Michael Töteberg and Leo A. Lensing, eds., *The Anarchy of the Imagination: Interviews, Essays, Notes*, trans. Krishna Winston (Baltimore/London: Johns Hopkins University Press, 1992), p. 100. [Fassbinder's article was first published in *Frankfurter Rundschau* (Frankfurt am Main), February 24, 1979.]

FASSBINDER, RAINER WERNER. "Hommage an Werner Schroeter," in Hans Helmut Prinzler and Eric Rentschler, eds., *Augenzeugen: 100 Texte neuer deutscher Filmemacher* (Frankfurt am Main: Verlag der Autoren, 1988), pp. 413–417

FELDMANN, SEBASTIAN. "Kommentierte Filmografie," in Sebastian Feldmann, et al., eds., *Werner Schroeter* (Munich: Hanser Verlag, 1980), pp. 85–192

FLINN, CARYL. *The New German Cinema: Music, History and the Matter of Style* (Berkeley: University of California Press, 2003)

FOUCAULT, MICHEL. "Sade: Sergeant of Sex," in Paul Rabinow and James D. Faubion, eds., *Aesthetics, Method, and Epistemology: Essential Works of Michel Foucault (1954–1984)*, Vol. 2, trans. Robert Hurley (New York: The New Press, 1994), p. 224. [Originally published as "Sade sergent du sexe / Michel Foucault; propos recueillis par Gérard Dupont," in *Cinématographe* (Paris), no. 16 (1975).]

FOUCAULT, MICHEL. "Passion According to Werner Schroeter," in Sylvère Lotringer, ed., *Foucault Live: Collected Interviews, 1961–1984*, trans. Lysa Hochroth and John Johnston (New York: Semiotext(e), 1989, 1996). [Discussion recorded by Gérard Courant in Paris on December 3, 1981.]

GALT, ROSALIND, AND SCHOONOVER, KARL. *Queer Cinema in the World* (Durham, NC: Duke University Press, 2017)

GARCÍA BARDÓN, XAVIER. "EXPRMNTL. An Expanded Festival. Programming and Polemics at EXPRMNTL 4, Knokke-le-Zoute, 1967," in *Cinema Comparat/ive Cinema* (Barcelona), vol. 1 no. 2 (2013), pp. 57–58. www.ocec.eu/cinemacomparativecinema/index.php/en/15-n-2-forms-in-revolution/133-exprmntl-an-expnded-festival-programming-and-polemics-at-exprmntl-4-knokke-le-zoute-1967

GRAFE, FRIEDA. "Schauplatz für Sprache: *Neurasia*," in *Filmkritik* (Munich), no. 159 (March 1970), pp. 136–137

HALLIGAN, BENJAMIN. *Desires for Reality: Radicalism and Revolution: Western European Film* (New York: Berghahn, 2016)

HEIN, BIRGIT. *Film im Underground. Von seinen Anfängen bis zum unabhängigen Kino* (Frankfurt am Main/Berlin/Vienna: Verlag Ullstein, 1971)

HEIN, BIRGIT. "Film in the Underground," trans. Daniel Hendrickson, in Nanna Heidenreich, Heike Klippel, and Florian Krautkrämer, eds., *Film als Idee. Birgit Heins Texte zu Film/Kunst* (Berlin: Vorwerk, 2016)

HIGHBERGER, CRAIG B. *Superstar in a Housedress: The Life and Legend of Jackie Curtis* (New York: Chamberlain Bros./ Penguin, 2005)

INDIANA, GARY. "Scattered Pictures: The Movies of Werner Schroeter," *Artforum* (New York), vol. 20 no. 3 (March 1982), pp. 46–56

JELINEK, ELFRIEDE. "Werner Schroeter als Person" (website posting, April 13, 2010), www.elfriedejelinek.com/fwernera.htm

KEHR, DAVE. "Werner Schroeter, German Film and Stage Director, Dies at 65," *New York Times*, April 10, 2010. www.nytimes.com/2010/04/21/arts/artsspecial/ 21schroeter.html

KLEISER, PAUL B. "*Willow Springs*: Gespräch mit Magdalena Montezuma und Werner Schroeter," in *Filmkritik* (Munich), no. 201 (September 1973), pp. 408–415

KOMAR, KATHLEEN. "'Es war Mord': The Murder of Ingeborg Bachmann at the Hands of an Alter Ego," *Modern Austrian Literature* (Houston, TX), vol. 27 no. 2 (1994), pp. 91–112

KUHLBRODT, DIETRICH. "Erfahrene Erfahrung: Über den Umgang mit Werner Schroeter, will sagen seinen Filmen," in Sebastian Feldmann, et al., eds., *Werner Schroeter* (Munich: Hanser Verlag, 1980), pp. 7–42

KUHLBRODT, DIETRICH. "Magdalena Montezuma," in Hans-Michael Bock, ed., *CineGraph. Das Lexikon zum deutschsprachigen Film* (Munich: Edition text + kritik, 2006), pp. E1–E4

KUZNIAR, ALICE A. *The Queer German Cinema* (Stanford, CA: Stanford University Press, 2000), pp. 113–138: "'The Passionate Evidence' of Werner Schroeter's *Maria Malibran* and *Der Rosenkönig*"

LANGFORD, MICHELLE. *Allegorical Images: Tableau, Time and Gesture in the Cinema of Werner Schroeter* (Bristol, UK: Intellect, 2006)

MANDT, CHRISTINA. *Unscreenings, Unwritings: Gender in Contemporary Adaptation Practice* (New Brunswick, NJ: Rutgers University, 2016)

PLUTA, EKKEHARD. "Das denaturierte Gesamtkunstwerk: Der Filmemacher Werner Schroeter," in *Medium: Zeitschrift für Medienkritik* (Berlin), no. 10 (1974), n.p.

PRAUNHEIM, ROSA VON. "Mit herzlichen Gruß an Champagner-Schroeter," in *Filmkritik* (Munich), no. 265 (January 1979), pp. 2–5. For an English translation, see Rosa von Praunheim, "With Fond Greetings to Champagne Schroeter," in Eric Rentschler, ed., *West German Filmmakers on Film: Visions and Voices* (New York: Holmes & Meier, 1988), pp. 191–195

QUANDT, JAMES. "Magnificent Obsession," in *Artforum* (New York), vol. 50 no. 9 (May 2012), pp. 252–262

RODE, CARLA. "Ein Sizilianer bei VW: Zu Werner Schroeters preisgekröntem Film *Palermo oder Wolfsburg*," in *Der Tagesspiegel* (Berlin), April 11, 1980

SCHMID, EVA M. J., AND SCURLA, FRANK, eds. *Werner Schroeter. Filme 1968–1970*. Documentation issued by Volkshochschule Recklinghausen/Studienkreis Film-Filmclub Ruhr-Universität Bochum, 1970. Unpaginated.

SCHROETER, WERNER (Interview), "Gegen das Rohe und Brutale steht die Verfeinerung," in *Artechock* (Munich), April 15, 2010. www.artechock.de/film/text/interview/s/ schroeter_2010.html

SCHROETER, WERNER (Interview), "Werner Schroeter: Ich suche mich im Fremden," in *Welt am Sonntag* (Berlin), April 12, 2009. www.welt.de/kultur/theater/article3543521/ Ich-suche-mich-im-Fremden.html

SCHROETER, WERNER, WITH CLAUDIA LENSSEN. *Tage im Dämmer, Nächte im Rausch. Autobiographie* (Berlin: Aufbau Verlag, 2011)

SCHROETER, WERNER. "On the Necessity of Utopia: Remarks by the Director Werner Schroeter," *Diese Nacht*, DVD liner notes, Filmgalerie 451 (2010)

SCHÜTTE, WOLFRAM. "Kopfsymphonie über Wahnsinn," in *Frankfurter Rundschau* (Frankfurt am Main), April 1, 1982

SCHÜTTE, WOLFRAM. "Werner Schroeter," trans. Jeremy Roth and John King (Munich: Goethe-Institut, 1988/1991). Reprinted in *Willow Springs & Tag der Idioten*, DVD liner notes (Filmmuseum München, 2014)

SIEGLOHR, ULRIKE. *Imaginary Identities in Werner Schroeter's Cinema. An Institutional, Theoretical, and Cultural Investigation* (PhD Dissertation, University of East Anglia, September 1994)
SYKORA, KATHARINA. *Figurenspiele. Texte zum Film* (Marburg: Schüren, 2013), pp. 90–94: "Kino-Ikon. Magdalena Montezumas Amalgam aus Leinwand und Maske"
WENDERS, WIM. "Die phantastischen Filme von Werner Schroeter über künstliche Leute," in Michael Töteberg, ed., *Emotion Pictures: Essays und Filmkritiken, 1968–1984* (Frankfurt am Main: Verlag der Autoren, 1986)
WENDERS, WIM. "Filme von Werner Schroeter," *Filmkritik* (Munich), no. 149 (May 1969), pp. 318–319
WITTE, KARSTEN. "Ansichten eines Engels: Über *Palermo oder Wolfsburg*," in *Die Zeit* (Hamburg), March 21, 1980. www.zeit.de/1980/13/zum-andenken-eines-engels
WITTE, KARSTEN. "Versteckte Zeichen und Signale: Werner Schroeters Filme," in *Frankfurter Rundschau* (Frankfurt am Main), January 5, 1991
WORTHMANN, MERTEN. "Fragen Sie das Universum," in *Die Zeit* (Hamburg), October 17, 2008. www.zeit.de/2008/43/Schroeter-Interview

Contributors

CHRISTINE NOLL BRINCKMANN is Professor Emeritus at Zurich University, Switzerland, where she founded the Department of Film Studies in 1989. Brinckmann's main fields of research have been classical Hollywood narrative cinema, American documentary film, viewer empathy, the aesthetics of experimental film, camera positions, and color in film. Her collection of essays *Die anthropomorphe Kamera und andere Schriften zur filmischen Narration* was published in 1997 by Chronos. Her book *Color and Empathy: Essays on Two Aspects of Film* was published in English by Amsterdam University Press in 2015. She has also published English-language essays on experimental cinema in *Millennium Film Journal* and on Hollywood pre-Blacklist cinema in *The Wiley-Blackwell History of American Film, Vol. 3*.

EDWARD DIMENDBERG is Professor of Humanities and European Languages and Studies at the University of California, Irvine. He is the author of *Film Noir and the Spaces of Modernity* (2004) and *Diller Scofidio + Renfro: Architecture after Images* (2013). During the 2018–19 academic year as a fellow of the J.S. Guggenheim Memorial Foundation and the Getty Research Institute he will be completing a book entitled *The Los Angeles Project: Architectural and Urban Theories of the City of Exception* and a critical edition of the 1935 urban geography of Los Angeles by Anton Wagner.

STEFAN DRÖSSLER is a film historian, programmer, and specialist in film reconstruction. In the 1980s Drössler became founding director of the Bonner Kinemathek, and artistic director of the Bonn International Silent Film Festival, which he still runs today. Since 1999 he has been the Director of Filmmuseum München, where he has restored and reconstructed more than 100 films, including works by Orson Welles, Walther Ruttmann, Robert Reinert, G.W. Pabst, Werner Schroeter, and others. He has lectured on Welles, film restoration, silent cinema, and the history of 3-D movies at festivals, universities, and cinematheques in Europe, America, and Asia. He is supervising editor of the DVD label *Edition Filmmuseum*, and regularly publishes articles in film programs, catalogues, magazines, DVD booklets, and books.

CARYL FLINN is Professor of Screen Arts & Cultures at the University of Michigan. She is the author of *New German Cinema: Music, Memory, and the Matter of Style* (which includes a chapter on Schroeter), *Brass Diva: The Life and Legends of Ethel Merman* (both University of California Press), *Strains of Utopia* (Princeton), and most recently, *The Sound of Music* (BFI Film Classics, 2015). She has published articles on film music, gender, and camp in various anthologies and journals. Among her current projects are examining kitsch and researching deaf cultures and film.

GERD GEMÜNDEN is the Sherman Fairchild Professor of the Humanities at Dartmouth College, where he teaches in the departments of German Studies, Film and Media Studies, and Comparative Literature. He is the author of *Framed Visions: Popular Culture, Americanization, and the Contemporary German and Austrian Imagination* (1998), *A Foreign Affair: Billy Wilder's American Films* (2008), and *Continental Strangers: German Exile Cinema, 1933–1951* (2014). His volumes as editor include *Wim Wenders: Einstellungen* (1993), *The Cinema of Wim Wenders* (1997), *Germans and Indians: Fantasies, Encounters, Projections* (2002), *Dietrich Icon* (2007), and *Culture in the Anteroom: The Legacies of Siegfried Kracauer* (2012). He is currently completing a monograph on the Argentine director Lucrecia Martel.

ROY GRUNDMANN is Associate Professor of Film Studies and co-founder of the Cinema and Media Studies Major at Boston University. He is the author of *Andy Warhol's Blow Job* (Temple University Press), the editor of *A Companion to Michael Haneke* (Wiley-Blackwell), and a co-editor of *The Wiley-Blackwell History of American Film, Vols. 1–4*, as well as the updated 2-volume paperback edition *American Film History: Selected Readings, Vol. 1, Origins to 1960*, and *Vol. 2, 1960 to the Present*. Grundmann's essays have appeared in numerous journals, including *Cinemaya*, *Millennium Film Journal*, *Afterimage*, *The Velvet Light Trap*, and *Montage A/V*, as well as *Cineaste*, where Grundmann is also a Contributing Editor. Grundmann has curated retrospectives on Andy Warhol, Michael Haneke, and Matthias Müller.

GERTRUD KOCH teaches Cinema Studies at Freie Universität Berlin and has been a Visiting Professor at Brown University and numerous other international universities. She was a research fellow at Kulturwissenschaftliches Institut in Essen, the Getty Research Center in Los Angeles, and many other institutions. Monographs: with Hauke Brunkhorst, *Herbert Marcuse zur Einführung* (Hamburg: Junius Verlag GmbH, 1987), *"Was ich erbeute, sind Bilder". Zur filmischen Repräsentation der Geschlechterdifferenz* (Frankfurt am Main: Stroemfeld, 1988), *Die Einstellung ist die Einstellung. Zur visuellen Konstruktion des Judentums* (Frankfurt am Main: Suhrkamp, 1992), *Siegfried Kracauer zur Einführung* (Hamburg: Junius Verlag GmbH, 1996 [English: Princeton, NJ: Princeton University Press, 2000]), *Breaking Bad* (Berlin: Diaphenes, 2015 [English trans., Diaphenes, 2017]), *Die Wiederkehr der Illusion. Film und die Künste, der Gegenwart* (Berlin: Suhrkamp, 2016), *Zwischen Raubtier und Chamäleon. Texte zu Film, Medien, Kunst und Kultur*, Judith Keilbach and Thomas Morsch, eds. (Munich: Verlag Wilhelm Fink, 2016). Koch is co-editor and a member of the editorial board of various German and international journals, including *OCTOBER*, *Constellations*, *Philosophy & Social Criticism*, *Mimesis*, and *Zeitschrift für Medienwissenschaft*.

MICHELLE LANGFORD is Senior Lecturer in Film Studies at UNSW, Sydney. Her research spans the cinemas of Germany and Iran. She is the author of *Allegorical Images: Tableau, Time and Gesture in the Cinema of Werner Schroeter* (Intellect, 2006) and editor of *The Directory of World Cinema Germany* (Intellect, 2012, 2013). Her research on Iranian cinema has appeared in leading film studies journals, including *Camera Obscura*, *Screen*, and *Screening the Past*. She is currently working on a book entitled *Allegory in Iranian Cinema: The Aesthetics of Poetry and Resistance*.

FATIMA NAQVI is Professor of German and Film Studies at Rutgers University. She has written books on the perception of victimhood in Western European culture between 1968 and the new millennium (*The Literary and Cultural Rhetoric of Victimhood,* Palgrave, 2007), the films of Michael Haneke (*Trügerische Vertrautheit,* Synema, 2010), and the intersection of architecture and educational discourse in the works of Thomas Bernhard (*How We Learn Where We Live*, Northwestern, 2016). She has held visiting professorships at the Karl-Franzens-Universität Graz and Harvard University.

MARC SIEGEL is Professor of Film Studies at the Johannes Gutenberg University in Mainz. His research and publications focus primarily on experimental film and queer studies. His book *A Gossip of Images* is forthcoming from Duke University Press.

FRANKIE VANARIA is a PhD student in the American & New England Studies program at Boston University. His research interests concern Hollywood and Latin American cinema, and the relationship between the two, as explored through the lens of continental philosophy.

Acknowledgments

The present volume of essays is based in part on the international, interdisciplinary conference, "Cinema, Opera, Art: The Passion of Werner Schroeter," organized at Boston University in September 2012, in conjunction with a comprehensive retrospective of Schroeter's films at the Harvard Film Archive. I would therefore first like to thank the various individuals and organizations who have made the conference at Boston University possible. As it provided a significant foundation for much of the scholarship featured in this collection, their financial, logistical, and intellectual support has also indirectly contributed to the publication of this volume. In particular, I would like to thank Dean Thomas Fiedler at the Boston University College of Communication and Paul Schneider, Chair of the Department of Film and Television, for their generous financial support and their enthusiasm for the project. Special thanks also go to the German Academic Exchange Service (DAAD), New York, the Boston University Center for the Study of Europe, the Boston University Humanities Foundation, and the Boston University Distinguished Professorship in the Core Curriculum for their generous financial contributions. I am grateful to Detlef Gericke Schoenhagen, former Director of the Goethe-Institut, Boston, who made the Goethe-Institut a splendid host venue for the conference. My heartfelt thanks also go to Karin Oehlenschläger, Programming Director at the Goethe-Institut, and to Matthias Feldman, who both provided important logistical support leading up to and during the conference. Further logistical support was provided by the staff of the Boston University College of Communication, in particular by Allison Ludlam Hoyt, Maureen Mahoney, Kim Relick, and Nathaniel Taylor. My very special thanks go to the conference manager, Colin Root, whose organization skills significantly contributed to the success of this event.

I would like to thank the following individuals for their stimulating contributions to the conference, which in turn also helped shape many of the essays in this volume: Ken Eisenstein, John Gianvito, Saul Levine, James Quandt, Eric Rentschler, and Charles Warren.

At the Harvard Film Archive, which held the retrospective of Schroeter's films and worked closely in conjunction with the conference, I would like to thank Haden Guest, Director, and David Pendleton, Programmer. David was one of Schroeter's biggest fans. His expertise and enthusiasm informed both the HFA series and the conference. David's untimely death made it impossible for him to contribute an essay to this volume. We, the contributors, dedicate this book in loving memory of him.

I would like to thank several academic institutions and cultural centers for their generous financial support for bringing this book to publication and for continuing to assure that the proceedings of our Boston University conferences on film and media can be shared with a wider audience. My thanks go to Dean Thomas Fiedler and the Boston University College of Communication, to the Boston University Center for the Humanities for their BUCH Publication Grant, and to the Goethe-Institut, Boston, for their financial contribution to the publication.

At the Austrian Film Museum, Vienna, my special thanks go to former director Alexander Horwath for his enthusiasm for this project and for accepting it into the renowned series of publications commissioned by the Film Museum. I would also like to thank the new director, Michael Loebenstein, and his team, Andrea Glawogger, Eszter Kondor, and Georg Wasner for their expert skills in shepherding the manuscript to publication. My thanks also go to Gabi Adébisi-Schuster for her careful and detailed graphic design. My special thanks go to our London-based American copy editor, Catherine Surowiec, for her extremely thoughtful and detailed editing of the manuscript. My thanks also go to Frankie Vanaria at Boston University for help with preparing parts of the manuscript.

I am particularly grateful to Stefan Drössler, Director of the Filmmuseum München, who is overseeing the archiving, preservation, and digital reissuing of Werner Schroeter's films. He not only lent his invaluable professional expertise about Schroeter's cinema to our 2012 Boston University conference, but has contributed the most detailed, comprehensive, and authoritative filmography of Schroeter's work to date. He has also provided vital logistical support in obtaining stills from numerous Schroeter films for this publication. My thanks also go to the Stiftung Preussischer Kulturbesitz and to Hans-Peter Frentz at the bpk-Bildagentur for making further images available from the estate of Digne Meller Marcovicz. I would also like to thank Frieder Schlaich from Filmgalerie 451 and Christoph Hahnheiser for kindly making available their images of several of Werner Schroeter's films.

Finally, my loving thanks go to Mark Hennessey, who once again has been a source of tremendous patience as well as personal and logistical support.

Roy Grundmann

TEXT CREDITS

The editor and publisher would like to thank Gérard Courant for granting permission to reproduce the copyrighted material in the article "Passion According to Werner Schroeter," trans. John Johnston, in Michel Foucault, ed. Sylvère Lotringer, *Foucault Live: Interviews, 1961–1984* (New York: Semiotext(e), 1989, 1996), pp. 313–321. Originally published in Gérard Courant, ed., *Werner Schroeter* (Paris: Goethe-Institut / Cinémathèque Française, 1982)

For all materials every effort has been made to trace copyright holders and to obtain their permission for the use of copyrighted material. The publisher apologizes for any errors or omissions in the above list, and would be grateful if notified of any corrections that should be incorporated in future reprints or editions of this book.

Image Credits

AUSTRIAN FILM MUSEUM – 28; 38, 115–116, 129–138, 142–152 (Frame Enlargements)

BPK-BILDAGENTUR – 9, 43 (bottom), 108, 195, 213; All: © bpk / Digne Meller Marcovicz

DEUTSCHE KINEMATHEK – 32, 120, 125; All: © Rodolfo Alcaraz

FILMARCHIV AUSTRIA – 158, 167, 176 (2nd row); All: © Black Forest Films

FILMGALERIE 451 – 55 © Elfi Mikesch; 201 © Thomas Plenert; 207 © Digne Meller Marcovicz; Back cover © Elfi Mikesch
Film stills from the Filmgalerie 451 DVDs *Palermo oder Wolfsburg, Abfallprodukte der Liebe – Poussières d'amour,* and *Diese Nacht (Nuit de chien):* 48, 164, 172, 176 (top, 3rd & 4th row), 185–190

FILMMUSEUM DÜSSELDORF – 53 (top) © Black Forest Films

FILMMUSEUM MÜNCHEN – 15 (middle & bottom), 33, 34, 36 (top & 2nd row left), 41 (top), 43 (top), 45, 50, 51, 53 (bottom), 86, 89, 179. Film stills from the Edition Filmmuseum DVDs published by Filmmuseum München #51 *Eika Katappa & Der Tod der Maria Malibran,* #61 *Der Bomberpilot & Nel Regno di Napoli*, and #71 *Willow Springs & Tag der Idioten*:
15 (top), 17, 20–23, 30, 41 (2nd & 3rd row), 60, 62, 65, 67, 70, 74, 75, 77, 96–105, 107, 112

VIENNALE – 47

WORCESTER ART MUSEUM, MASSACHUSETTS, USA / BRIDGEMAN IMAGES – 61

FilmmuseumSynemaPublikationen

Available English Language Titles

The book series under the imprint FilmmuseumSynemaPublikationen, jointly edited by the Austrian Film Museum and SYNEMA—Society for Film and Media, offers richly illustrated books on the work of independent filmmakers and on topics of film history and theory. All titles are distributed internationally by Columbia University Press (**cup.columbia.edu**). In the German-language area please also see **www.filmmuseum.at**.

Volume 30
ROBERT BEAVERS
Edited by Rebekah Rutkoff
Vienna 2017, 224 pages
ISBN 978-3-901644-69-6

In a career spanning five decades, Robert Beavers has distinguished himself as one of the most important American avant-garde filmmakers. This volume contains critical investigations of Beavers' most important films and a collection of the filmmaker's own writings. Occupying a unique space between poetry and philosophy, his aphoristic meditations vivify his own work and generously illuminate the art of film. The essay contributors include Tom Chomont, Don Daniels, Luke Fowler, Haden Guest, Kristin M. Jones, James Macgillivray, Gregory J. Markopoulos, Ricardo Matos Cabo, Jonas Mekas, René Micha, Susan Oxtoby, Rebekah Rutkoff, P. Adams Sitney, and Erik Ulman.

Volume 28
ALAIN BERGALA
THE CINEMA HYPOTHESIS. TEACHING CINEMA IN THE CLASSROOM AND BEYOND
Translated from the French by Madeline Whittle
Vienna 2016, 136 pages
ISBN 978-3-901644-67-2

Alain Bergala's *The Cinema Hypothesis* is a seminal text on the potentials, possibilities, and problems of bringing film to schools and other educational settings. It is also the passionate confirmation of a love for cinema and an attempt to think of art-education differently. The book stages a dialogue between larger concepts of cinema and a hands-on approach to teaching film. Its detailed insights derive from the author's own experiences as a teacher, critic, filmmaker and advisor to the French Minister of Education. Bergala, who also served as chief editor of *Cahiers du cinéma*, promotes an understanding of film as an autonomous art form that has to be taught accordingly. Confronting young people with cinema can create friction with established norms and serve as a productive rupture for both institution and pupil: perhaps more than any other art form, the cinema enables a lived, intimate experience of otherness. "The Cinema Hypothesis *is actually an erudite and absorbing deliberation on cinema's receding cultural status, and a passionate appeal for its rescue ...*". (Fandor) – "The Cinema Hypothesis *must be of considerable interest to those involved in teaching cinema on any level.*" (Sight & Sound)

Volume 26
JEAN-MARIE STRAUB & DANIÈLE HUILLET
Edited by Ted Fendt
Vienna 2016, 256 pages
ISBN 978-3-901644-64-1

Jean-Marie Straub and Danièle Huillet have distinguished themselves as two of Europe's most inventive, generous and uncompromising filmmakers. In classics such as *Not Reconciled, Moses and Aaron, Class Relations, Antigone,* and *Sicilia!*, they developed unique approaches to film adaptation, performance, sound recording, cinematography, and translation, working throughout Germany, Italy and France since the early 1960s. This book is the first English-language "primer" on Straub and Huillet and features original essays by Claudia Pummer, John Gianvito, Harun Farocki, Jean-Pierre Gorin, Ted Fendt, and Barbara Ulrich, as well as François Albera's career-spanning interview with the two filmmakers. *"A must for anyone with an interest for intellectual and experimental art film."* (epd film) – *"An immensely useful tool for framing and enhancing the duo's films."* (Cinema Scope)

Volume 24

BE SAND, NOT OIL
THE LIFE AND WORK OF AMOS VOGEL

Edited by Paul Cronin
Vienna 2014, 272 pages
ISBN 978-3-901644-59-7

An émigré from Austria who arrived in New York just before the Second World War, Amos Vogel was one of America's most innovative film historians and curators. In 1947 he created *Cinema 16*, a pioneering film club aimed at audiences thirsty for work "that cannot be seen elsewhere," and in 1963 was instrumental in establishing the New York Film Festival. In 1974 he published the culmination of his thoughts, the book *Film as a Subversive Art*. In the words of Martin Scorsese: "The man was a giant." This is the first book about Vogel. "*An indispensable study. If the book is invaluable for gathering together numerous never-before-collected or previously unpublished pieces by Vogel himself, the newly commissioned essays by various scholars are every bit as welcome.*" (Film Comment)

Volume 23

HOU HSIAO-HSIEN

Edited by Richard I. Suchenski
Vienna 2014, 272 pages
ISBN 978-3-901644-55-0

Hou Hsiao-hsien is the most important figure in Taiwanese cinema, and his sensuous, richly nuanced films reflect everything that is vigorous and genuine in contemporary film culture. Through its stylistic originality and historical gravity, Hou's body of work opens up new possibilities for the medium. This volume includes contributions by Olivier Assayas, Peggy Chiao, Jean-Michel Frodon, Shigehiko Hasumi, Jia Zhang-ke, James Quandt, and many others as well as conversations with Hou Hsiao-hsien and some of his most important collaborators over the decades. "*Delicious is a good word for this book, an absolute necessity for every serious cinephile.*" (David Bordwell)

Volume 19

JOE DANTE

Edited by Nil Baskar and Gabe Klinger
Vienna 2013, 256 pages
ISBN 978-3-901644-52-8

In the often dreary landscape of Hollywood's blockbuster era, the cinema of Joe Dante has always stood out as a rare beacon of fearless originality. Blending humor with terror and trenchant political satire with sincere tributes to "B" movies, the "Dante touch" is best described as a mischievous free-for-all of American pop culture and film history. This first English language book on Dante includes a career-encompassing interview, a treasure trove of never-before-seen documents and illustrations, and new essays by Michael Almereyda, J. Hoberman, Bill Krohn, John Sayles, and Mark Cotta Vaz, among many others. "*The closest we currently have to a full-blown autobiography, the book does an admirable job as a single-volume overview.*" (Sight & Sound)

Volume 17

A POST-MAY ADOLESCENCE
LETTER TO ALICE DEBORD

By Olivier Assayas
Vienna 2012, 104 pages
ISBN 978-3-901644-44-3

Olivier Assayas is best known as a filmmaker, but cinema makes only a late appearance in his book. This reflective memoir takes us from the massive cultural upheaval that was May 1968 in France to the mid-1990s when Assayas made his first film about his teenage years. The book also includes two essays on the aesthetic and political legacy of Guy Debord, who played a decisive role in shaping the author's understanding of the world. *"Assayas' voice is clear, urgent, and persuasive. For him the matter at hand, the subject that keeps slipping away, is the story of how he came to know the work of Guy Debord. This is nothing less than the story of his life."* (Film Quarterly)

Volume 16
OLIVIER ASSAYAS
Edited by Kent Jones
Vienna 2012, 256 pages
ISBN 978-3-901644-43-6

Over the past few decades, French filmmaker Olivier Assayas has become a powerful force in contemporary cinema. Between such major works as *Irma Vep, Les Destinées, Summer Hours, Carlos* and *Clouds of Sils Maria*, he has charted an exciting path, strongly embracing narrative and character and simultaneously dealing with the 'fragmentary reality' of life in a global economy. This richly-illustrated monograph includes a major essay by Kent Jones, contributions from Assayas and his most important collaborators, as well as 16 individual essays on each of the filmmaker's works.

Volume 15
SCREEN DYNAMICS
MAPPING THE BORDERS OF CINEMA
Edited by Gertrud Koch, Volker Pantenburg, and Simon Rothöhler
Vienna 2012, 184 pages
ISBN 978-3-901644-39-9

This volume attempts to reconsider the limits and specifics of film and the traditional movie theater. It analyzes notions of spectatorship, the relationship between cinema and the "uncinematic", the contested place of installation art in the history of experimental cinema, and the characteristics of the high definition image. Contributors include Raymond Bellour, Victor Burgin, Vinzenz Hediger, Tom Gunning, Ute Holl, Ekkehard Knörer, Thomas Morsch, Jonathan Rosenbaum and the editors. "Screen Dynamics *is a thorough and provocative survey of the fields with which the generations growing up with these technologies will engage."* (Film International)

Volume 11
GUSTAV DEUTSCH
Edited by Wilbirg Brainin-Donnenberg and Michael Loebenstein
Vienna 2009, 252 pages
ISBN 978-3-901644-30-6

According to Viennese filmmaker Gustav Deutsch, "film is more than film." His own career proves that point. In addition to being an internationally acclaimed creator of found footage films, he is also a visual artist, an architect, a researcher, an educator, an archaeologist, and a traveler. This volume traces the way in which the cinema of Gustav Deutsch transcends our common notion of film. Essays by Nico de Klerk, Stefan Grissemann, Tom Gunning, Beate Hofstadler, Alexander Horwath, Wolfgang Kos, Scott MacDonald, Burkhard Stangl, and the editors.

Volume 9
FILM CURATORSHIP
ARCHIVES, MUSEUMS, AND THE DIGITAL MARKETPLACE
By Paolo Cherchi Usai, David Francis, Alexander Horwath, and Michael Loebenstein
Vienna 2008, 240 pages
ISBN 978-3-901644-24-5
OUT OF PRINT (2ND EXTENDED EDITION IN PLANNING)

This volume deals with the rarely-discussed discipline of film curatorship and with the major issues and challenges that film museums and cinémathèques are bound to face in the Digital Age. *Film Curatorship* is an experiment: a collective text, a montage of dialogues, conversations, and exchanges among four professionals representing three generations of film archivists and curators.

Volume 6
JAMES BENNING
Edited by Barbara Pichler and Claudia Slanar
Vienna 2007, 264 pages
ISBN 978-3-901644-23-8

James Benning's films are among the most fascinating works in American cinema. He explores the relationship between image, text and sound while paying expansive attention to the "vernacular landscapes" of American life. This volume traces Benning's artistic career as well as his biographical journey through the United States. With contributions by James Benning, Sharon Lockhart, Allan Sekula, Dick Hebdige, Scott MacDonald, Volker Pantenburg, Nils Plath, Michael Pisaro, Amanda Yates, Sadie Benning, Julie Ault, Claudia Slanar and Barbara Pichler.

Volume 5
JOSEF VON STERNBERG
THE CASE OF LENA SMITH
Edited by Alexander Horwath and Michael Omasta
Vienna 2007, 304 pages
ISBN 978-3-901644-22-1

The Case of Lena Smith, directed by Josef von Sternberg, is one of the legendary lost masterpieces of the American cinema. Assembling 150 original stills and set designs, numerous script and production documents as well as essays by eminent film historians, the book reconstructs Sternberg's dramatic film about a young woman fighting the oppressive class system of Imperial Vienna. The book includes essays by Janet Bergstrom, Gero Gandert, Franz Grafl, Alexander Horwath, Hiroshi Komatsu and Michael Omasta, a preface by Meri von Sternberg, as well as contemporary reviews and excerpts from Viennese literature of the era.

Volume 4
DZIGA VERTOV
THE VERTOV COLLECTION AT THE AUSTRIAN FILM MUSEUM
Edited by the Austrian Film Museum, Thomas Tode, and Barbara Wurm
Vienna 2006, 288 pages
ISBN 3-901644-19-9

For the Russian filmmaker and film theorist Dziga Vertov KINO was both a bold aesthetic experiment and a document of contemporary life. This book presents the Austrian Film Museum's comprehensive Vertov Collection, including many unpublished documents and writings such as his extensive autobiographical "Calling Card" from 1947.